AA004286

ICDS 2018

The Twelfth International Conference on Digital Society

March 25 – 29, 2018

Rome, Italy

ICDS 2018 Editors

Lasse Berntzen, University College of Southeast, Norway
Martijn Hartog, The Hague University of Applied Sciences -The Hague, The Netherlands

Printed from e-media with permission by:

Curran Associates, Inc.
57 Morehouse Lane
Red Hook, NY 12571

Some format issues inherent in the e-media version may also appear in this print version.

Printed by Curran Associates, Inc. (2018)

International Academy, Research, and Industry Association (IARIA)
412 Derby Way
Wilmington, DE 19810

Phone: (408) 893-6407
Fax: (408) 527-6351

petre@iaria.org

Additional copies of this publication are available from:

Curran Associates, Inc.
57 Morehouse Lane
Red Hook, NY 12571 USA
Phone: 845-758-0400
Fax: 845-758-2633
Email: curran@proceedings.com
Web: www.proceedings.com

ICDS 2018

Forward

The twelfth edition of The International Conference on Digital Society (ICDS 2018) was held in Rome, Italy, March 25 - 29, 2018.

Nowadays, most of the economic activities and business models are driven by the unprecedented evolution of theories and technologies. The impregnation of these achievements into our society is present everywhere, and it is only question of user education and business models optimization towards a digital society.

Progress in cognitive science, knowledge acquisition, representation, and processing helped to deal with imprecise, uncertain or incomplete information. Management of geographical and temporal information becomes a challenge, in terms of volume, speed, semantic, decision, and delivery.

Information technologies allow optimization in searching an interpreting data, yet special constraints imposed by the digital society require on-demand, ethics, and legal aspects, as well as user privacy and safety.

The event was very competitive in its selection process and very well perceived by the international scientific and industrial communities. As such, it is attracting excellent contributions and active participation from all over the world. We were very pleased to receive a large amount of top quality contributions.

The accepted papers covered a large spectrum of topics related to advanced networking, applications, social networking, security and protection, and systems technologies in a digital society. We believe that the ICDS 2018 contributions offered a panel of solutions to key problems in all areas of digital needs of today's society.

We take here the opportunity to warmly thank all the members of the ICDS 2018 technical program committee as well as the numerous reviewers. The creation of such a broad and high quality conference program would not have been possible without their involvement. We also kindly thank all the authors that dedicated much of their time and efforts to contribute to the ICDS 2018. We truly believe that thanks to all these efforts, the final conference program consists of top quality contributions.

This event could also not have been a reality without the support of many individuals, organizations and sponsors. In addition, we also gratefully thank the members of the ICDS 2018 organizing committee for their help in handling the logistics and for their work that is making this professional meeting a success.

We hope the ICDS 2018 was a successful international forum for the exchange of ideas and results between academia and industry and to promote further progress on the topics of digital society.

We also hope that Rome provided a pleasant environment during the conference and everyone saved some time for exploring this beautiful city.

ICDS 2018 Chairs

ICDS Steering Committee
Lasse Berntzen, University College of Southeast, Norway
Åsa Smedberg, Stockholm University, Sweden
Azi Lev-On, Ariel University, Israel
Jaroslaw Kozlak, AGH University of Science and Technology, Krakow, Poland

ICDS Industry/Research Advisory Committee
Enrico Francesconi, Institute of Legal Information Theory and Techniques - Italian National Research Council (ITTIG - CNR), Italy
Sunil Choenni, Dutch Ministry of Security & Justice / Rotterdam University of Applied Sciences, Netherlands
Korina Velazquez, Comisión Especial de Acceso Digital - Cámara de Diputados, Mexico
Schubert Foo, Wee Kim Wee School of Communication and Information, Singapore

ICDS 2018

COMMITTEE

ICDS Steering Committee
Lasse Berntzen, University College of Southeast, Norway
Åsa Smedberg, Stockholm University, Sweden
Azi Lev-On, Ariel University, Israel
Jaroslaw Kozlak, AGH University of Science and Technology, Krakow, Poland

ICDS Industry/Research Advisory Committee
Enrico Francesconi, Institute of Legal Information Theory and Techniques - Italian National Research Council (ITTIG - CNR), Italy
Sunil Choenni, Dutch Ministry of Security & Justice / Rotterdam University of Applied Sciences, Netherlands
Korina Velazquez, Comisión Especial de Acceso Digital - Cámara de Diputados, Mexico
Schubert Foo, Wee Kim Wee School of Communication and Information, Singapore

ICDS 2018 Technical Program Committee

Chiniah Aatish, University of Mauritius, Mauritius
Habtamu Abie, Norwegian Computing Center, Norway
Ricardo Afonso, Federal University of Alagoas (UFAL), Brazil
Shaftab Ahmed, Bahria University, Pakistan
Mohamad Ibrahim Al Ladan, Rafik Hariri University, Lebanon
Laura Alcaide Muñoz, University of Granada, Spain
Cristina Alcaraz, University of Malaga, Spain
Salvador Alcaraz, Universidad Miguel Hernández, Spain
Alexandre Alvaro, UFSCar - Sorocaba, Brazil
Olatz Arbelaitz Gallego, University of the Basque Country (UPV/EHU), Donostia, Spain
Kambiz Badie, ICT Research Institute, Iran
Sebastiano Bagnara, Institute of Cognitive Sciences and Technologies - Italian National Research Council in Rome, Italy
Mortaza S. Bargh, Research and Documentation Centre of the Dutch Ministry of Security and Justice, Netherlands
Ilija Basicevic, University of Novi Sad, Serbia
Najib Belkhayat, ENCG Business School - Cady Ayyad University, Marrakech, Morocco
Lasse Berntzen, University College of Southeast Norway, Norway
Aljosa Jerman Blazic, SETCCE Ltd. / IT association at Chamber of commerce, Slovenia
Mahmoud Brahimi, University of Msila, Algeria
Justin F. Brunelle, The MITRE Corporation, USA
Mikhail Bundin, Lobachevsky State University of Nizhni Novgorod (UNN), Russia
Alberto Caballero Martínez, Universidad Católica San Antonio de Murcia, Spain
Vinicius Cardoso Garcia, Universidade Federal de Pernambuco, Brazil
Maria Chiara Caschera, CNR-IRPPS, Italy
Sunil Choenni, Rotterdam University of Applied Science (HR), The Netherlands
Yul Chu, University of Texas Rio Grande Valley (UTRGV), USA

Dharmendra Shadija, Sheffield Hallam University, UK
Andreiwid Sheffer Corrêa, Federal Institute of Sao Paulo, Brazil
Patrick Siarry, Université Paris-Est Créteil, France
João Marco C. Silva, High-Assurance Software Lab. | INESC TEC & University of Minho, Portugal
Georgios Ch. Sirakoulis, Democritus University of Thrace, Greece
Åsa Smedberg, Stockholm University, Sweden
Dimitrios Stratogiannis, National Technical University of Athens, Greece
Chandrasekaran Subramaniam, Sri Krishna College of Engineering and Technology, India
Dennis Tachiki, Tamagawa University, Tokyo, Japan
Shigeaki Tanimoto, Chiba Institute of Technology, Japan
Julien Tscherrig, HumanTech Institute, HEIA-FR, Switzerland
Chrisa Tsinaraki, EU JRC, Italy
Umut Turksen, Coventry University, UK
Jürgen Umbrich, WU Vienna | Institute for Information Business, Austria
David Valle Cruz, Universidad Autónoma del Estado de México, Toluca, Mexico
Korina Velazquez, Civismo Digital Mx, Mexico
Nikos Vrakas, University of Piraeus, Greece
Jui-Pin Yang, Shih Chien University, Taiwan
Yingjie Yang, De Montfort University, UK
Nilay Yavuz, Middle East Technical University, Ankara, Turkey
Joaquín Sergio Zepeda Hernández, Universidad Autónoma Metropolitana, Mexico
Qiang Zhu, University of Michigan, USA
Ewa Ziemba, University of Economics in Katowice, Poland
Jovana Zoroja, University of Zagreb, Croatia
Anneke Zuiderwijk - van Eijk, TU Delft, The Netherlands

Copyright Information

For your reference, this is the text governing the copyright release for material published by IARIA.

The copyright release is a transfer of publication rights, which allows IARIA and its partners to drive the dissemination of the published material. This allows IARIA to give articles increased visibility via distribution, inclusion in libraries, and arrangements for submission to indexes.

I, the undersigned, declare that the article is original, and that I represent the authors of this article in the copyright release matters. If this work has been done as work-for-hire, I have obtained all necessary clearances to execute a copyright release. I hereby irrevocably transfer exclusive copyright for this material to IARIA. I give IARIA permission or reproduce the work in any media format such as, but not limited to, print, digital, or electronic. I give IARIA permission to distribute the materials without restriction to any institutions or individuals. I give IARIA permission to submit the work for inclusion in article repositories as IARIA sees fit.

I, the undersigned, declare that to the best of my knowledge, the article is does not contain libelous or otherwise unlawful contents or invading the right of privacy or infringing on a proprietary right.

Following the copyright release, any circulated version of the article must bear the copyright notice and any header and footer information that IARIA applies to the published article.

IARIA grants royalty-free permission to the authors to disseminate the work, under the above provisions, for any academic, commercial, or industrial use. IARIA grants royalty-free permission to any individuals or institutions to make the article available electronically, online, or in print.

IARIA acknowledges that rights to any algorithm, process, procedure, apparatus, or articles of manufacture remain with the authors and their employers.

I, the undersigned, understand that IARIA will not be liable, in contract, tort (including, without limitation, negligence), pre-contract or other representations (other than fraudulent misrepresentations) or otherwise in connection with the publication of my work.

Exception to the above is made for work-for-hire performed while employed by the government. In that case, copyright to the material remains with the said government. The rightful owners (authors and government entity) grant unlimited and unrestricted permission to IARIA, IARIA's contractors, and IARIA's partners to further distribute the work.

Table of Contents

Mobile and User-friendly Two-Factor Authentication for Electronic Government Services Using German Electronic Identity Card and a NFC-enabled Smartphone

Michael Massoth
Department of Computer Science
Hochschule Darmstadt – University of Applied Sciences
Darmstadt, Germany
E-mail: michael.massoth@h-da.de

***Abstract*— A mobile, secure and user-friendly two-factor authentication using the German electronic identity (eID) card will be presented. The new approach shall be used for the mobile online-authentication of citizens in order to get access onto high trust level electronic government services. One part of the innovation is the use of a Near Field Communication (NFC) enabled Android smartphone as ubiquitous NFC card reader. The new approach implements a mobile, as well as a stationary authentication solution for citizens. The high trust level of the mobile online-authentication will be reached by a strong two-factor authentication with the German eID card and the corresponding 6-digit Personal Identification Number (PIN).**

Keywords-mobile authentication; identity management; strong two-factor authentication; high trust level.

I. INTRODUCTION

Due to the rapid increase of digitalization within our industry and society, more and more businesses and government agencies are offering online services where a citizen can access anywhere, anytime, using the online function of the German National electronic Identity (eID) Card. Citizens shall be able to communicate with the administration simply and securely around the clock online in order to perform necessary administrative tasks. This saves costs, the way to administration, waiting times, paper and postage. Citizens and users can identify themselves not only on the Internet, but also at vending machines and the self-service terminals in public authorities. Therefore a mobile and strong two-factor authentication using the German electronic identity (eID) card will be presented in this paper. The new approach shall be used for a quick mobile online-authentication of citizens in order to get access onto all high trust level electronic government services.

The paper is structured as follows. In Section II, the online authentication process with the German eID card and the problems of previous solutions are discussed. Section III presents some related work. Section IV introduces the new mobile AusweissApp2 for Android in Germany. The new mobile authentication approach with the citizen service app is shown in Section V. In Section VI, the new stationary authentication approach with a Quick Response (QR) code is presented in detail. Section VII gives a security evaluation of the REST-interface. Section VIII presents a security evaluation of the HTTS-interface. Section IX ends this paper with a conclusion and outlook on future work.

II. ONLINE AUTHENTICATION WITH GERMAN ID CARD

The new German National Identity Card was introduced in 2010, Dec 1st, in smart card format and with a contactless chip, see Figure 1. With this activated chip, the citizen and eID card holder can use the eID function (online function). With the eID function, the citizen can prove her or his identity in a simple, secure and quick manner on the Internet or at vending machines. The eID card chip transmits the personal data using secure connections once the user authorizes such a transmission by entering the corresponding 6-digit PIN. So a strong two-factor authentication (property and knowledge) will take place. For realization of the electronic authentication, a trusted and secure channel between the chip and the service provider will be established, using an authenticated Diffie-Hellmann key agreement protocol. Both communication parties know with whom they interact (reciprocal authentication).

The German National Identity Card offers maximum security for the personal data on the chip. This applies to both the physical security features of the document and the security technologies protecting the personal data on the chip. The eID function significantly improves data security and reduces the amount of personal data collected (data minimization). The German eID system fulfills certain strong requirements described in the technical guidelines and security advices, published by the German Federal Office for Information Security (BSI), see [1] and [2]. The security and privacy details of the German eID system were addressed in various papers and articles, see, e.g., [3] and [4].

Figure 1. German National eID Card

In order to use the activated eID function, the citizen need a NFC [10] card reader (available from various retailers) and a client software, such as AusweisApp2, which ensures a secure connection between the eID chip and the Internet service provider so that data can be exchanged in encrypted form [13]. The online authentication process with the eID card (using the example of a web service) will be explained step-by-step below:

(1) The card holder opens the provider's web service requiring online authentication.

(2) The service transmits the authentication request to the eID server.

(3) A secure channel is established between the eID server, the client software (e.g., AusweisApp2), the card reader and the ID card's chip, and the authenticity of the service provider and the authenticity and integrity of the eID card (protection against forgery) are checked.

(4) The client software shows the card holder the service provider's authorization certificate and the requested personal data categories. The eID card holder decides which personal data he/she wishes to transmit.

(5) By entering the 6-digit PIN the eID card holder confirms the transmission of his/her data.

(6) The eID card data are sent to the eID server.

(7) The eID server sends an authentication response and the eID card data to the service.

(8) The authentication response and the ID card data are retrieved. The service checks the authentication results and decides whether the authentication was successful. A response is then sent to the user and/or the service is provided.

The consumer research study of GfK, determined in May 2015, stated, that only 5% of all Germans used their eID card for online authentication services within the past 12 months [6]. Also, the "AusweisApp2" (for stationary Windows and Mac OS) was only downloaded about 180,000 times from Dec 2014 to May 2015. There are probably two main reasons for that disappointing result: First, there are only few services (55 commercial and 109 from administrations, in May 2015) with eID support available on the market. Thus, the citizen and users may not see a significant benefit in using eID. Second, for the online authentication there is a special NFC card reader needed which can cost between 30 (basic) to 160 (comfort) Euros. As interim conclusion: The necessity to purchase such an expensive NFC card reader was and is a high blocking factor for the citizens and users to make use of the online authentication function of the German eID card.

III. RELATED WORK

Other countries in Europe also provide mobile authentication solutions for their citizens and users. In Austria for example a new system called "Identity Austria" (IDA) will be introduced. With the new IDA system it will be possible for an Austrian citizen to recall and display official documents and ID cards such as a driving license, passport, e-card or approval form, on the mobile phone without having to carry the different ID cards. The cards and documents are just displayed but not stored on the smartphone. The requested data can be accessed via a centralized high-security server in the Ministry of the Interior and with the consent of the person concerned via an encrypted Internet connection. First field tests has taken place in summer 2017.

The predecessor project was "My Identity App" (MIA) [6] and was developed by the Österreichische Staatsdruckerei GmbH. MIA combines electronic formats of traditional printed ID documents and electronic identities (eID) into a platform-independent smartphone app embedded in an ID ecosystem. Authentication of MIA against the backend is performed by means of a client certificate, which is stored on the users' smartphone. All data transfers are secured using Transport Layer Security (TLS). There are no data stored on the smartphone. Personal data and digital formats of documents and ID cards are always retrieved from a trusted high-security server of a cloud backend infrastructure. A strong two-factor authentication, e.g., with a generated one-time transaction number and a biometric fingerprint, could be performed if required for authentication and proof of identity within an online service.

In Switzerland, there is so far no national eID card available, but Swisscom provides a Mobile ID solution for secure mobile authentication via the smartphone [7]. The Swisscom Mobile ID is a public key infrastructure (PKI)-based secure authentication service that enables users of business applications to access secure accounts, platforms, applications and cloud services. Mobile ID is an application that is not installed on the smartphone, but on the subscriber identity module (SIM) card over-the-air. This makes the application work on any popular smartphone. First, the mobile phone number must be entered for registration. The Swisscom's database is then checked to ascertain whether this mobile phone number is under contract with Swisscom. Then the users home address is displayed. This has to be confirmed by the user. A Mobile ID is already preinstalled on all Swisscom SIM cards as a SIM toolkit (STK) applet, which can only be accessed by the mobile provider "over the air" (OTA) via the correct identification key. Additionally an RSA key is generated, which binds the SIM card to the specific device and thus makes it a safety token. Furthermore, a user-specific Mobile ID PIN is defined, which the user must enter each time when the RSA key, which is stored on the SIM card, is to be accessed. If the user wants to log on to a website, a four-digit number is displayed on the website. At the same time, a message is sent via the SMS channel, which contains the login location and the four-digit number. If both are matching, then the user is prompted to enter his personal Mobile ID PIN. After the correct Mobile ID PIN has been entered, a message is sent back to the sender and the login is successful.

Otterbein et al. [8] presented a new approach with "derived" identities on mobile phones. They analyzed and evaluated different kinds of hardware-based security solutions in order to protect sensitive data at the smartphone.

IV. NEW MOBILE AUSWEISAPP2 FOR ANDROID IN GERMANY

The new mobile AusweisApp2 for Android was released officially on 27th April 2017 at Google Playstore. With that client software the online identification can be used with an android smartphone or tablet (version 4.3 and higher) without an additional NFC card reader. To do so, the smartphone or tablet must have an NFC interface in the first place. The second requirement for the NFC-enabled smartphone is the support of the communication function "Extended Length". This function must be supported by both the NFC chip inside the smartphone and the firmware of the respective device manufacturer. In the third place, the NFC chip must have a sufficient field strength, which ensures that the contactless eID card is supplied with sufficient power to read the stored data. Since 3rd July 2017 the open source code of the AusweisApp2 Android release (1.12.2) is available on Github under the European Union Public License (EUPL). With the new BSI-certificated mobile AusweisApp2 it is now possible to implement a mobile two-factor authentication for online services using the German eID card and a NFC-enabled Android smartphone, as demonstrated in the following sections.

V. MOBILE AUTHENTICATION WITH CITIZEN SERVICE ACCOUNT APP

The mobile two-factor authentication using the German eID card and a NFC-enabled Android smartphone as ubiquitous NFC card reader will be presented as prove of concept, demo and practical development experience, shown in Figure 2. The new approach shall be realized for a typical electronic government service with trust level "high".

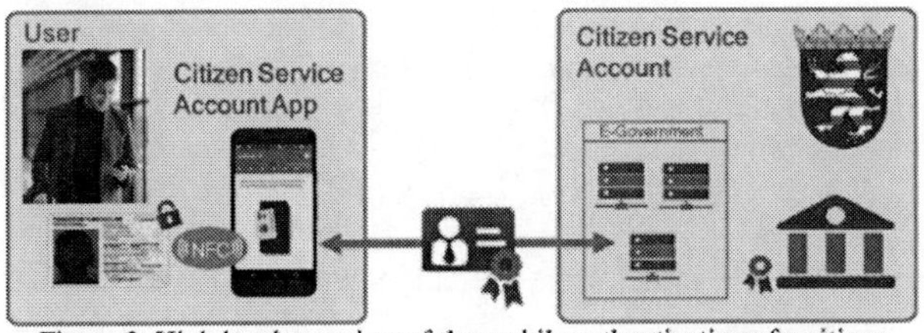

Figure 2. High level overview of the mobile authentication of a citizen

Hereby a Linux-based virtual machine from Hochschule Darmstadt (- University of Applied Sciences) is used as server platform in the backend. A Tomcat web server was installed on this site, which serves as a container for all developed web applications. A MariaDB SQL [15] database is used to store the authentication procedures, as well as the additional data of the particular e-government service. The PKI-infrastructure and the eID-Server of the Bundesdruckerei GmbH (Berlin), or as alternative the media transfer AG (Darmstadt), could be used for live testing. To enable platform-independent communication with various terminals, a Representational State Transfer (REST) [12] server based on the Jersey framework was developed as a server application. The task of the REST interface basically consists of two parts. On the one hand, it is used to authenticate a customer, using the new German eID card. It can also be used to process and terminate the particular electronic government services with trust level "high". Further applications are possible and could be integrated into the backend architecture. The approach of a successful authentication is shown in Figure 3 below, see step (1)-(4):

Step (1): The App asks you to hold your identity card behind the back of your smartphone and to enter the 6-digit PIN of your German eID card. [Figure 3a]

Step (2): The Android smartphone uses NFC to read your private data contactless from your activated eID chip. [Figure 3b]

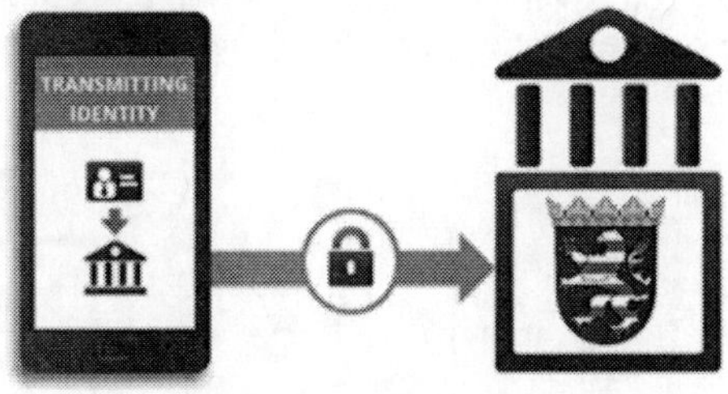

Step (3): Transmits your encrypted personal data to the citizen service account server. [Figure 3c]

Step (4): After successful transmission you have completed the proof of your identity. [Figure 3d]

Figure 3. Step-for-step approach for mobile authentication

The Citizen Service Account App interacts with the server via the following five essential steps:

- Request of an Authentication and Session Token
- Transmission of the Transaction Number (TAN) after successful authentication using the ID card
- Request of the user's read-out ID card data
- Transfer of the input form data
- Confirmation of the vehicle decommissioning

For this purpose, a REST client has been implemented as prototype and proof of concept, which is able to address the specified REST API of our server. The required data between the app and the server are exchanged in JSON format [17].

VI. STATIONARY AUTHENTICATION OF A CITIZEN WITH QUICK RESPONSE (QR) CODE

The complete process of online authentication of the citizen can also be done with a stationary QR code solution. The high level overview is shown in Figure 4 below:

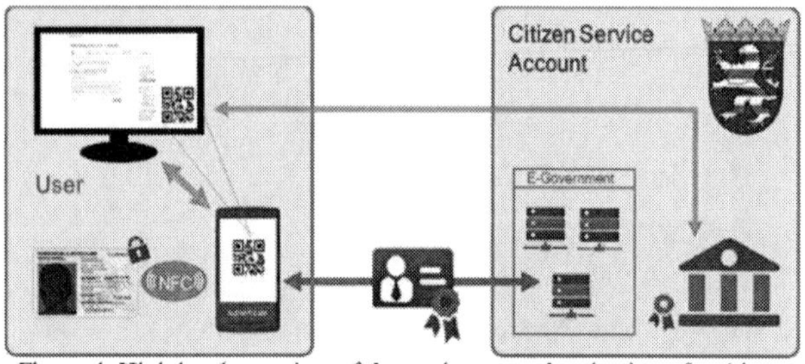

Figure 4. High level overview of the stationary authentication of a citizen

The corresponding step-by-step process for the stationary authentication of a citizen with the quick response code (QR) solution is shown in Figure 5 below:

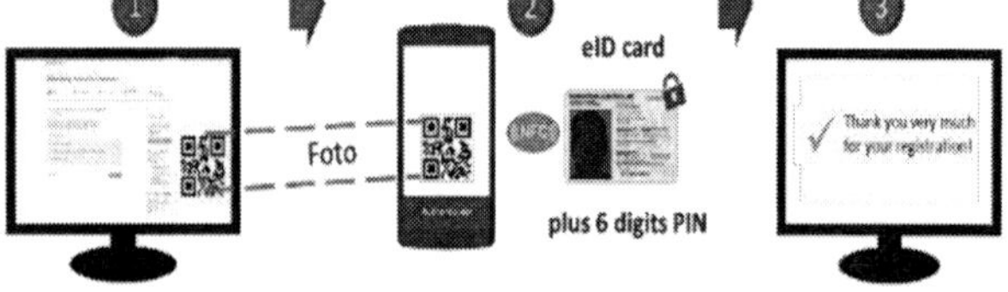

Figure 5. Step-by-step process for the stationary authentication of a citizen

In the stationary authentication approach the user performs the actual login process via the website of the e-government service account and uses the Citizen Service Account App only to scan the generated QR and set the displayed TAN into the corresponding field in the website.

As prerequisite the citizen has to download and install the citizen service account app first on a NFC-enabled Android smartphone. Then the step-by-step process for the stationary authentication of a citizen continues as following:

Step (1): The citizen opens the website of the e-government service account on the desktop PC or notebook and wants to register for the service account as a citizen for the first time.

Step (2): A QR code is then displayed on the website of the e-government service account. The citizen opens the service account app on its smartphone and scans the QR code of the website. It thus establishes a link between the smartphone's service account app and the browser-based website on the PC. He then legitimates himself with the German eID of his ID card and the corresponding 6-digit PIN.

Step (3): After successful authentication the process is terminated in the browser of the PC or Notebook.

Rest–Server: To enable a platform-independent communication with various terminals, a REST server based on the Jersey framework [16] was developed as a server application. The task of the REST interface basically consists of two parts. On one hand, it is used to authenticate a customer, using the new ID card. It can also be used to log off a vehicle after successful authentication. Further applications are possible and could be integrated into the e-government architecture.

REST contains the following five core principles:

- Unique identification (e.g., http://example.com/customers/1234)
- Links / Hypermedia (for example links and forms)
- Standard methods (GET, POST, PUT, DELETE, HEAD, OPTIONS)
- Resources and Representations (Set data format for output, such as XML, JSON)
- Stateless communication (no savings of session status)

VII. SECURITY EVALUATION OF THE REST-INTERFACE

Possible attack vectors and threats against the REST-interface are:

A. *Distributed-Denial-of-Service (DDoS) attack:*

A DDoS attack on a system with a REST interface is aimed at exploiting the limit of the API keys. Often developers do not set a limit on requests to the API when implementing the REST interface. If an attacker finds out such a REST interface, he is able to paralyze the system with frequent requests.

B. *Cross Site Request Forgery (CSRF) attack:*

In a CSRF attack, a user is given a command for a web application (e.g., in the form of a link in a guest book) by an attacker. If the user follows this link, the command is sent to the web application and executed in the context of that user. If the user is logged on to the web application, the user's trust relationship with the web application is exploited and the command is executed with the rights of the user.

C. *Countermeasure Cross Site Request Forgery (CSRF):*

As a safeguard against a CSRF attack, a secret token can be introduced that is difficult to guess by the attacker. Each time the web application views the page, that token is passed as a parameter in URLs or as a hidden field on forms (double submit cookies). For each client request, the web application checks whether the transmitted token matches the value stored for the session. If an error occurs, the requested call is rejected. Without knowledge of this token an attacker cannot adjust a valid HTTP request. For high-security web applications, consider creating the token for each request so that each time the web application is called, a new token is sent to the client, which must then be used in the subsequent request [19].

VIII. SECURITY EVALUATION OF THE HTTPS-INTERFACE

All HTTPS connections of the prototype are implemented and realized with TLS 1.2. The current version TLS 1.2 is specified in RFC 5246. Unlike its predecessor Secure Sockets Layer (SSL), TLS uses the cryptographically more secure keyed-hash message authentication code (HMAC) method to calculate message authentication code (MAC) values. TLS also uses a modified key generation method, which provides greater robustness against attacks on hash values used in key generation as pseudo-random number generators. TLS has also extended the amount of alert messages, with all extensions classified as fatal alerts. Examples of such extensions are the warnings that an unknown Certification Authority (CA) has been specified, or that a decryption operation has failed.

One possible attack vector and threat against the HTTPS-interface shall be discussed here in more detail. The Browser Reconnaissance and Exfiltration via Adaptive Compression of Hypertext (BREACH) attack is a security exploit against HTTPS when using HTTP compression. [18]

The BREACH attack was discovered in 2013. This type of data theft exploits the data compression and data encryption used by websites to speed up page load times, save bandwidth, and secure data during transmission. While the BREACH attack does not directly address SSL security, it compromises the privacy goals of SSL because HTTPS is used only to encrypt page headers and disclose other content. Hackers use a combination of brute-force attacks and divide-and-conquer methods in BREACH attacks to gain access to credentials, email addresses, and other sensitive and personal information from SSL-enabled sites. BREACH attacks work with all versions of the SSL and TLS protocol and with any type of ciphers collection, as long as the following conditions are met:

- The web application is served via HTTP-level compression and contains user-provided data and a static secret in the HTTP response text.
- The attacker knows what he is looking for and is able to monitor the traffic between the user and the web application to get the length of the HTTP responses.
- The attacker can persuade the user to visit a malicious scripting site and then inject a man-in-the-browser malware that can send requests to the target site.

By injecting plain text into an HTTPS request and observing the length of the compressed HTTPS responses, an attacker is able to iteratively guess and derive plaintext secrets from an SSL stream. [18]
BREACH attacks only require a few thousand queries and can be completed in less than 60 seconds. There is no practical way to turn off the attack.

Some countermeasures in order to give a higher protection against BREACH attacks are:

- One possible safeguard is to disable HTTP compression. This leads to reduced performance and increased bandwidth usage.
- Other measures include the separation of secrets and user input or a limitation of the rate limit for queries to the server. Most protections against BREACH attacks are application-specific or require improved information security practices to handle sensitive data.
- As a further preventive measure, security management for web applications can be implemented and a web application firewall can be used to detect and block malicious clients. [18]

In the following subsections, we discuss some additional countermeasures in order to protect the implemented HTTPS and TLS1.2 connections.

A. *Countermeasure TLS backward compatibility (TLS):*

Incorrect configuration of the TLS 1.2 interface allows entry into the connection. If the connection is broken, there is the potential for man-in-the-middle attacks and phishing attacks. A correct configuration of the extensive TLS connection ensures long-term protection against these intrusion attempts.

By default, TLS 1.2 allows backward compatibility with older versions of TLS. Older versions of TLS offer more vulnerabilities and poorer cryptographic properties. It is advisable to only accept TLS 1.2 and to block all clients with older versions in case of a handshake at the beginning of the connection.

B. *Countermeasure Cipher Suites (TLS):*

The range of cipher suites is large at TLS 1.2, but some are no longer safe. The BSI recommends either Galois / Counter Mode (GCM) or Cipher Block Chaining (CBC). Both are currently considered safe and must continue to be supported until at least 2023. The TLS connection should be set to GCM at least for machine-to-machine connection. With GCM, the real key is never transferred and the temporary key is destroyed. This means that even if an attacker breaks the connection and obtains the private key, unlike CBC, he cannot make the content. Furthermore, the BSI recommends the Elliptic Curve Digital Signature Algorithm (ECDSA) which uses elliptic curve cryptography. ECDSA is recommended here due to the short keys and good performance.

C. *Countermeasure DDoS on HTTPS:*

It is strongly recommended, that the IP range allowed for HTTPS connections shall be truncated, so that only the IP addresses of legitimate connection partners will remain.

IX. CONCLUSION AND OUTLOOK

The new approach and solution has implemented a mobile strong two-factor authentication with German eID card and the corresponding 6-digit PIN, whereby a NFC-enabled Android smartphone will be used. The new mobile solution overcomes the need to buy an expensive NFC card reader. Instead, the NFC-enabled Android smartphone will be used as ubiquitous NFC card reader.

The new approach shall be used for the quick mobile authentication of citizens in order to get access onto electronic government services with trust level "high", like, e.g., the citizen service account.

Advantages for the citizens and users are:

- Mobile and stationary web-based use
- Identification within seconds
- Easily proof of the citizens identity with legal security
- Without biometry, texting, and media breaks.
- Replacement of expensive card reader
- Save the way to the government agency and the long waiting times,

Advantages for the government:

- Sovereign digital identity data
- Strong two-factor authentication suitable for all government services with trust level "high" (and below)
- No media disruption
- High processing speed
- Cost savings and reductions
- High satisfaction of citizens and users

Future work: The new approach will be implemented and used for the de-registration of a vehicle as off the road.

ACKNOWLEDGMENTS

This work was supported by the Hessian Ministry of the Interior and Sports (HMdIS, Government of the Federal State of Hessen) [14], Project "Mobiles Servicekonto Hessen".

REFERENCES

[1] Bundesamt für Sicherheit in der Informationstechnik (BSI): Advanced Security Mechanisms for Machine Readable Travel Documents and eIDAS Token (2015). https://www.bsi.bund.de/SharedDocs/Downloads/EN/BSI/Publications/TechGuidelines/TR03110/BSI_TR-03110_Part-2-V2_2.pdf. Last accessed 06th Dec 2017.

[2] Bundesamt für Sicherheit in der Informationstechnik (BSI): Technische Richtlinie 03112 – Das eCard-API-Framework (2014). https://www.bsi.bund.de/DE/Publikationen/TechnischeRichtlinien/tr03112/index_htm.html. Last accessed 06th Dec 2017.

[3] Bender, J., Dagdelen, Ö., Fischlin, M. and Kügler, D.: "Security analysis of the pace key-agreement protocol." International Conference on Information Security. Springer Berlin Heidelberg (2009).

[4] Bender, J., Dagdelen, Ö., Fischlin, M., and Kügler, D.: "The PACE— AA protocol for machine readable travel documents, and its security." International Conference on Financial Cryptography and Data Security. Springer Berlin Heidelberg (2012).

[5] http://www.gfk.com, last access 9th Dec 2017. GfK SE (2015) Fünf Prozent nutzen den elektronischen Personalausweis. http://www.gfk.com/insights/news/fuenf-prozent-nutzen-elektronischen-personalausweis. Last accessed: 06th Dec 2017.

[6] Österreichische Staatsdruckerei GmbH, MIA – My Identity App. https://www.mia.at. Last accessed 06th Dec 2017.

[7] Swisscom Mobile ID, https://www.swisscom.ch/de/business/mobile-id/overview.html. Last accessed 06th Dec 2017.

[8] Florian Otterbein, Tim Ohlendorf, and Marian Margraf: "Mobile Authentication with German eID", IFIP Summer School 2016.

[9] http://www.egov4dev.org/success/definitions.shtml, last access 4th Dec 2017.

[10] http://nearfieldcommunication.org/, last access 6th Dec 2017.

[11] http://www.investopedia.com/terms/q/quick-response-qr-code.asp, last access 7th Dec 2017.

[12] REST: www.restapitutorial.com/lessons/whatisrest.html, last access 9th Dec 2017.

[13] AusweisApp2 can be downloaded for free at: www.ausweisapp.bund.de, last access 7th Dec 2017.

[14] https://english.hessen.de, last access 6th Dec 2017

[15] https://mariadb.org, last access 8th Dec 2017

[16] https://jersey.github.io, last access 8th Dec 2017.

[17] http://www.json.org, last access 8th Dec 2017.

[18] „Akamai BREACH-Attack" [Online]. Available: https://www.akamai.com/de/de/resources/breach-attack.jsp Last access 11st Dec 2017

[19] BSI, Prevention of Cross-Site Request Forgery https://www.bsi.bund.de/DE/Themen/ITGrundschutz/ITGrundschutzKataloge/Inhalt/_content/m/m04/m04403.html Last access 11st Dec 2017

Smart Cities, Big Data and Smart Decision-making

Understanding "Big Data" in Smart City Applications

Lasse Berntzen, Marius Rohde Johannessen
Department of Business, History and Social Sciences
University College of Southeast Norway
Horten, Norway
e-mail:{lasse.berntzen; marius.johannessen}@usn.no

Rania El-Gazzar
Department of Business and Law
University College of Southeast Norway
Hønefoss, Norway
e-mail: rania.el-gazzar@usn.no

Abstract—**Smart decision making is based on data combined with analytics to improve decision-making. This paper examines several application areas of smart cities, and related data sources used for decision-making. In many cases, systems may make decisions on their own. Such systems may play an important role in the development of smart cities. In other cases, the data can be combined with historical data or other open data sources to play a role as the foundation for decision-making. Our findings are presented as an analytical framework, which will be used for further empirical studies into this domain.**

Keywords-smart decision-making; smart cities; big data; sensors; analytics.

I. INTRODUCTION

This paper presents an analytical framework for smart or (intelligent) decision making in the context of smart cities. The framework is based on a review of literature, white papers and news sources covering the topic, as well as empirical data from a study on air quality monitoring. The analytical framework shows areas in need of further study and forms the basis for future research projects.

Smart decision-making uses a systematic approach to data collection and applies logical decision-making techniques instead of using intuition, generalizing from experience, or trial and error.

"Smart cities" is a multifaceted concept and has been defined in many different ways; more than 100 definitions of smart cities have been analyzed by the International Telecommunication Union (ITU)'s focus group on smart sustainable cities [1][2]. The mandatory requirement for smart cities is to improve quality of life and achieve sustainable development (economic, social, and environmental) through the use of Information and Communications Technology (ICT) and intelligence [3]. Definitions emphasized the technological aspect of a smart city as being "a technologically interconnected city" or Internet of Things (IoT) using big data is promoted to achieve the efficiency and intelligence in managing cities' resources [4][5].

A smart city is a city that is characterized as an "instrumented, interconnected, and intelligent" [6]-[8]. This can be conceptualized as three layers, as shown in Figure 1.

These characteristics are enabled by use of ICT, which constitute the heart of a smart city [9]. The "instrumentation" layer does data acquisition through sensor-based systems that provide real-time data through sensors, meters and cameras, but also from social media and open data sources. The instrumentation layer enables capturing and filtering data from various sources for timely response. The inputs from the instrumentation layer are integrated and transformed into event-related information at the "interconnection" layer to provide rich insights for decision-making. The interconnection layer provides all forms of collaboration among people, processes, and systems to enable a holistic view supporting decision-making. At the "intelligence" layer, business intelligence and analytics are applied to the information provided by the interconnection layer and other city-relevant data and, then, the analyzed information is visualized to understand the city requirements and city policies, hence, make informed decisions and take actions. The intelligence layer is focused on deep discovery, analyses, and forecasting. These three layers that build up the smartness in a smart city are constructed by smart technology solutions and ICT infrastructure, such as IoT, big data, and Internet.

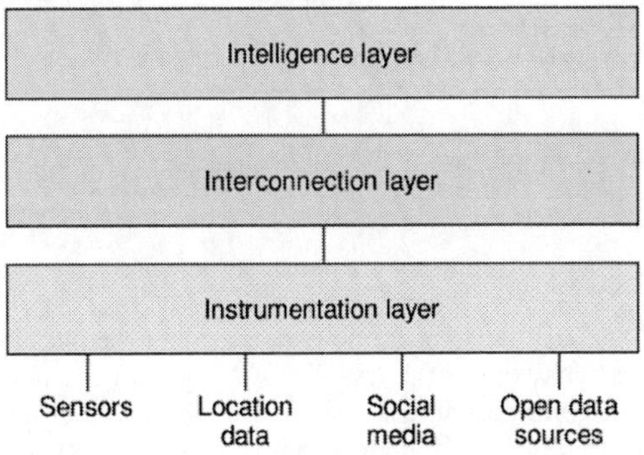

Figure 1. Three-layer model.

Regarding the intelligence layer that is concerned with decision-making, a review of studies on smart city and decision-making resulted in nine articles. This indicates that smart city and decision-making is an area that deserves further investigation on how to make a big impact from big data [10].

In this paper, we elaborate on smart or intelligent decision-making in the context of smart cities. Smart decision-making relies on data and analytics to make better decisions. By using autonomous systems, the decisions can be implemented in real time. Human intervention can be reduced to oversee the decisions and take over if the system is malfunctioning.

The main focus of this paper is on the instrumentation layer, and the data sources used by this layer. The data is refined through the interconnection layer and processed by the intelligence layer to enable decision-making. The three-level model provides a systematic approach to collecting facts and applying logical decision-making techniques, instead of generalizing from experience, intuition (guessing), or trial and error.

The rest of the paper is structured as follows: Section 2 discusses methodology. Section 3 focuses on the instrumentation layer, including identification of common data sources. Section 4 describes some selected smart city application areas. Section 5 presents our analytical framework. Section 6 contains our conclusion, some limitations, and ideas for future work.

II. METHODOLOGY

The purpose of this paper is to begin exploring how typical application areas of smart cities use, analyze and visualize data. Data analysis and visualization is essential for decision-making and intelligence in smart cities [6]-[8]. However, our literature review reveals little research in this area.

Figure 2 shows how data is analyzed and visualized. The analytics typically stores data for future use, e.g., for predictions. The visualization is used for human decision-making.

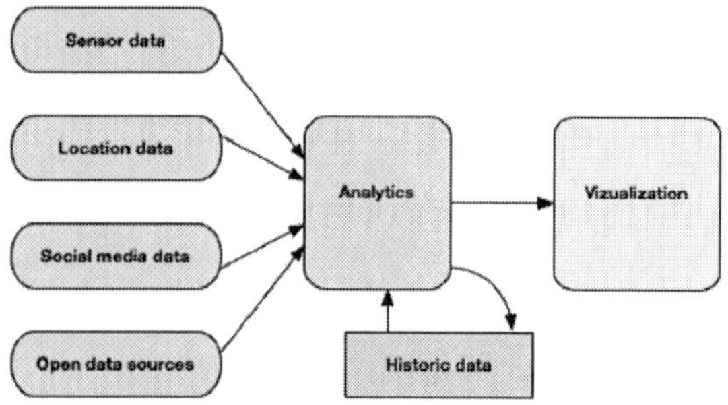

Figure 2. From data to decisions.

Thus, an analytical framework outlining the possible data sources, analytical and visualization techniques could be a valuable contribution to decision-making, as well as for future studies in this domain. Our research question for this study is "*Which data sources are applicable to the different application areas of smart cities*?"

Data collection was done through several iterations. Initially, we planned on conducting this study as a pure literature review. However, there are few studies of this area so far. We were only able to identify nine research papers (referenced in Table 1), using the search phrases "smart city" and "decision-making" in the title. Thus, we had to rely on additional data sources and conduct a document analysis of industry white papers, as well as industry, technology and regular news sources. In addition, we applied existing empirical data from a previous study on air quality monitoring.

This exploratory approach led us to three themes, which we summarize in Section 3, Table 1. Further, the examined news sources and white papers identified eight application areas of data analysis in smart cities; parking, speed monitoring, public transport, traffic, environmental monitoring, energy management, waste handling, and crime prevention. For analysis, we have applied literature, findings from the air quality monitoring study, as well as data from industry to map potential data sources for each of the eight categories. This allowed us to create an initial framework of data sources for the eight identified categories.

III. DATA FOR DECISION-MAKING

At the instrumentation layer, data for decision-making may originate from many different sources. Laney [11] defines big data as data having high volume, high velocity and/or high variety. High volume refers to large amounts of data demanding both specialized storage and processing. High velocity refers to streams of real-time data, e.g., from sensor networks or large-scale transaction systems. Finally, high variety is about dealing with data from different sources having different formats.

Big data may originate from sensors. Another important source for big data is the world-wide-web. Web mining can be used to retrieve unstructured data (text) related to everyday events happening in a city. In this context social media, such as Facebook and Twitter can provide information about problems and citizen sentiments. Many government organization and private companies offer open data sets online that can be used for analysis and decision- making.

Marr [12] argues that the real value of big data is not in the large volumes of data itself, but in the ability to analyze vast and complex data sets beyond anything we could ever do before. Due to recent advances in data analysis methods and cloud computing, the threshold for using big data has diminished.

A. *Sensors*

Sensors and sensor networks are important for smart decision-making. Sensors provide real time information about weather, traffic, air quality, energy consumption, water consumption, and waste. Data from sensor networks are structured and easy to process. According to Cambridge dictionary, the word "sensor" means a device that is used to record that something is present or that there are changes in something. IoT is an infrastructure with interconnected units that may among other things act as sensor platforms. Botterman [13] defines IoT as:

"A global network infrastructure, linking physical and virtual objects, through the exploitation of data capture and communication capabilities. This infrastructure includes existing and evolving Internet and network developments. It will offer specific object-identification, sensor and connection capability as the basis for the development of independent federated services and applications. These will be characterized by a high degree of autonomous data capture, event transfer, network connectivity and interoperability". (p.12).

B. Location data

Location data places an object in a specific position. Location is important both for stationary and mobile objects. For mobile objects, location data comes from the Global Positioning System (GPS) or from triangulation of radio signals, e.g., belonging to a mobile network.

C. Social media

Another possible data source for smart decision-making is social media. Social media has been defined differently among scholars [14]. However, we adopt the definition by Kaplan and Haenlein [15]: "Internet-based applications that build on the ideological and technological foundations of Web 2.0, and that allow the creation and exchange of User Generated Content" (p.62).

Data retrieved from social media will mostly be unstructured (text, images, video), but also structured meta-data providing additional information, e.g., tags containing author, content type, title, date/time and location. Unstructured data from social media may provide insight in the perceptions and sentiments of smart city citizens.

D. Open Data Sources

Open data is data that can be freely used, reused and redistributed by anyone - subject only, at most, to the requirement to attribute and share alike. Open data has the following characteristics [16]:

- Availability and access: The data must be available as a whole and at no more than a reasonable reproduction cost, preferably by downloading from the Internet. The data must also be available in a convenient and modifiable form.
- Reuse and redistribution: The data must be provided under terms that permit re-use and redistribution.
- Universal participation: Everyone must be able to use, re-use and redistribute - there should be no discrimination against fields of endeavor or against persons or groups.
- Interoperability: The ability to interoperate - or intermix - different datasets (i.e., one piece of open material contained therein can be freely intermixed with other open materials).

E. Decision-making in Smart Cities

In the context of smart city, decision-making has been given less attention in the literature; Google Scholar found nine articles discussing decision-making in smart cities (See Table 1). The nine articles investigated various aspects of the three layers described earlier.

Studies related to interconnection layer have highlighted various collaboration aspects that are important for smart cities. Ojasalo and Tähtinen [17] proposed a model of an open innovation platform for public sector decision-making in a city. The authors identified three different kinds of relationships that are present and partly interwoven in open innovation platforms (i.e., governing, sparring, and collaboration). The proposed model helps organizing the three types of relationships of an innovation platform with the city's decision-making and external actors, by combining different decision-making cultures between the public and private sector.

TABLE I. MAPPING LITERATURE TO SMART CITY LAYERS

Ref.	Instrumentation layer	Interconnection layer	Intelligence layer	Others
[17]		X		
[18]			X	
[19]			X	
[20]			X	
[21]	X			
[22]	X			
[23]	X	X	X	
[14]				X
[22]				X

At the intelligence layer, Eräranta and Staffans [18] discussed knowledge creation and situation awareness in collaborative urban planning practice, and how digitalization changes it. The authors argued that smart city planning is not only a data-driven super linear scaling practice, but an integrative and collaborative learning process facilitated by face-to-face interaction, advanced analyses and visualizations of available data, ongoing processes, and local history and stories. The authors brought in collaboration at the intelligence layer.

At the intelligence layer, Passe et al. [19] attempted to understand human behavior and decision-making about the built environment within an expanding range of spatial, political, and cultural contexts. The authors emphasized the importance of participation by a broad range of stakeholders in making decisions for the future of smart cities. The authors argued for the need to consider social dynamics in addition to building-occupant interactions, which requires investigating multiple scales and types of data to create new methodologies for design and decision-making processes. This approach moves data collection, analysis, design, and decision-making away from hierarchical relationships and utilizes the expertise of all stakeholders.

Also at the intelligence layer, Honarvar and Sami [20] talked about the various sensors embedded in different places of smart cities to monitor and collect data about status of cities. Mining such data to extract valuable knowledge creates a challenge because various sources of data in smart cities are big, independent, heterogeneous and no semantic is integrated and annotated to them. The authors proposed an approach to leverage linked open data and semantic web technologies, data mining mechanisms, and big data processing platforms.

At the instrumentation layer, Khan et al. [21] emphasized the role of citizen participation as an important data source for social innovation and co-creating urban regeneration proposals through innovative IT systems. Those IT systems can use open government data, visualize urban proposals in 3D models and provide automated feedback on the feasibility of the proposals. Using those IT systems as a communication platform between citizens and city administrations offers an integrated top-down and bottom-up urban planning and decision-making approach to smart cities. In the same line, Foucault and Moulier-Boutang [22] proposed a governance model called "Smart City – organological". The model consists of an adaptive device built around a differentiation of smart sensors and tags to improve human decision-making. The device is taking into account both "physical sensors" and "economic and social sensors" to capture the explicit or implicit needs.

At the level of the three layers, Nathali Silva et al. [23] worked on an area of concern regarding the continuous growth of the complex urban networks that is challenged by real-time data processing and intelligent decision-making capabilities. The authors proposed a smart city framework based on big data analytics. The framework operates on three levels: instrumentation layer (data generation and acquisition level), interconnection layer (collecting heterogeneous data related to city operations, data management and processing level), and intelligence layer (filtering, analyzing, and storing data to make decisions and events autonomously, and initiating execution of the events corresponding to the received decisions).

Some other topics were studied in the literature, e.g., Gang and Yang [24] studied design issues to improve the intelligence layer of city emergency management. Kurniawan et al. [25] investigated the development and optimization possibilities of Makassar City smart operation room. The authors used fuzzy multi-criteria decision-making to illustrate the project priority rank and further to determine the alternative optimal option in conducting the project.

IV. Application Areas

In order to understand more about data sources and decision-making techniques, we have examined some common application areas connected to smart cities (See Table 2). The first four areas are connected to transport:

- Smart parking
- Speed monitoring
- Smart public transport
- Smart traffic

The rest of the application areas represent the broadness of the smart city concept:

- Environmental monitoring
- Energy management
- Waste handling
- Crime prevention

A. Smart Parking

Smart parking assists drivers to find a nearby parking spot. The information provided to the driver can have many different forms, from public displays placed next to roads to mobile apps directing the driver to a free parking spot [26][27][28].

Smart parking data is sensor based. Outdoor sensors may be magnetic sensors located in capsules embedded in the ground, detecting the presence of a car, or cameras detecting if a parking spot if free or not. Indoor parking spots may instead have infrared or ultrasound sensors to detect the presence of cars.

Smart parking may also include payment solutions based on mobile phone apps, use of SMS, or dedicated devices like SmartPark™ [29]. The payment solutions may give the user the opportunity to pay for time actually used instead for paying for a fixed time period.

Smart parking sensor data provides information to city planners and car park companies about the occupancy of parking spots over time. The collected information can be used for decision-making regarding the construction of new parking sites, and to decide on pricing.

B. Vehicle Speed Monitoring

Vehicle speed monitoring warn drivers about their driving speed. The idea is to make drivers slow down if they are driving at excess speed. Speed monitoring units may be stand-alone, but state-of-the art units are connected to the Internet and provides real-time information on driving habits [30].

Several technologies have been demonstrated for vehicle speed monitoring including use of cameras, RADAR, LIDAR, and underground sensors [31]. A measurement station is put in a fixed position, and excess speed is shown on a display device.

Another approach is to install mandatory units in all vehicles. The driver can then be alerted of excess speed directly by the unit. Such units can also upload speed data through some kind of network [31].

(Some GPS devices warns the driver about excess speed, but such data are not relevant, since data are not uploaded for use by traffic authorities.)

Vehicle speed monitoring data can be used by traffic authorities and police to decide on traffic control locations. Such data can also be used to implement speed reducing measures, such as speed bumps or traffic lights, and even control such measures in day-to-day operations.

C. Smart Public Transport

One important measure to reduce environmental footprint is to reduce car traffic, in particular the use of private cars. A well-developed public transport infrastructure can be an incentive to reduce traffic load. Car owners may also be discouraged by the toll charges or congestion charges implemented in many cities.

Smart public transport uses technology to provide public transport users with a better user experience [32]. Use of sensors and GPS technology can provide real time data on arrivals and departures of public transport vehicles.

Smart ticketing solutions may use smart cards or mobile phones equipped with Near Field Communication (NFC) to make ticketing more efficient from a user point of view [33].

Online route planners may help users choose the most efficient route from one location to another location.

The data collected from smart public transport can be used for real time situation reports and may also be used by public transport planners to adjust time tables, change routes, create new routes, and adjust fares.

Social media may be mined to find citizen perceptions of the public transport system.

D. Smart Traffic

Smart traffic is about using technology to ensure more efficient traffic management. Traffic management may use road lights and signs to optimize traffic flow in real time [34]. Commercial car navigation systems provide information on fastest and shortest routes. Some navigation systems collect information from other cars real time to detect bottlenecks and provide alternative routes.

Data may come from sensors embedded in the roads. The most common technique is to detect traffic density by embedding coils under the road surface to pick up passing cars. Alternatives are to use camera or radar technology to detect traffic.

Data may also come from the vehicles themselves, by using radio transmissions or a cellular network [35].

The data collected may be used by the city-administration for road-planning, adjusting intervals of traffic lights. Data can also be used by transport companies to decide on best schedules for pick-ups and deliveries.

Mining social media may provide some information on how citizens experience traffic situation.

E. Air Quality Monitoring

Monitoring air quality and other environmental parameters is important for decision-making. Some cities are enforcing restrictions on traffic when pollution levels reach a certain threshold [36].

In most cases, the air quality monitoring is done by fixed monitoring stations located throughout the city, but may also be done by mobile handheld units, or units installed in cars.

Measurements include gases: CO, CO_2, NO_X, and dust particles, normally 2,5 PM and 10 PM.

Collected data can be combined with other data sources, e.g., meteorological data, to provide real time situation reports and make forecasts for future pollution levels. Data can be visualized and be made available to the public. Such data is particularly valuable for citizens with respiratory problems.

Social media may be mined to find citizen perceptions of air quality.

F. Energy Management

Smart power grids contribute to better energy management and reduced environmental footprint. An essential part of the smart grid is smart meters. Smart meters are devices that continuously measure power consumption of households and buildings. Household appliances can communicate with the smart meter to schedule activities when the load on the power grid is low. The smart meters also communicate with energy management systems to optimize energy consumption [37]. Buildings can also take part in energy production through use of solar panels and other alternative energy sources.

Sensor data may be combined with location data and open data sources to make forecasts. Social media data plays a minor role in the context of energy management.

G. Waste Handling

Sorting waste materials for recycling has become common practice. Garbage collection can be improved by only collecting waste when necessary. "Intelligent" waste containers can report their state of becoming full and get included in the schedule of trucks collecting the waste [38][39][40].

The recycling process itself can provide valuable data on types and amounts.

Data from the waste collection process can be used to decide on container size and pick-up patterns. Data may also be made public to show timeliness and efficiency of the waste handling, from garbage collection through recycling.

Social media data mining can be used to detect sentiments about the garbage collection.

H. Crime Prevention

Crime prevention is about allocating police resources to areas most likely to get victims of crime, but also to find out where to establish surveillance by video cameras and other means.

Data used for crime prevention will mostly be former reported crimes combined with open data sources, e.g., demographic data, property values, income levels of citizens, street light coverage, etc. [41][42].

Social media may be mined to find indications of unreported crimes.

TABLE II. MAPPING APPLICATIONS TO DATA SOURCES

Application areas	Data sources			
	Sensor data	**Location data**	**Open data**	**Social media data**
Smart parking	X	X	-	-
Speed monitoring	X	x	-	-
Smart public transport	X	X	-	x
Smart traffic	X	x	-	x
Air quality monitoring	X	x	X	x
Energy management	x	x	x	-
Waste handling	X	X	-	x
Crime prevention	-	X	X	x

X major data source
x minor data source
- not applicable

V. ANALYTICAL FRAMEWORK

The purpose of our case studies is to examine data sources and methods used to analyze data. Seven examples of smart city applications show the importance of sensor data, but also the opportunities of using open data sets combined with sensor data to improve analysis and enable forecasting. Web mining and social media has limited use in these cases, but can be used to alert city administration about potential problems and sentiments.

The crime prevention case does not rely on sensor data, but on reports of crimes. Combining different open data sets can provide better insight related to crime prevention. The reported crimes can provide patterns, but combining data sets may shed light on underlying factors, like property values, incomes, absence of street lights and other factors.

In this study, we have examined mainly the instrumentation and interconnection layers, finding a set of data sources used in different smart city application areas, as shown in Table 2.

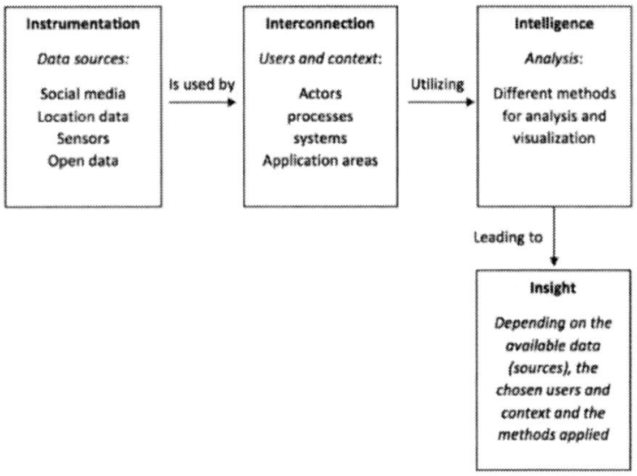

Figure 3. Analytical framework.

When we map these finings to the three layers in Table 1, we have the outline of an analytical framework as shown in Figure 3. The resulting analytical framework may guide future research efforts in the field. Existing research and white papers provide examples of how big data can be applied for decision making, but as our framework shows, there is a need for both synthesizing existing studies as well as conducting new empirical studies to create a roadmap for decision-makers. This roadmap would list relevant data sources and analytical techniques for different users and contexts. The framework forms a possible foundation for future studies in this area.

VI. CONCLUSION, LIMITATIONS AND FUTURE WORK

In this paper, we used eight typical application areas of smart cities to explore their use of data. We examined relevant data sources, and their use. Data collected from sensors are very important for seven of the chosen application areas. Open data is often a valuable supplement to collected data. In some cases, location data are combined with other types of data. Social media data mining may play a role to show user perceptions and sentiments.

The collected data need to be processed and analyzed to be useful for decision-making.

Data will often be used for automatic decision-making. In seven of the chosen application areas, we found examples of data used for automatic decision-making:

- Smart parking: Automatic update of displays directing drivers to available parking spots.
- Speed monitoring: Automatic regulation of traffic lights, or even photographing speeding vehicle to issue a speed ticket.
- Smart public transport: Automatic updates of screens showing arrival and departure times.
- Smart traffic: Automatic control of signs and traffic lights to redirect traffic.
- Air quality monitoring: Automatic alerts to citizens in the areas, through signs or SMS service.
- Energy management: Automatic start of household appliances, based on grid load.
- Waste handling: Automatic updates of garbage truck schedules based on amount of garbage in each container.

For strategic and long-term decisions done by humans, the results of the processing and analysis need to be visualized in a meaningful way, e.g., through graphs, bar charts, pie charts often combined with a map or even embedded in a Geographic Information System (GIS) front-end.

This paper studied application areas of smart cities to examine use of (big) data. The study is not exhaustive. We used example of application areas from literature, but as "smart cities" have ambiguous definitions, we may have overlooked some areas. Further, as we had to start examining white papers from industry it is likely we have missed interesting data from relevant sources even after our rigorous search in the most well-known big data/analytics companies.

In the future, we intend to investigate how data can be analyzed using different methods and techniques, so that we can present a comprehensive model of possible combinations of data sources, actors and contexts, and analytical techniques.

REFERENCES

[1] ITU-T. *Focus Group on Smart Sustainable Cities.* [Online]. Available from: https://www.itu.int/en/ITU-T/focusgroups/ssc/Pages/default.aspx [retrieved: 2018.02.04].

[2] ITU-T Focus Group on Smart Sustainable Cities. "*Smart sustainable cities: An analysis of definitions.* [Online]. Available from: https://www.itu.int/en/ITU-T/focusgroups/ssc/Documents/website/web-fg-ssc-0100-r9-definitions_technical_report.docx, 2014. [retrieved: 2018.02.04].

[3] A. Vesco and F. Ferrero, Eds., Handbook of Research on Social, Economic, and Environmental Sustainability in the Development of Smart Cities. IGI Global, pp. xxv-xxxi, 2015.

[4] Deloitte. *Smart Cities: Big Data.* [Online]. Available from: https://www2.deloitte.com/content/dam/Deloitte/fpc/Documents/services/systemes-dinformation-et-technologie/deloitte_smart-cities-big-data_en_0115.pdf, 2015. [retrieved: 2018.02.04].

[5] F. Bonomi, R. Milito, P. Natarajan, and J. Zhu, "Fog Computing; A Platform for Internet of Things and Analytics," in Big Data and Internet of Things: A Roadmap for Smart Environments, N. Bessis and C. Dobre, Eds. Studies in Computational Intelligence, 546, Springer, pp. 169–186, 2014.

[6] V. Albino, U. Berardi, and R. M. Dangelico,. "Smart Cities: Definitions, Dimensions, Performance, and Initiatives," Journal of Urban Technology, 22(1), pp. 3–21, 2015.

[7] IBM. *A vision of smarter cities.* [Online]. Available from: https://www-03.ibm.com/press/attachments/IBV_Smarter_Cities_-_Final.pdf, 2010. [retrieved: 2018.02.04].

[8] M. Kehoe et al., Smarter Cities Series: A Foundation for Understanding the IBM Approach to Smarter Cities, IBM Redguides for Business Leaders, pp. 1–30, 2011.

[9] E. Negre and C. Rosenthal-Sabroux, "Smart Cities: A Salad Bowl of Citizens, ICT, and Environment," in Handbook of Research on Social, Economic, and Environmental Sustainability in the Development of Smart Cities, A. Vesco and F. Ferrero, Eds., IGI Global, pp. 61-78, 2015.

[10] H. Chen, R. H. L. Chiang, and V. C. Storey, "Business Intelligence and Analytics: From Big Data to Big Impact," MIS Quartely, 36(4), pp. 1165–1188, 2012.

[11] D. Laney, 3D Data Management: Controlling data, volume, velocity, and variety. Technical Report. META Group, 2001.

[12] B. Marr, Big Data – Using Smart Big Data Analytics and Metrics to Make Better Decisions and Improve Performance. John Wiley & Sons Ltd, 2015.

[13] M. Botterman, Internet of Things: An Early Reality of the Future Internet, Workshop Report, European Commission, Information Society and Media Directorate, 2009.

[14] J. W. Treem and P. M. Leonardi, 7 Social Media Use in Organizations Exploring the Affordances of Visibility, Editability, Persistence, and Association. Communication Yearbook, 36, pp. 143–189, 2012.

[15] A. M. Kaplan and M. Haenlein, "Users of the world, unite! The challenges and opportunities of Social Media," Business Horizons, 53(1), pp. 59–68, 2010.

[16] Open Knowledge International. *Open Data Handbook.* [Online] http://opendatahandbook.org/guide/en/what-is-open-data/ [retrieved: 2018.02.04].

[17] J. Ojasalo and L. Tähtinen, "Integrating Open Innovation Platforms in Public Sector Decision Making: Empirical Results from Smart City Research," Technology Innovation Management Review, 6(12), pp. 38–48, 2016.

[18] S. Eräranta and A. Staffans, "From Situation Awareness to Smart City Planning and Decision Making," Proceedings of the 14th International Conference on Computers in Urban Planning and Urban Management (CUPUM 2015), J. Ferreira and R. Goodspeed, Eds., Paper 197, pp. 1-17, 2015.

[19] U. Passe et al., "Methodologies for Studying Human-Microclimate Interactions for Resilient, Smart City Decision-Making, " Proceedings of the 32nd International Conference on Passive and Low Energy Architecture, P. La Roche and M. Schiler, Eds., pp. 1735-1742, 2016.

[20] A. R. Honarvar and A. Sami, "A Multi-source Big Data Analytic System in Smart City for Urban Planning and Decision Making," International Conference on Internet of Things and Big Data, Doctoral Consortium (DCIT), pp. 32-36, 2016.

[21] Z. Khan et al., "Developing Knowledge-Based Citizen Participation Platform to Support Smart City Decision Making: The Smarticipate Case Study," Information, 8, 47, pp. 1-24, 2017.

[22] J.-P. Foucault and Y. Moulier-Boutang, "Towards economic and social 'sensors': Condition and model of governance and decision-making for an organological Smart City," International Conference on Smart and Sustainable City and Big Data (ICSSC), pp. 106-112, 2015.

[23] B. Nathali Silva, M. Khan, and K. Han, Big Data Analytics Embedded Smart City Architecture for Performance Enhancement through Real-Time Data Processing and Decision-Making. Wireless Communications and Mobile Computing, pp. 1–12, 2017.

[24] L. I. Gang and L. I. Yang, "Construction of Emergency Decision-making Intelligence System Against the Background of Smart City," Journal of Library Science in China, 3(4), 2016.

[25] F. Kurniawan, A. P. Wibawa, Munir, S. M. S. Nugroho, and M. Hariadi, "Makassar Smart City Operation Center Priority Optimization using Fuzzy Multi-criteria Decision-making," 4th International Conference on Electrical Engineering, Computer Science and Informatics (EECSI), pp. 1-5, 2017 .

[26] Smart Parking Ltd. *Company website.* [Online]. http://www.smartparking.com [retrieved: 2018.02.04].

[27] Fybr. *Company website.* [Online]. http://www.fybr.com [retrieved: 2018.02.04].

[28] WorldSensing. *Company website.* [Online]. https://www.worldsensing.com/industries/parking-operators/ [retrieved: 2018.02.04].

[29] SmartPark. *Company website.* [Online] https://smartpark.co.nz [retrieved: 2018.02.04].

[30] C. H. Schaffer, Customer Success Is Key – How a small manufacturer transformed an Internet of Things (IoT) solutions provider and unlocked $2 million is SaaS revenue. (Kindle edition) amazon.com, 2015. [retrieved: 2017.12.01].

[31] G. Kirankumar, J. Samsuresh, and G. Balaji, "Vehicle Speed Monitoring System [VSM] (Using RuBee Protocol)," IACSIT International Journal of Engineering and Technology, Vol. 4, No. 1, pp. 107-110, 2012.

[32] R. M. John et al., "Smart public transport system," International Conference on Embedded Systems (ICES), pp. 166-170, 2014.

[33] P. Chowdhury, P. Bala, and D. Addy, "RFID and Android based smart ticketing and destination announcement system," Advances in Computing Communications and Informatics (ICACCI), pp. 1-5, November 2016.

[34] R. Hawi, G. Okeyo, M. Kimwele, "Smart Traffic Light Control using Fuzzy Logic and Wireless Sensor Network," Computing Conference, London, pp. 450-460, 2017.

[35] K. Kumarmanas, S. Praveen, V. Neema, and S. Devendra, "An Innovative Device for Monitoring and Controlling Vehicular Movement in a Smart City," Symposium on Colossal Data Analysis and Networking (CDAN), pp. 1-3, 2016.

[36] A. Florea et al., "Low cost mobile embedded system for air quality monitoring - air quality real-time monitoring in order to preserve citizens' health," Sixth International Conference on Smart Cities, Systems, Devices and Technologies, (SMART), IARIA, pp. 5-12, 2017.

[37] C. Meinecke, Potentiale und Grenzen von Smart Metering. Springer. 2015.

[38] F. Folianto, Y. S. Low, W. L. Yeow, "Smartbin: Smart Waste Management System," IEEE Tenth International Conference on Intelligent Sensors, Sensor Networks and Information Processing (ISSNIP), pp. 1-2, 2015.

[39] A. S. Wiaya, Z. Zainuddin, and M. Niswar, "Design a smart waste bin for waste management," 5th International Conference on Instrumentation, Control, and Automation (ICA), pp. 62-66, 2017.

[40] H. Poddar, R. Paul, S. Mukherjee, B. Bhattacharyya, "Design Of Smart Bin For Smarter Cities," International Conference on Innovations in Power and Advanced Computer Technologies [i-PACT2017], IEEE Press, pp. 1-6, 2017.

[41] F. Wang, Ed., Geographic Information Systems and Crime Analysis, Idea Group Publishing, 2005.

[42] S. Chainey and J. Ratcliffe, GIS and Crime Mapping, Wiley, 2005.

Preconditions for the Structural Deployment of (Digital) Technology for Healthcare in a Participatory Society

Validation of methodological and practical challenges

Martijn Hartog
eSociety Institute
The Hague University of Applied Sciences
The Hague, The Netherlands
m.w.hartog@hhs.nl

Bert Mulder
eSociety Institute
The Hague University of Applied Sciences
The Hague, The Netherlands
a.w.mulder@hhs.nl

Abstract—**This article describes the threats and practical challenges of diversity in target groups and the models for the adoption for technology for healthcare in The Netherlands. With the sense of urgency created by the participatory society, in which citizens are responsible for their own direction for health, government and the quality of life within The Netherlands, digital solutions become more and more part of the society and relationship between citizens and governmental bodies. Its mere focus is on validation methodological approaches and practical challenges in order to stimulate vitality and healthy independent living for a longer period of time.**

Keywords-healthcare; digital technology; quality of life; participatory society; methodology; practical challenges.

I. TARGET GROUPS IN A DIGITAL PARTICIPATORY SOCIETY

The development of the participation society makes 'own direction' and 'own responsibility' increasingly important for residents. The described interventions are aimed at taking care for health and quality of life yourself. However, equipping citizens for the participation society is not self-evident. Because 'own direction' and 'own responsibility' of citizens presuppose that they act themselves, they must have sufficient motivation, knowledge, skills and potential for action. In that context, the Scientific Council for Government Policy [1], introduces the term 'doing ability' next to 'thinking ability'. The Council states that citizens need 'doing ability' to be able to set goals, to formulate steps and implement them. Most online sources now facilitate knowledge and thereby stimulate 'thinking ability'. Stimulating 'doing ability' is something else. For example, there are initiatives to make road maps available online [1], for living a longer vital, health and independent life.

According to the National Social Media Research, the use of social media is intensive: ten million Dutch people use WhatsApp and Facebook, of which 80% daily; more than seven million use YouTube, of which 20% daily [2]. In 2016, The Netherlands has the relatively largest number of online shops [3], and the largest number of online therapies. This high degree of digitization of the Netherlands and the Dutch people means that the active use of digital solutions at the urban level is a real possibility - the use of the internet is spread so widely that all population groups of all ages (up to 75 years) are online. That creates opportunities but also challenges. Recent research by Stichting Pensioenfonds Zorg en Welzijn (PGGM) among 30,000 professional care workers shows that only 10% of them use digital resources in their work. In the consulting rooms of general practitioners, patients do not very often suggest e-health [4].

The next section describes the possible models of technology. Section three will threat the methodological and practical challenges in the applicability of health models focussing on participation. The final section will conclude on the awareness and motivation of possible solutions.

II. MODELS FOR THE ADOPTION OF TECHNOLOGY

The literature describes a number of models for the adoption of technology. Some are too general (such as Venkatesh's Technology Acceptance Model) while others focus more on organizations [5]. Such models do not focus on the practical introduction into a larger urban environment. An interesting model for gaining insight into aspects of adoption is the 'eHealth Value Framework for Clinical Adoption and Meaningful Use' (in short: 'eHealth Value Framework') of the University of Victoria in Canada [6]. Originally developed to map the aspects of adoption of Electronic Patient Dossier (EPD) systems, it is sufficiently generic to get an overview of the aspects that are important in stimulating a diversity of applications on an urban scale.

In addition to implementation itself, there is a broader context for the deployment of technology at the urban level, an interest that extends beyond the current project. For the stimulation of health in urban environments, literature refers to its own character in size, density, diversity and complexity and advocates a tailor-made approach that does justice to this [7]. In 'theory of smart cities', Harrison and Donnelly [8] describe how new technology creates 'making the invisible visible' and thereby creates the possibility for a new way of (more real time) thinking about the city.

Harrison and Donnelly [8] also propose to think in an 'urban information model' as a way to structure and classify the many different types of information contained or flowing in the network. This makes it possible to describe urban development's statistically not only on a macro level, but also through new observations and new models on a more individual level. The recent collaboration between the Municipality of The Hague and the Statistics Netherlands (CBS) as an Urban Data Centre, is in line with this notion. Another possibility is the Extramural Leids Academic Network (ELAN) data network, in which General Practitioners information is made available anonymously.

III. VALIDATION: METHODOLOGICAL AND PRACTICAL CHALLENGES

The project explicitly aims to validate the results to show whether and to what extent the chosen interventions contribute to longer independent living. Here, a number of methodological challenges are described that must be taken into account when realizing this ambition.

Validating single applications is easier than validating the effect of multiple applications at the urban level. Validating is easiest in the situation where an individual client uses a single intervention for a clearly defined (health care) need, e.g., added value of digital glucose meters in diabetes sufferers, use of apps in people with sleep problems or home automation in elderly people who live independently. Much evidence-based research focuses on such direct applications.

Validating the effect of multiple applications on an urban scale is more complex. This complexity arises from the multidimensional character of concepts such as: 'longer independent at home', 'quality of life', 'social strength' or 'vitality'. In addition, this complexity is created by the scale of applications: longer independent at home is not only realized by individual users but equally strongly in groups of users such as client systems, or in the social networks of neighbourhoods or districts. In both cases, the number of factors that contribute to an improvement in quality is often much greater than a single (digital) technology that is used. A direct causal relationship is particularly difficult to demonstrate. This, therefore, requires new or different analysis techniques and smart use of epidemiological analyses. The dimensions of positive health try to give new frameworks in which measurements can be made. This is in line with the observation that the added value as determined by professionals is not always that of users. For example, there is no evidence-based long term research for the effect of online 'brain training', but it does noticeably contribute to the feeling of rehabilitation patients that they 'do something' and for that reason it is sometimes included in the treatment regime (personal communication from a rehabilitation doctor and -psychologist). It is a fundamental question, which is also described by the Council for Public Health and Society [9].

With regard to e-health, the National Competence Centre for eHealth (Nictiz) outlines the dilemma in its report 'Evaluation of eHealth technology: in the context of policy', the broad definition of e-health, the diverse nature of the stakeholders and their different need for evidence [10]. In the report, several methodological approaches are described in which way an investigation could be designed. This includes a number of specific methodological solutions (such as the use of Social Return on Investment (SROI) [11]). There are other statistical possibilities (such as the N = 1 method [12]) to be able to determine validity in complex situations, but these can only be taken into account when determined which form of validation is required: when is healthy and vitally longer independent living successful?

IV. CONCLUSION

A number of conclusions can be drawn:

- There are existing and available digital and technological solutions that can support independent living for longer.
- A reasonable number of those solutions have been examined and found useful.
- Each user has his or her own needs that can and must be customized.
- The urban scope of the project creates a number of specific challenges.
- Validation requires attention through methodological complexity.

The fact that digital solutions deliver added value is in itself insufficient precondition for success. The project is preferred to encourage the use of 'existing' solutions among residents, which means that such solutions not only have to 'exist', but that citizens must know them and be able to use them. This presupposes the creation of awareness and motivation, making knowledge and skills available and facilitating the possible solutions to actually purchase, pay, install and use:

- Awareness - information via media, professionals and organizations.
- Motivation - indicating added value.
- Knowledge - explanation and courses tailored, direct and online.
- Skills - instruction, direct and online.
- Practical use - financing, installation, management and maintenance.

For example, the use of digital solutions is always supported by a coherent set of activities. If these are not present and use is still desirable, compensation will have to be made for this. Three scenarios can be distinguished when stimulating digital solutions:

- Stimulating a broad approach aimed at the use of digital solutions in general by the entire population.
- Stimulating a specific target group to use specific digital solutions.

- Or a mix of both.

REFERENCES

[1] Scientific Council for Government Policy (WRR), "Knowing is not doing. A realistic perspective on self-reliance", The Hague, April 2017.

[2] Newcom Research, "National Social Media Research", 2016.

[3] Kompass Benelux, retrieved December, 2017 from <https://retailtrends.nl/news/44759/nederland-heeft-relatief-meeste-webwinkels>

[4] Smarthealth, "Newsroom: onderzoek 30.000 zorgmedewerkers, 10% past eHealth toe", retrieved January 2018 from <http://www.smarthealth.nl/2017/01/31/ehealth-mhealth-nieuws-week-5-2017/>

[5] T. Greenhalgh et al., "Diffusion of innovations in service organizations: systematic review and recommendations", Milbank Q, vol. 82, no. 4, pp. 581–629, 2004.

[6] University of Victoria, Human and Social Development, "eHealth Value Framework for Clinical Adoption and Meaningful Use", retrieved January 2018 from <http://ehealth.uvic.ca/methodology/models/valueFramework.php>

[7] D. Vlahov et al., "Urban as a determinant of health", Journal of Urban Health, vol. 84, no. 1, pp. 16–26, 2007.

[8] C. Harrison and L. Donnelly, "A Theory of Smart Cities", *Proceedings of the 55th Annual Meeting of the ISSS, Hull, UK*, pp. 1–15, 2011.

[9] Council for Public Health and Society (RVS), "Without context no evidence – on the illusion of evidence based practice in health care", retrieved December 2017 from <https://www.raadrvs.nl/publicaties/item/zonder-context-geen-bewijs>

[10] National Competence Centre for eHealth (Nictiz), "Evaluation of eHealth technology: in the context of policy", May 2017; Esteves, A. M. et al., "Social impact assessment: the state of the art", Impact Assessment and Project Appraisal, vol. 30, no. 1, pp. 34–42. 2012.

[11] R. Millar and K. Hall, "Social Return on Investment (SROI) and Performance Measurement", Public Management Review, vol. 15, no. 6, pp. 923–941, 2013.

[12] E. Schuringa et al., "The N = 1 statistics behind the patient follow system at FPC Dr. S. van Mesdag". GGzet Wetenschappelijk, vol. 2, pp. 70–77, 2011.

IoT Digital Enterprise Platform based on Cloud Metering and Big Data Services

Kalthoum Zaouali
National School of
Engineering of Tunis-ENIT
University Tunis El Manar
Tunis, Tunisia
e-mail:
zaoualikalthoum@gmail.com

Mohamed Lassaad Ammari
Department of Electrical
and Computer Engineering
Laval University
Quebec, Canada
e-mail:
mlammari@gel.ulaval.ca

Amine Choueib
Chifco Company
Tunis, Tunisia
e-mail:
amine.chouaieb@chifco.com

Ridha Bouallegue
Innov'Com Laboratory
Higher School of Communication
Carthage University
Tunis, Tunisia
e-mail:
ridha.bouallegue@supcom.rnu.tn

***Abstract*—The use of Internet of Things (IoT) results in more connected and smarter environments, while enabling energy consumers and providers to reduce costs thanks to advanced metering management. The demand of data traffic has recently grown as fast as the number of connected devices and smart-meters. In order to meet the explosive growth of big-data, new technologies are required to improve the existing metering infrastructure. In this paper, we propose an open IoT digital enterprise platform for smart-metering applications focused on allowing open access to big-data and cloud services. We investigate the main issues and challenges of smart-metering big-data analytics as a free business service. Referring to some major information technology architectures, we introduce our suggested architecture that can help enterprises deploy their specific big-data framework for smart objects, smart-meters, smart-homes, smart-buildings, smart-factories, smart-cities or smart-grids. This is done by adding smart-metering cloud services based on an advanced metering infrastructure.**

Keywords–Big-data; Cloud; Digital enterprise; IoT; Smart-metering.

I. INTRODUCTION

Since software is the center of technology, the industrial revolution ought to open up new horizons, dimensions, challenges, opportunities and business areas, thus freeing data and benefiting from it. Companies attempt to cut costs and make software an enabler for future success and for an industrial and digital economic revolution [1].

We are still in the early stage of realizing the vastness of customers' requirements like the infinity universe, the hugeness of data size, their deep knowledge and their streaming. We aim to broaden the data dimension as an infinite space (data from varying sources) and to ensure the data management coming from every physical signal, social media and satellite [2]. Accordingly, our new challenge is to deal with such a huge volume of knowledge available in digital platforms. The data processing is no longer enough; it is necessary to access this vast amount of data and transform the mining of information in order to create new values for companies, customers, societies, as well as the environment [3]. Therefore, connecting people, indoor and outdoor with technology in real-time helps customers conceive their business life and make sense of its impact on the economy, the society and the environment [4].

It is essential to draw customers' attention to new services they do not know and have not utilized yet and then fit them to their own objectives and requirements. For instance, controlling the energy generation according to demand is a major issue and a main objective of energy vendors [5]. The target of the offered service is to help this specific customer align an energy demand and supply it through a cloud-based IoT platform offering the opportunities of networking, processing and storing data, based on scalability, flexibility, and performance capabilities [6] [7].

Smart-meters data satisfy the basic aspects characterizing big-data as volume, variety and velocity (3'V) [8]. The big-data technology provides a real-time analysis and deals with consuming smart-meters data correlated with weather information and other readings of external behavior [9]. Using big-data capabilities, we have to manage the huge amount of data captured by smart-meters in frequent time periods. Hence, advanced analytics allows companies to extract the available information and knowledge from the massive volume of data to gain new insights reinforcing their proactivity in taking analytical actions. Smart-metering big-data management using analytical algorithms may achieve substential values needed to make decision for monitoring and prevention [10] [11]. A key to decision-making improvement is the variety of data sources.

A manufacturing company hopes to improve maintenance and ensure real-time supervision and predictive analytics for factory productivity optimization and business and operation visibility [12]. Our contribution is to propose an open IoT digital enterprise platform for smart-metering applications based on open standards to support and integrate different devices and platforms in order to help energy markets to bring solutions quickly. The advanced smart-metering systems can be integrated with an IoT platform and big-data cloud services ensuring advanced smart-meters data management and analytics. Indeed, our suggested platform can optimize the production factory capacity by predicting failures and consumption based on the correlations between historical data and real-time data.

The remainder of this paper is organized as follows. Section II discusses the background and issues of smart-metering big-data management. In Section III, we mention some leading big-data reference architectures. Our proposed IoT big-data digital enterprise platform for smart-metering applications is described in Section IV. Finally, conclusion and some future work are drawn in Section V.

II. BACKGROUND AND ISSUES OF SMART METERING BIG-DATA MANAGEMENT

Several IoT standards and protocols have been elaborated to construct IoT devices satisfying some requirements, such as batteries' power supply and limiting in-memory processing capacity where there is no continuous power supply. Major IoT systems offer private services that are exclusively allocated to particular vendors [13]–[16]. In addition, some IoT systems are unable to be extended or combined due to their limited capabilities of sensing, memory storage, or analytics functionalities [17]–[19]. The IoT protocols have to optimize these constrains and to provide an open smart space infrastructure connecting every type of vendors' devices with a free access to open data, open standards, and open cloud services [20]–[22]. Our challenge is to provide an open smart-metering big-data system with a free access to open big-data and cloud services.

In [23], a green IoT platform was developed to demonstrate the interest of open data and open Application Programming Interfaces (APIs) for a public IoT smart-city infrastructure to maximize the Swedish society benefits. A lot of business applications are based on the IoT technology. Now, the urgent requirements for enterprises are acquisition, storage management, and processing the huge amount of heterogeneous data generated by large distributed sensor networks [24] [25]. The IoT data in cloud platforms are characterized by multi-source high heterogeneity data acquired from different distributed sensors including structured, unstructured and semi-structured data types. The communication between IoT devices in a smart environment generates a massive volume of real-time and stream data. As a consequence, its multi-dimension processing in cloud needs a flexible scalability of storage, and compression schemes [26] [27]. Supported by wireless sensor networks, the IoT, cloud computing, social networks and smart engines, big-data systems can offer many benefits for business enterprises and societies by potentially acquiring, storing, analyzing a huge amount of data. Big-data can provide and implement an ecosystem of convergence and collaboration based on various services across several fields, networks and business processes and rules [28]–[31]. Cai et al. [32] proposed a functional IoT framework based on big-data storage systems in cloud computing and defined the big-data processing modules' capabilities and challenges for several industrial applications. This IoT storage system surfs cloud platforms and tracks significant information to enable any enterprise to assure inter-operation, intelligence and innovation. Ahmad et al. [33] envisioned the basic role of integrating the IoT with social networking to understand human behaviors using big-data analytics based on the Hadoop ecosystem. The authors suggested a system architecture for real-time big-data processing and analytics consisting of IoT devices, social IoT servers and applications. This social IoT system is able to improve users' behaviors by providing feedbacks sent as an alert message. The human dynamics theory describes real-time human behaviors in social areas offering an intelligent environment.

Big-data offer the possibility to find most similar users who have similar interests and tastes utilizing an item-based collaborative filtering technique that calculates the similarity between items and recommends the item which an active user previously preferred. This technique has been successfully applied in several IoT contexts to analyze IoT devices and services and to exploit the relations between users, resources and recommended tags. Mashal et al. [34] put forward a hyper-graph model for an IoT service recommendation that would facilitate the integration of IoT services that users would expect. The recommendation problem was modeled as a tripartite graph with hyper-edges among users, devices, and services. The correlations between these three parties defined the heterogeneous relationships and behaviors in the IoT service recommendation. To ensure open and secure services in IoT scenarios with lower processing load and to remotely configure fine-grained access control policies, scalability and flexibility, Simone Cirani et al. [35] suggested an IoT-Oauth-based-Authorization-Service (OAS) architecture targeting IoT applications based on HTTP and on constrained application protocol services to offer an open authorization framework integrated using the OAS.

Several companies are competing for developing advanced energy management solutions based on cloud platforms, smart-metering technologies, and advanced analytics tools. The authors in [36], provided an overview of the big-data background, components and technologies including the Hadoop framework, the data center, cloud computing and the IoT. Thus, the advanced analytics techniques will play a crucial role in the future smart-metering progress that will require efficiency in stream data analytics, integrating advanced machine-learning capabilities and the competence of decision-making techniques [37].

However, there are major issues for the smart-meters big-data management. The first issue is the storage of the huge "volume" of data. High availability is realized by ensuring data reading and data writing anywhere, avoiding joins and transactions, and tolerating redundancies, such as Hadoop Distributed File Systems (HDFS), highly distributed databases (NOSQL), and NewSQL databases. The second issue concerns "velocity" and massive data processing. As a solution, it is recommended to move processing to data using the in-memory processing standard. The third big-data issue results in the "variety" property of data collection from different sources, formats and types that can provide homogenization and data fusion. Different types of original data, such as smart-meters measurement data, weather data, geographical information data and marketing data, are collected and extracted from different sources, such as connected smart- meters, Web applications, relational back-end systems, data stream, social media and other forms of data-sets in the cloud. Data should be extracted and stored in distributed structures in memory waiting their processing. A new structure of the NoSQL database is created to manage the storage and retrieval of unstructured collected data with various format extensions. The "Spark" technology is used for "batch" and "μ-batch" processing, "storm" for streaming processing, and schema-less "NoSQL" databases as a distributed platform for massive data storage based on HDFS, using the Map-Reduce architectural pattern for parallel calculation of large data-sets, which is a programming model focusing on a simple hardware to perform complex jobs. Data processing is divided in many small activities run in different clusters and in the YARN framework for scheduling jobs and managing cluster resources [38] [39].

Due to the big-data 3'V, it is necessary to devise a new architecture for smart-meters big-data management with new technology features according to new demands. Before introducing our proposed architecture, let us investigate some big-data reference architectures developed by the major IT vendors.

III. Big-data Reference Architectures

The construction of the proposed smart-metering big-data analytics architecture is referred to various big-data reference architectures defined as consistent conceptual models. These technical references can provide an understanding of big-data structures, services and capabilities to explore our specific big-data system interoperability, extendibility, and portability. We will discuss surveyed big-data platforms, such as Microsoft, Oracle, IBM and SAP to perceive the main components of a big-data architecture.

A. IBM Big-Data Architecture

The process of big-data analytics starts with data discovery and exploration. Data are figured from different sources to incorporate and discover a new data value. The IBM big-data platform [40] [41] allows indexing, searching and navigating diverse sources of big-data represented in different formats (structured, semi-structured, or unstructured). To generate the accurate analytics applications, processing data and complex analytics models are executed both to deprive replicated data and to provide fast and multiple analytic iterations. For an effective analysis, a game-changing analytics platform provides tools for the exploration, analysis, management and storage of both structured and unstructured data. Real-time analysis can offer the opportunity of analyzing data as it is being generated insight to make decisions and actions before storing data on physical disks. The volume of the data stream depends on the dynamical variation in time. Therefore, the big-data platform should be able to manage these increasing volumes of data as well as to analyze data in motion. To consume efficiently the big-data, the accelerators as tool sets and the library of analytical packages are used to reduce the analytic cycle time acquired to discover and process data, develop and deploy models, and analyze and visualize results. The data management is focused on data integration and governance including data quality, security, life cycle management, and master data management capabilities. These big-data requirements can be managed by Hadoop (unstructured data), stream computing (real time data), and data warehouse (structured data).

B. Microsoft Big-Data Architecture

The key components of the Microsoft big-data architecture [42] are data sources, data transformation, data infrastructure, and data usage. Big-data are collected from various sources classified by the 3'V big-data characteristics. Then, independent functional blocks are implemented to ensure data transformation and pre-processing, such as the collection block to pile up data from different types and forms, the aggregation block to aggregate collected data into a larger collection, the matching block to enhance information about each object, and the data mining block for both descriptive and predictive analytics. Transformed data are stocked in metadata to be utilized by multiple data infrastructure services. Under development, the results can be provided in various data usage formats, granularity and under different security considerations.

C. SAP Big-Data Architecture

The SAP big-data reference architecture includes ingestion, storage & processing, and consume components. Additional components are also added to manage the data life cycle, the infrastructure, security and data governance [43]. The SAP High-speed Analytical Appliance (SAP HANA) platform provides several advantages, such as serving big-data features to the business customers in order to improve their applications. The ingestion key component of the SAP HANA platform permits the acquisition of various data types (structured, semi-structured, and unstructured data) from different sources (sensors, relational back-end systems, data stream, social media, etc.). For data processing and storage functions, the SAP big-data platform investigates the potential between transactional and analytical processing abolishing the computing time latency by using in-memory computing and an engine for real-time simulation and planning cycles. Other components, such as graph engine and spatial or location data processing are also integrated in the SAP big-data architecture. An integrated Hadoop platform supports the treated data through a distributed file system. The Hadoop real-time platform offers to users efficient data processing and storage as benefits of real-time processing. The consume component supports the analytics functions, such as dashboards, reports, exploration, charting and visualization, and applications including machine learning and predictive and native HANA applications & services. Within the SAP HANA platform, the infrastructure management provides the security and life cycle management of a data object using common services for data security and governance.

D. Oracle Big-Data Architecture

The Oracle big-data reference architecture proposes an incorporated big-data platform based on Hadoop and Oracle NoSQL database technologies to acquire, process, and analyze big-data using decision-making techniques. As an infrastructure service component, the Oracle big-data architecture suggests hardware, a network, connectivity, an operating system, virtualization, storage, security, and management. Data sources support the data streams, the NoSQL /Tag-values and the relational and unstructured databases. The information-provisioning component provides big-data processing including information discovery, data conversion and massive unstructured data and stream processing. The data warehouse and the operational database are used to store processing data. The information analysis component recovers the analytics applications as descriptive (reporting / dashboards) and predictive analytics (statistical analysis, semantic analysis, data mining, text mining, in-DB Map/Reduce and spatial) [44].

E. Discussion

Through the review of big-data architectures and the descriptive Table I, several components can identify big-data system. As a result, we can consider three common ones. The first one is the big-data management and storage component which investigates (i) structured, semi-structured and unstructured data, (ii) volume, variety, velocity and variability, and (iii) SQL and NoSQL and distributed file systems. The second one is the big-data analytics and application interfaces studying descriptive, predictive, spatial, real-time, interactive and batch analytics, besides reporting and dashboards. The third component is the big-data infrastructure as well as in-memory data grids, operational databases, analytic databases, relational databases, flat files, content management systems and horizontal scalable architectures. Other components can support these three main components, namely the user usage, landscape management, the modeling & life cycle management, and the data governance as security, compliance, etc.

Our architecture is in fact based on these three components. In addition to what is existing in big-data platforms, we have integrated the cloud-based IoT big-data platform and the smart-metering cloud services.

IV. Proposed IoT Big-data Digital Enterprise Platform

Our integrated architecture is built to involve data management and help IT organization to develop applications that support digital transformations with analytic capabilities. It helps to free IT data and to spend the majority of data sources for more consumed operations. The proposed IoT big-data digital enterprise platform, represented by Figure 1, allows the access to a leverage data in many ways, such as digital data management, flexible data management or incorporated integration.

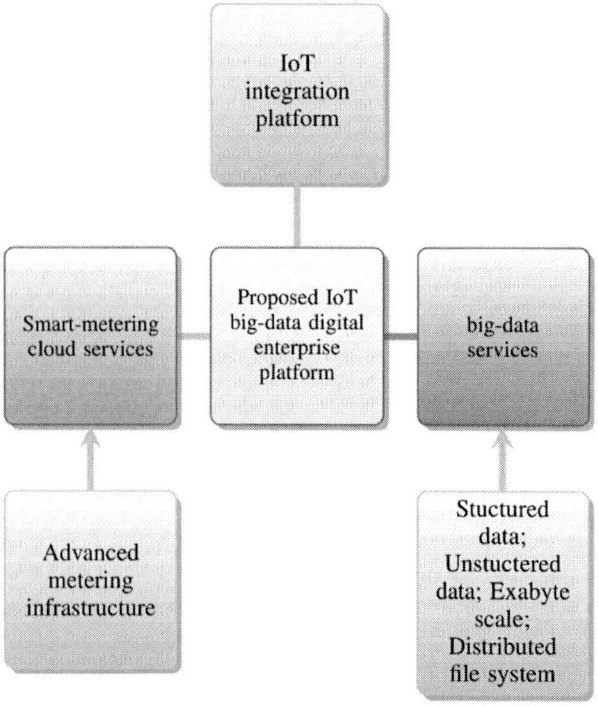

Figure 1. Proposed IoT big-data digital enterprise platform for smart-metering applications

Indeed, our suggested platform permits data processing and access to handle the huge amount of data collected by widely deployed sensors, as well as a solution for the advanced smart-meters to interact with the platform. For real-time data, such as weather data, data from sensors and smart-meters, production and consumption data, we propose to use external data storage in an effort to measure energy consumption. With our solution, we can increasingly manage the data from a variety of sources that can be real-time data from databases which contain user details, user energy consumption data, user equipment, weather API or collected data from social media. The big challenge is to take control of the data stream and to use it in more efficient ways. This can be realized through connectivity up in the space with big-data.

In our architecture, we can filter and extract the data in which we need in other tasks, like machine learning, and to train and test our intelligent system. Also, we analyze the collected data and clearly present it to facilitate understanding our data content in charts and graphics formats in order to support rapid and confident decisions. Our integrated IoT big-data platform imports multi-store tables, which enables new partition tables in memory or file systems. It is possible to move across the stores using big queries or in-memory processing capabilities. The solution allows providers or customers easy access to applications. The different cloud services offered by our integrated platform are shown and described in Figure 2 . This integrated platform consists of IoT

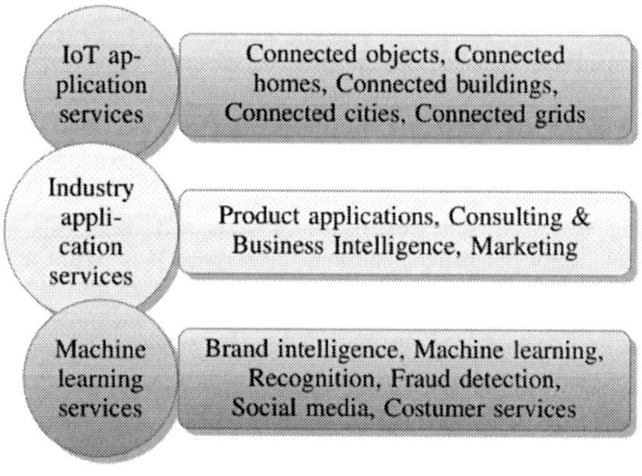

Figure 2. Cloud-based IoT big-data platform services

applications services for connected objects, homes, buildings, cities and grids in order to ensure industry application services like product applications, consulting and business intelligence, and marketing. The advanced analytics of these services is done by integrating machine learning services, such as brand intelligence, machine learning, recognition, fraud detection, social media and customer services, so as to attribute new values to big-data.

Figure 3 illustrates in detail our proposed IoT big-data digital enterprise platform that ensures many functionalities:

- Smart devices and gateways: To substantiate and manage several connected devices and smart-meters based on different communication protocols. The Advanced Metering Infrastructure (AMI) uses various networking models to manage and control the communication with the smart-meters in the field. The AMI head end system involves software applications and databases for smart-meters data acquisition and storage. It promises real-time monitoring of the AMI network of smart-meters. Furthermore, the AMI head end system enables utilities to take advantage of the accurate measurement devices available in the market in order to measure customers' energy consumption, configure smart-meter parameters, and check these smart devices via firmwares.
- IoT integration platform: To apply analytics at the edge and to enable low-latency decision making.

TABLE I. BIG-DATA REFERENCE ARCHITECTURES

	Big-data management and storage components	Big-data analytics and application interface components	Big-data infrastructure components	Supporting components
IBM architecture	*** Data Integration and Governance:** Data integration, Data quality, Life cycle management, Master data management; *** Accelerators**; *** Hadoop**; *** Stream computing**; *** Data warehouse**.	*** IBM big-ata platform:** - Visualization and discovery: Indexing, Searching, Navigation; - Application development; *** Analytics applications:** - Business Intelligence /Reporting; - Exploration/ Visualization; - Industry applications; - Functional applications; - Content analytics - Predictive analytics.	*** IBM big-data platform:** - Systems management	*** Data Integration and Governance:** - Security
Microsoft architecture	*** Data Sources:** - Data Objects; Variety; Velocity; Volume; *** Data transformation:** - Collection; Aggregation; Matching.	- Data Minning: Descriptive / Predictive.	*** Data infrastructure:** - Conditioning - Storage & Retrieval; *** Security**; *** Management**	***Data Usage:** - Network Operators / Telecom; - Industries/Businesses; - Government: Health & Fin. Institution; - Academia.
SAP architecture	*** SAP HANA in-memory:** - Transactional; Analytical; Graph; Spatial; Text & Social media processing; Extended storage; Planning and simulation; *** Hadoop Platform:** Processing & storage; *** Modeling & Life cycle management**.	*** Analytics:** Exploration, Dashboards, Reports, Charting, Visualization; *** Applications:** - Machine learning & predictive; - Native HANA applications & services; *** Modeling & Life cycle management**.	*** SAP HANA platform:** - Data objects management; - Data objects security.	- Landscape management; - Modeling & Life cycle management - Data governance: Security; Compliance; Audits.
Oracle architecture	*** Information provisioning:** - Data processing and discovery: Information discovery; Conversion data; Processing of massive unstructured and streaming data; - Operational database and data warehouse; *** Data sources:** Distributed file system; Data streams; NoSQL/Tag-value; Relational; Faceted unstructured; Spatial/relational.	*** Information analytics:** - Descriptive analytics: Reporting; Dashboards; - Predictive analytics: Statistical analysis; Data minning; In-DB Map-Reduce; Semantic analysis; Text mining; Spatial	*** Infrastructure services:** Hardware; Operating System; Storage; Security; Network; Connectivity; Virtualization; Management.	

- Big-data management, advanced analytics & machine learning: To enable deep business insights and business intelligence by integrating IoT big-data processing and advanced analytics utilizing machine learning and business rules for decision making.
- Big-data enterprise applications: To permit the integration with enterprise and IoT big-data analytics applications in order to ensure the development and deployment of enterprise applications with low complexity, authorization, data security and data governance.

Our proposed architecture is based on open standards to support and integrate different devices and platforms in order to help energy markets to bring solutions quickly. Every enterprise can freely select its IoT technology protocols. The advanced smart-metering systems can be integrated with IoT platform and big-data cloud services ensuring advanced smart-meters data management and predictive analytics. The big-data analytics can facilitate the integration and deployment of various utility applications.

V. CONCLUSION AND FUTURE WORK

Big-data will be more and more a complex distributed data environment with dynamic acquisition necessitating a strong orchestration of the inter-process and its dependencies. Software enablement for enterprises will make a sense of big-data orchestration by providing not only an available storage system but also to integrate the big-data analytics in their concerning business framework. In this paper, we have proposed an open IoT enterprise platform for smart-metering applications focused on allowing an open access to big-data and cloud services. This platform seems to be a digital enterprise platform offering both specific services deployed in the cloud and external open services offered by big-data to improve and satisfy the customers' requirements. Furthermore, several issues, such as scalability, flexibility, interoperability and availability should be considered in this digital enterprise platform. As a future work, we will study some aspects of our proposed architecture, such as multi-vendor interoperability, low cost, low power consumption and security, which require considerable attention from energy communities.

ACKNOWLEDGMENT

This work is part of a PhD thesis supported by "PASRI-MOBIDOC" Project financed by the EU, "Chifco" company, "Innov'COM" laboratory, and National School of Engineering of Tunis-ENIT.

REFERENCES

[1] S. Fang and et al., "An integrated system for regional environmental monitoring and management based on internet of things," IEEE Transactions on Industrial Informatics, vol. 10, no. 2, May 2014, pp. 1596–1605.

[2] S. K. Sowe, T. Kimata, M. Dong, and K. Zettsu, "Managing heterogeneous sensor data on a big data platform: Iot services for data-intensive science," in Proc. IEEE 38th Int. Computer Software and Applications Conf. Workshops, Jul. 2014, pp. 295–300.

[3] J. Yin, Y. Tang, W. Lo, and Z. Wu, "From big data to great services," in Proc. IEEE Int. Congress Big Data (BigData Congress), Jun. 2016, pp. 165–172.

[4] Y. Nakamura and et al., "Novel heterogeneous computing platforms and 5g communications for iot applications," in Proc. IEEE/ACM Int. Conf. Computer-Aided Design (ICCAD), Nov. 2017, pp. 874–879.

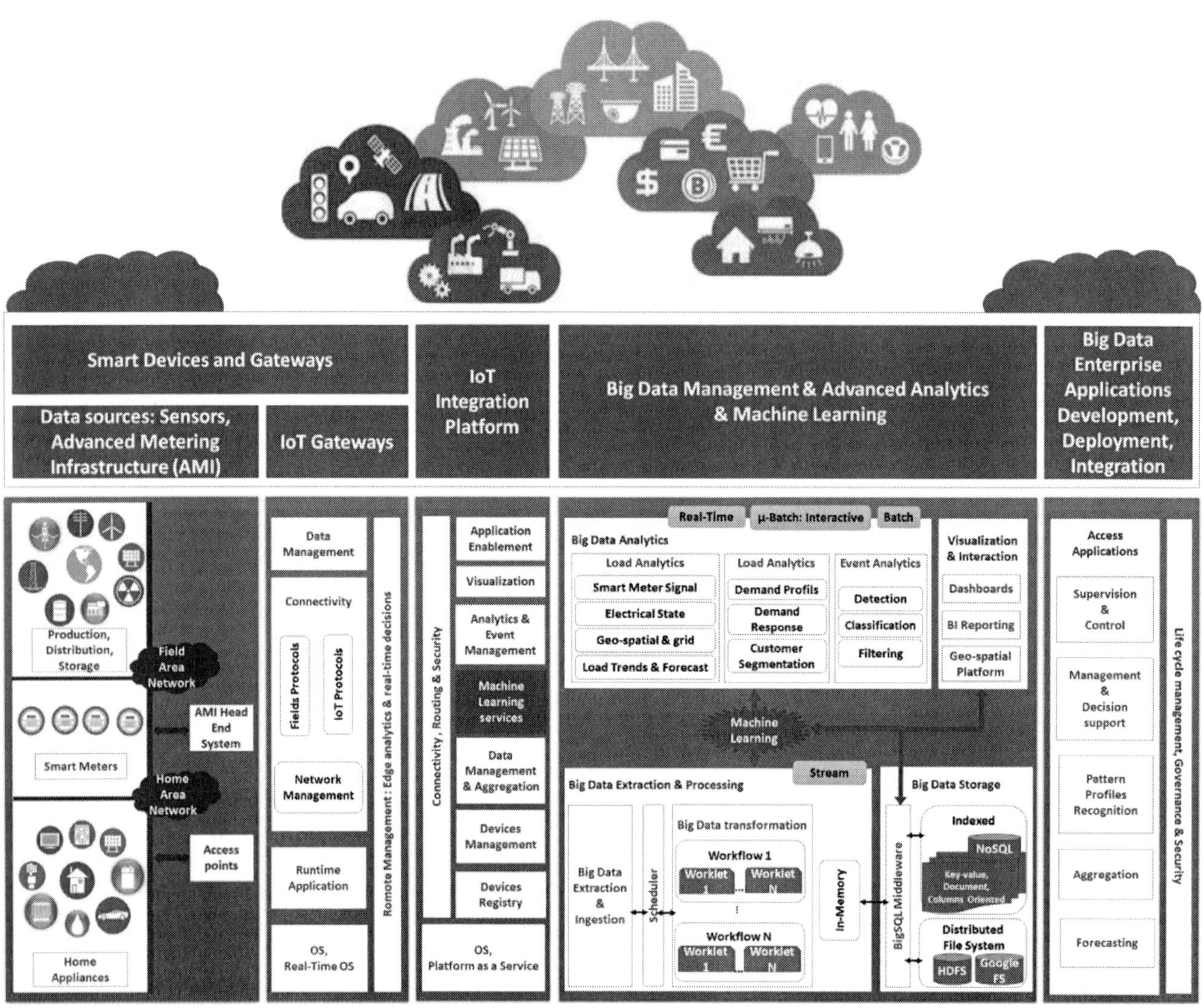

Figure 3. Detailed description of the suggested IoT big-data digital enterprise architecture based on smart-metering services

[5] F. D. Garcia, F. P. Marafo, W. A. d. Souza, and L. C. P. d. Silva, "Power metering: History and future trends," in Proc. Ninth Annual IEEE Green Technologies Conf. (GreenTech), Mar. 2017, pp. 26–33.

[6] D. de la Bastida and F. J. Lin, "Openstack-based highly scalable iot/M2M platforms," in Proc. Physical and Social Computing (CPSCom) and IEEE Smart Data (SmartData) 2017 IEEE Int. Conf. Internet of Things (iThings) and IEEE Green Computing and Communications (GreenCom) and IEEE Cyber, Jun. 2017, pp. 711–718.

[7] N. Dalcekovi, S. Vukmirovi, I. Kovacevi, and J. Stankovski, "Providing flexible software as a service for smart grid by relying on big data platforms," in Proc. Computers and Communications (ISNCC) 2017 Int. Symp. Networks, May 2017, pp. 1–6.

[8] J. Hu and A. V. Vasilakos, "Energy big data analytics and security: Challenges and opportunities," IEEE Trans. Smart Grid, vol. 7, no. 5, 2016, pp. 2423–2436.

[9] X. Peng, M. Bessho, N. Koshizuka, and K. Sakamura, "Dcrdl: An energy management rule definition language for context-based device control in smart buildings," in Proc. IECON 2015 - 41st Annual Conf. of the IEEE Industrial Electronics Society, Nov. 2015, pp. 000 279–000 285.

[10] S. Singh and A. Yassine, "Mining energy consumption behavior patterns for households in smart grid," IEEE Transactions on Emerging Topics in Computing, vol. PP, no. 99, 2017, p. 1.

[11] T. Y. Ku, W. K. Park, and H. Choi, "Iot energy management platform for microgrid," in Proc. IEEE 7th Int. Conf. Power and Energy Systems (ICPES), Nov. 2017, pp. 106–110.

[12] F. Tao and Q. Qi, "New it driven service-oriented smart manufacturing: Framework and characteristics," and Cybernetics: Systems IEEE Transactions on Systems, Man, vol. PP, no. 99, 2017, pp. 1–11.

[13] W. Dai and et al., "Tnguard: Securing iot oriented tenant networks based on sdn," IEEE Internet of Things Journal, vol. PP, no. 99, 2018, p. 1.

[14] G. Marques, N. Garcia, and N. Pombo, "A survey on iot: Architectures, elements, applications, qos, platforms and security concepts," in Advances in Mobile Cloud Computing and Big Data in the 5G Era. Springer, Jan. 2017. [Online]. Available: http://dx.doi.org/10.1007/978-3-319-45145-9-5

[15] J. Chin, V. Callaghan, and I. Lam, "Understanding and personalising smart city services using machine learning, the internet-of-things and big data," in Proc. IEEE 26th Int. Symp. Industrial Electronics (ISIE), Jun. 2017, pp. 2050–2055.

[16] J. Tian, A. Chin, and M. Karg, "Digital services in the automotive industry," IT Professional, vol. 18, no. 5, Sep. 2016, pp. 4–6.

[17] H. El-Sayed and et al., "Edge of things: The big picture on the

integration of edge, iot and the cloud in a distributed computing environment," IEEE Access, vol. PP, no. 99, 2017, p. 1.

[18] D. Yuan, J. Jin, J. Grundy, and Y. Yang, "A framework for convergence of cloud services and internet of things," in Proc. IEEE 19th Int. Conf. Computer Supported Cooperative Work in Design (CSCWD), May 2015, pp. 349–354.

[19] A. Zimmermann and et al., "Digital enterprise architecture - transformation for the internet of things," in Proc. IEEE 19th Int. Enterprise Distributed Object Computing Workshop, Sep. 2015, pp. 130–138.

[20] Y. Mehmood and et al., "Internet-of-things-based smart cities: Recent advances and challenges," IEEE Communications Magazine, vol. 55, no. 9, 2017, pp. 16–24.

[21] B. Levin, "Big data ecosystem reference architecture," Microsoft Corporation, 2013.

[22] E. Biliri and et al., "Big data analytics in public safety and personal security: Challenges and potential," in Proc. Technology and Innovation (ICE/ITMC) 2017 Int. Conf. Engineering, Jun. 2017, pp. 1382–1386.

[23] B. Ahlgren, M. Hidell, and E. C. H. Ngai, "Internet of things for smart cities: Interoperability and open data," IEEE Internet Computing, vol. 20, no. 6, Nov. 2016, pp. 52–56.

[24] S. Kubler and et al., "Open iot ecosystem for sporting event management," IEEE Access, vol. 5, 2017, pp. 7064–7079.

[25] S. K. Sharma and X. Wang, "Live data analytics with collaborative edge and cloud processing in wireless iot networks," IEEE Access, vol. 5, 2017, pp. 4621–4635.

[26] W. Shi and S. Dustdar, "The promise of edge computing," Computer, vol. 49, no. 5, 2016, pp. 78–81.

[27] L. Baresi, L. Mottola, and S. Dustdar, "Building software for the internet of things," IEEE Internet Computing, vol. 19, no. 2, 2015, pp. 6–8.

[28] W. Tan, Y. Fan, A. Ghoneim, M. A. Hossain, and S. Dustdar, "From the service-oriented architecture to the web api economy," IEEE Internet Computing, vol. 20, no. 4, 2016, pp. 64–68.

[29] C. Hochreiner, S. Schulte, S. Dustdar, and F. Lecue, "Elastic stream processing for distributed environments," IEEE Internet Computing, vol. 19, no. 6, 2015, pp. 54–59.

[30] X. Xu, Q. Z. Sheng, L.-J. Zhang, Y. Fan, and S. Dustdar, "From big data to big service," Computer, vol. 48, no. 7, 2015, pp. 80–83.

[31] J. M. Schleicher, M. Vögler, S. Dustdar, and C. Inzinger, "Application architecture for the internet of cities: Blueprints for future smart city applications," IEEE Internet Computing, vol. 20, no. 6, 2016, pp. 68–75.

[32] H. Cai, B. Xu, L. Jiang, and A. V. Vasilakos, "Iot-based big data storage systems in cloud computing: Perspectives and challenges," IEEE Internet of Things Journal, vol. PP, no. 99, 2016, p. 1.

[33] A. Ahmad, M. M. Rathore, A. Paul, and S. Rho, "Defining human behaviors using big data analytics in social internet of things," in Proc. IEEE 30th Int. Conf. Advanced Information Networking and Applications (AINA), Mar. 2016, pp. 1101–1107.

[34] I. Mashal, O. Alsaryrah, and T. Y. Chung, "Analysis of recommendation algorithms for internet of things," in Proc. IEEE Wireless Communications and Networking Conf, Apr. 2016, pp. 1–6.

[35] S. Cirani, M. Picone, P. Gonizzi, L. Veltri, and G. Ferrari, "Iot-oas: An oauth-based authorization service architecture for secure services in iot scenarios," IEEE sensors journal, vol. 15, no. 2, 2015, pp. 1224–1234.

[36] A. F. Mohammed, V. T. Humbe, and S. S. Chowhan, "A review of big data environment and its related technologies," in Proc. Int. Conf. Information Communication and Embedded Systems (ICICES), Feb. 2016, pp. 1–5.

[37] D. Alahakoon and X. Yu, "Smart electricity meter data intelligence for future energy systems: A survey," IEEE Trans. Ind. Informat., vol. 12, no. 1, 2016, pp. 425–436.

[38] Z. Asad, M. A. R. Chaudhry, and D. Malone, "Greener data exchange in the cloud: A coding-based optimization for big data processing," IEEE Journal on Selected Areas in Communications, vol. 34, no. 5, 2016, pp. 1360–1377.

[39] A. Farahzadia, P. Shams, J. Rezazadeh, and R. Farahbakhsh, "Middleware technologies for cloud of things - a survey," CoRR, vol. abs/1705.00387, 2017. [Online]. Available: http://arxiv.org/abs/1705.00387

[40] P. O'Sullivan, G. Thompson, and A. Clifford, "Applying data models to big data architectures," IBM Journal of Research and Development, vol. 58, no. 5/6, 2014, pp. 18–1.

[41] P. J. Meaney and et al., "The ibm z13 memory subsystem for big data," IBM Journal of Research and Development, vol. 59, no. 4/5, 2015, pp. 4–1.

[42] Y. Demchenko, C. Ngo, and P. Membrey, "Architecture framework and components for the big data ecosystem," Journal of System and Network Engineering, 2013, pp. 1–31.

[43] R. K. Chawda and G. Thakur, "Big data and advanced analytics tools," in Colossal Data Analysis and Networking (CDAN), Symposium on. IEEE, 2016, pp. 1–8.

[44] J. P. Dijcks, "Oracle: Big data for the enterprise," Oracle white paper, 2012, p. 16.

Carbon Emission Trading for Community Contribution

Ichiro Satoh

National Institute of Informatics
2-1-2 Hitotsubashi Chiyoda-ku Tokyo 101-8430 Japan
Email: ichiro@nii.ac.jp

Abstract—**The reduction of greenhouse gas (GHG), including CO_2 , has been recognized as the task to be solved by the world. This paper presents an approach to enable citizens to use carbon emission credits or allowances for community contribution, e.g., schools and non-profit organizations. It assigns a small amount of carbon emission credits or allowances to RFID tags or barcodes attached to specific products and show how must credits that tag is worth like coupon for mitigating GHG emissions. People, including students, who want to support communities, including schools, collect these tags or barcodes and then redeemed the credits assigned to them to offset the GHG emitted from their communities. The approach was constructed and evaluated with real customers and real carbon credits with real communities.**

Keywords-Carbon emission credit; Carbon emission allowance; RFID tag; Barcode.

I. INTRODUCTION

The reduction of greenhouse gas (GHG), including CO_2 , has been recognized as a common task to be solved by the world. Public organizations, e.g., schools, museums, civil halls, community centers, and local governments, are required to work for public purposes, but they are not avoid to emit greenhouse gases for their activities like commercial activities. For example, schools need to consume energy for lighting and heating in their buildings. Although they should reduce their GHG emissions as much as possible, their missions are to provide people, including local communities and students with services as much as possible. In public sectors, approaches to reducing GHG emitted from communities may be different from those from commercial sectors. This paper proposes an approach to helping public communities, e.g., schools and non-profit organizations, to offset their GHG emissions. The approach assigns a specified amount of carbon emission credits to RFID tags or barcodes attached to specific products and show how must credits that tag or barcode is worth like coupons. People, including students, who support public communities, including schools, collect these tags or barcodes and then redeem the credits assigned to them to offset the GHG emitted from their communities.

This paper proposes an approach to enable citizens to use carbon emission credits or allowances for community contribution, e.g., schools and non-profit organizations, where carbon emission credits or allowances are economical values and can be traded [6]. The key idea behind it is to assign a small amount of carbon emission credits or allowances to RFID tags (or barcodes) attached to specific products by using RFID-tags [8][9], which was a scheme for reducing GHG emissions from the home and individual sectors and offsetting GHG emissions from public sectors, so that tags or barcodes can be worth like coupon for mitigating GHG emissions. People, including students, who want to support communities, including schools, collect these tags or barcodes and then redeemed the credits assigned to them to offset the GHG emitted from their communities. The approach was constructed and evaluated with real customers and real carbon credits with real communities.

The rest of the paper is organized as follows. Section II states the problems that the paper addresses and the requirements of the approach. Section III surveys related work. Section IV presents basic approach outlines the basic ideas of the approach. Section V describes the design and implementation of the approach and Section VI presents our experiences with the approach. Section VII discusses on the approach and Section VIII gives some concluding remarks.

II. PROBLEM STATEMENTS

We briefly outline conventional *carbon emission credits* before explaining our approach. Carbon emission credits are not carbon emission allowances, which are limits on emissions that are lowered over time. A government sets limits on the amount of CO_2 that companies are allowed to emit CO_2 . If a company emits an amount of CO_2 due to their activities below its limit, it can sell the excess capacity, which is the difference between the limit and the amount has emitted, to companies whose emissions are over their limits. They represent a certain volume of absorbed or reduced emissions by different people or organizations that have reduced excessive amount of GHG in the atmosphere in the short- or long-term. For example, developed countries or companies financially or technically support projects that aim to reduce GHG emissions in developing countries. They can, in turn, offset their emissions by credits generated from the projects. These projects might involve installing renewable energy technologies, implementing energy efficiency measures, or removing CO_2 from the atmosphere through carbon sequestration. Emission credits can be traded in voluntary markets to reduce overall GHG emissions while still allowing countries or companies that may have difficulty doing so to have outlets for transition. However, existing carbon emission credits and their trading have several problems:

- Carbon trading is usually provided through electric commerce systems, but existing trading systems are too complicated and difficult for end-users to sell or buy carbon credits for reasons unique to carbon credits. Since carbon credits are tradable, the systems must authenticate whether the creditors that demand credits to be transferred to them are the credits' current owners or their certificating agents. Carbon credits also have specified expiration dates, e.g., one or two years, for institutional reason for carbon credits. The price of the credits is based in part on the validation process and the sophistication of the fund or development company that acted as the sponsor of the carbon project. Therefore, fees for trading carbon credits tend to be expensive, where in Japan, a fee of 6,200 yen (about 72 US dollars) is charged for one carbon credit trading independently of the number of credits. Existing systems allow professional carbon traders to sell or buy large amounts of emission credits.
- The minimal units of existing trading credits are more than one hundred or one thousand tonnes of CO_2 . However, the amount of CO_2 an average person emits throughout his/her life for one year is less than one tonne. Each end consumer product should have less than one kilogram of credits. However, there are currently no approaches to trading small amount of carbon credits, e.g., one gram or one kilogram except for ours. However, each final settlement process in existing approach needs time and effort, because the process needs receive RFID tags, which are physical certificates for carbon credits. The approach proposed in this paper needs to reduce the cost of settlement process.
- Carbon credits can already be traded through e-commerce, but existing trading systems have been designed of professional traders, called *carbon providers* or *carbon agencies*. Since credits are virtual values, it is too difficult and complicated to authenticate whether the stakeholders that claim the credits are the credits' current owners or their certificating agents. Therefore, it almost impossible for communities and end consumers, in additions to small companies and NPOs/NGOs to sell or buy credits. Furthermore, current personal-level carbon emission trading has not been designed for communities. To support communities, carbon emission credits should be easily exchanged within communities.
- Carbon offsetting has gained some appeal mainly among end-consumers in western countries who have become aware and concerned about the potentially negative environmental effects of energy-intensive lifestyles and economies. However, existing schemes for carbon offsetting products assume they only support end-consumers so that they experience problems at companies. They lack any mechanism for transferring the carbon credits linked to the products to the consumers. Instead, dealers or manufacturers, who assign the credits to products, offset the credits on behalf of the consumers of the products. Therefore, the consumers have no chance of owning the credits and they do not know whether the credits have been properly offset by the dealers or manufacturers.

III. Related Work

There have been several attempts for trading small amount of carbon emission allowances instead of carbon emission credits. So, we survey carbon allowances. The notion of carbon emission allowances has been useful in existing schemes such as the European Union (EU) Emissions Trading Scheme (EUETS) for EU countries or similar schemes elsewhere [1]. Several countries, e.g., the U.K. and Ireland, have proposed schemes for carbon emission trading in the home/end user sector to Conferences of the Parties (COP) of the United Nations Framework Convention on Climate Change (UNFCCC). *Personal Carbon Trading* (PCT) is a general term referring to personal versions of *carbon emission trading* in the home/end user sector. The original notion of *Carbon emissions allowances* is an economical approach to reducing the amount of GHG emissions in industrial sector. The allowances are limits, often called *carbon emission caps*, where a government authority first sets limits on the amount of CO_2 that companies are allowed to emit. If a company emits an amount of CO_2 below its limit, it can sell the excess capacity, which is the difference between the limit and the amount of CO_2 that has really emitted, as carbon allowances to companies whose emissions are over their limits. If a company emits an amount of CO_2 beyond its limit, it must pay a penalty or buy carbon allowances from someone so that it can comply with its allowances.

On the other hand, PCTs support carbon emissions allowances allocated to individuals rather than companies. If individuals emit at a level above that permitted by their initial allocation, they need to purchase additional carbon emission allowances from those using less, creating a profit for those individuals who emit at levels below those permitted by their initial allocation. Several researchers and organizations have proposed different kinds of PCT in the last five to ten years.

- *Cap and Share* was originally developed by the Foundation for the Economics of Sustainability (Feasta) [2] and supported the use of fossil fuels. Individuals received certificates from the government and fuel suppliers required corresponding certificates equal to emissions from the use of fossil fuels to sell fuel.
- Personal allowance (PCA) was proposed by Hillman [4] and it was a proposed downstream carbon cap and trade policy instrument suggested for the U.K. There represented a mandatory policy whereby all individuals received an annual carbon emissions budget for their personal use. The PCA scheme only covered emissions under direct personal control, e.g., household energy use (electricity and gas) and private transport (not including public transport).
- Tradable Energy Quotas (TEQs)[3] assumed that individuals would receive certificates and if they used fewer certificates, they could sell their surplus. All fuels and electricity had *carbon ratings* in units. When individuals buy energy, their certificates are deducted according to the amount of CO_2 emitted from the use of that energy.
- Household carbon trading [5] was a yearly carbon emission cap to set for residential energy use based on emissions reduction targets. Allowances are allocated to each household on an equal per household allocation basis via utility service providers who place the allowances in each user's account.
- Tradable transport carbon permit [7] was a cap that was set for emissions from private transport. Allowances were allocated to all individuals to comply for free, but these were not any equal basis. Allowances are transferred to the regulating authority for every purchase of fuel to cover the CO_2 equivalent of a liter of fuel and cancelled. Participants bought and sold permits through intermediates like banks or buy them at gas stations.

Although the concept of PCT was expected to reduce the GHG emissions from homes and individual sectors, existing PCT have several serious problems that must be solved before applying schemes can be applied to the real world.

Since existing PCT has aimed at reducing GHG emitted from energy, i.e., their spending electric power from thermal power plants and refuelling their private cars, they have mismatches with existing carbon emission trading and carbon emission reduction schemes in companies, although reducing GHG emissions is a global issue. For example, suppose that a supermarket sells beverages or mineral water from room temperature shelves in addition to refrigerated shelves to reduce the amount of GHG emitted from electricity for the latter and to obtain surplus carbon emission allowances. When customers intentionally select and buy beverages or mineral water from normal temperature shelves, they should share the surplus allowances with the supermarket. Nevertheless, there is no way to share surplus allowances with supermarkets in existing carbon emission trading schemes, including PCT. Furthermore, existing approaches aimed at personal-level or company-level trading but not community-level.

IV. Basic Approach

Our previous paper [9] enabled a small amount of carbon emission credits or allowances attached to products or services to be transferred to consumers who buy these products or products. The approach proposed in this paper is to enable people to donate their own carbon emission credits/allowances to communities and the communities to mitigate their GHG emissions with the credits/allowances.@It provides communities with a method to collect a volume of RFID tags or barcodes as credits for the rights to claim credits with low costs in addition to the key ideas of our approach.

- The previous approach introduced RFID tags or barcodes as a certificate to claim carbon emission credits or allowances attached to products in in supply chains. It could directly use the RFID tags or barcodes that had already been attached to products.
- The approach proposed in this paper supports a donation of carbon emission credits or allowances to communities to mitigate their GHG emissions by giving the RFID tags or barcodes that are certificates to claim carbon emission credits or allowances.

A. RFID tags/barcodes as certificates in donating carbon emission credits

Whereas the previous approach introduced RFID tags (or barcodes) as certificates for carbon emission credits [8][9], the approach proposed in this paper is designed for certificating carbon emission credits. The former is assigned by the government, but the latter is voluntarily generated by certificated projects to reduce GHG. Therefore, the latter is essentially various. To claim credits dominated by RFID tags (or barcodes), we need to return these RFID tags (or barcodes) to the stakeholders that assigned credits to the tags (or barcodes). RFID tags (or barcodes) can be used as certificates for carbon emission credits. For example, when sellers want to attach carbon offsetting credits to products, they place RFID tags (or barcodes) on them that represent the credits for the products. Therefore, purchasers, who buy the products, tear the RFID tags (or barcodes) from them and return the tags to the sellers (or the stakeholders of the credits). When the sellers receive the RFID tags (or barcodes) from the purchasers, they transfer the credits to any accounts for payments that the purchasers specify. It is difficult to replicate or counterfeit RFID tags (or barcodes) whose identifiers are the same, because their identifiers are unique and embedded into them on the level of semiconductors.

B. Community-based collection/lump-settlement for certificates for carbon credits

When a purchaser has peeked an RFID tag (or barcode) from a product, which might have been attached to a product that he/she purchased, our approach permits the purchaser to resell the tag (or barcode) to others. Instead, the new holder of the tag can claim the credits attached to the tag from the stakeholder of these credits or resell them to someone else. Note that trading or donating RFID tags (or barcodes) corresponds to trading or donating carbon emission credits that can offset GHG emitted from the receivers. To offset GHG emitted from a community, e.g., school and council, according to the Kyoto protocol, holders of tags donate certified credits to the community by giving the RFID tags (or barcodes) assigned to credits to the community. Next, the community donate a volume of credits to the government via a complicated electronic commerce system or carbon agency.

C. Procedure

Figure 1 explains our approach to attach carbon credits to products with RFID tags (or barcodes), which involves seven steps:

1. A seller places an RFID tag (or barcode) on a product (or a volume of products) if the product has no tag.
2. It sets a certain amount of credits for offsets for a product and registers the amount and the identifier of the tag in a database.
3. It sells the product with the RFID tag to a purchaser.
4. The purchaser tears the tag from the product that it has bought.
5. It only gives its tags to a community, e.g., school and non-profit organization.
6. The community collects tags and sorts tags according to the sellers that their credits should be paid to, because the identifiers of the tags discover the sellers.
7. It returns the tags to their sellers.
8. The seller receives the tag and then finds the amount of credits coupled to the tag in the database.
9. It transfers the amount to the account specified by the community and removes information on the identifier from the database so that the tag can be reused.

Note that in our approach RFID tags can be reused even when their identifiers are static because the database removes information on the identifiers after the tags are returned.

V. Design and Implementation

The proposed approach enables sellers at steps in a supply chain to sell their products with RFID tags (or barcodes) coupled to carbon emission credits to customers, including raw materials and components. Anyone can access information about the credits attached to the products, because the credits are transferred to purchasers who return the tags themselves to the sellers. The sellers should provide information about the credits, e.g., their amounts, expiration dates, and sources. When customers can read RFID tags (or barcodes) with web-enabled terminals, they see information on the credits attached to the tags.

- Our approach requires each RFID tag (or barcode) to have its own unique read-only identifier. Most RFID tags (or barcodes) used in supply chain management already have such identifiers.
- To support carbon offsets, the amount of credits attached to a product need to be equivalent to the total or partial amount of CO_2 emissions resulting from the use or disposal of the products.

This approach assumes to have agents, called *carbon credit agents*, to enable customers to access the information. They have two databases. The first maintains credit accounts and the second maintains information about assigned credits. They can only be connected to certain RFID agents and other account agents through authenticated and encrypted communications.

Some readers may worry that returning RFID tags (or barcodes) to their stakeholders is more costly than returning the identifiers of tags (or barcodes) via a network. There are two flows that are opposite to each other between sellers and purchasers at each stage in real supply chains: the flows of products and the flows of receipts or containers for the products. Our approach can directly use the latter flow to return tags (or barcodes) from purchasers to sellers. Therefore, our cost and extra CO_2 emissions are small. Actually, returnable containers, which deliver parts or components from sellers and then return them to sellers, are widely used in real supply chains.

VI. Experiences

The proposed approach was already evaluated through a social experiment with real retailers, end consumers, local communities, e.g., elementary school, local government, and non-profit organizations. We asked an elementary school, called Kita-sunamachi, in Kouto-area of Tokyo. The school announced students that several beverage cans are sold in a super market, supermarket (Kitasuna branch of Ito-yokadou), which is one of the biggest in Tokyo area, with seals assigned with 300, 500, or 700 g carbon emission credits. It was carried out for two weeks from 9 am to 10 pm and more than five thousand goods were sold with carbon. Figure 2 shows beverage cans with barcodes in a showcase at the supermarket. In this experiment, the credits are called Japan Verified Emission Reduction (J-VER), where J-VER credits were generated from thinning

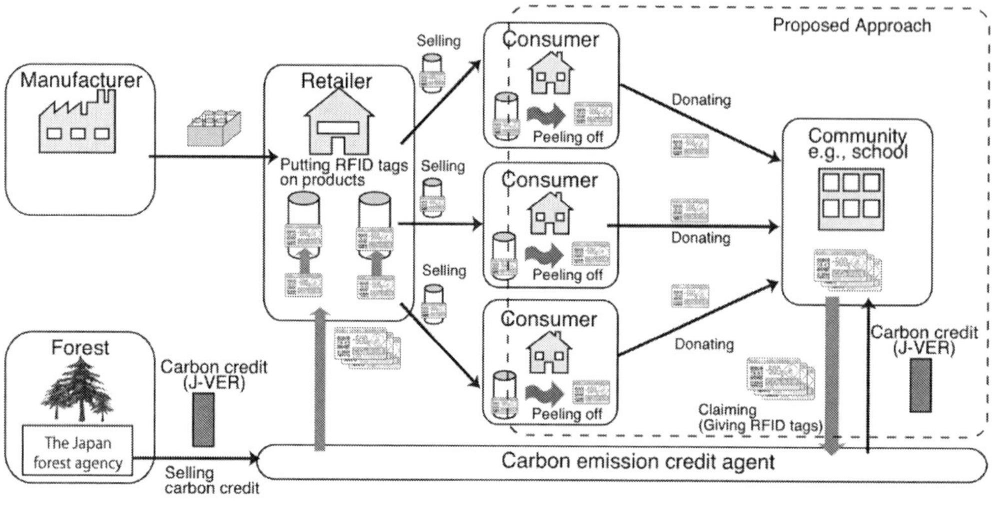

Figure 1. Community-based carbon credit attachment and settlement

forest and were traded on the domestic market and managed by the Forestry Agency.

Figure 2. Beverage with RFID tag (or barcodes) seal for carbon credits

When students bought the beverage cans, they should tear off the seals from cans and put them collecting boxes located at the school as shown in Fig. 3.

- The supermarket attached RFID tag seals on cans and sold them to real consumers, where each seal displayed small amount of its carbon emission credits.
- The customers bought cans with RFID tag seals like other items.
- They peeled the seals from the cans that they bought, where the seals could easily be unattached from products by them.
- Students, who had the seals, attached the seals on certain mount papers and return the seals on the mounts to boxes located at the school.
- The school collected seals from about three hundred students and returned to the supermarket and informed its carbon credit account.
- The supermarket read the identifiers of the seals and then transferred the carbon credits to the accounts.
- They could see the balances of their carbon account through a web site for carbon account management.

Figure 3. RFID tag/barcode seal collecting box

The supermarket totally sold 5320 cans, where the sales volumes of cans with carbon credits in two weeks was three times more than usual at the supermarket. Thirty-five percent of RFID tags or barcodes were returned to the supermarket by customers who claimed the credits. About 750 tags among them were donated to the school through our approach. There were many lessons learned from the experiment, but most problems in the experiment were not technical. For example, many consumers asked us about the notion of carbon credits so that we spent a lot of time to dealing with their questions. We could considerately reduce the cost of settlement of RFID tags, because the school collected many tags from students and returned a volume of the tags to the supermarket in comparison with our previous approach [8][9], which lacked any techniques for donations to third parties like the approach presented in this paper.

VII. Discussion

Our approach intended a supermarket to use carbon credits as an incentive to sell products. We expected end consumers to explicitly select products with more credits, which were in proportion to the amount of reduced CO_2 emissions. The approach also allowed existing RFID tags for logistics to be directly used as certificates for credits so that its environment cost was minimal. The approach had to be as simple as possible so that participating parties could easily understand how the approach worked and what they should to. The trading of RFID tags in the approach corresponded to the trading of credits. RFID tags could be used as monetary values, where money is generally considered to have three functions, as a medium of exchange, as units of accounts, and as stores of values. RFID tags in our approach could be exchanged because they were physical and tradable entities in the real world. The tags could be coupled to a certain number of credits. The tags were durable and able to be stored and the information stored in the tags could not easily be erased. The approach restricts sellers to assign more carbon credits to RFID tags than the amount of credits that they have because assigned credits are withdrawn from their carbon accounts. The approach permitted anyone to access information about credits, e.g., their amount, expiration dates, and sources via RFID tags and only the holders of the tags could claim the credits. The approach allowed purchasers, including end consumers, to claim credits by returning the tags coupled to them to the stakeholders of the tags without any complicated authentication mechanisms. End consumers did not need to read the RFID tags, because they could sell the tags to others, including sellers. The buying and selling of products is often done where networks and electronic devices may not be available, i.e., in warehouses, on streets, and in stores. Account agents need to be always connected to the system, but sellers and purchasers do not. The reader may worry whether the accuracy and correctness of carbon credits attached to products can be ensured at the supplier level. Consumers can select products according to the amount of carbon credits attached to them and they can know information about the credits through our identifiers assigned to small amounts of carbon credits.

VIII. Conclusion

We proposed a scheme to bridge the gap between personal- and company-level carbon emission credits or allowances and trading by using information technology, in particular RFID tags, barcodes, and telecommunication. The key idea underlying our approach was to combine offline and online approaches. The former was to introduce RFID tags (or barcodes) as physical certificates for the rights to claim carbon allowances, including carbon emission allowances and caps. The latter was to support the transfer of small amounts carbon emission allowances via e-commerce. When purchasers buy products with allowances for carbon offsets, they can claim the allowances by returning the RFID tags (or barcodes) coupled to the allowances to stakeholders, e.g., sellers or agencies, without the need for any complicated authentication. The approach could collect small amount of carbon credits by using communities, e.g., schools and non-profit organizations. The approach was designed to help communities to offset their GHG emissions. Finally, we would like to identify further issues that need to be resolved in the future. We plan to carry out more public experiments on the approach in other supply chains. We need to estimate the social cost in implementing and operating the approach.

References

[1] A. Brohe, "Personal Carbon Trading in perspective: potential pitfalls and compatibility with the EU ETS Framework," International Energy Agency Workshop, Paris, 2008.

[2] "The Foundation for the Economics of Sustainability (festa): Cap & Share: A fair way to cut greenhouse emissions," festa, 2008.

[3] D. Fleming, "Energy and the Common Purpose (Descending the Energy Staircase with Tradable Energy Quotas (TEQs)) ," The Lean Economy Connection, 2005.

[4] M. Hillman, "Carbon budget watchers," Town and Country Planning, Vol.67, No.9, 1998, pp. 305.

[5] D. Niemeier, et al., "Rethinking downstream regulation: California's opportunity to engage households in reducing greenhouse gases," Energy Policy, Vol.36, 2008, pp. 3436-3447.

[6] "Personal Carbon Trading," Y. Parag and T.Fawcett (eds), Routledge, 2010.

[7] C. Raux and G. Marlot, "A System of Tradable CO2 Permits Applied to Fuel Consumption by Motorists," Transport Policy, Vol. 12, No. 3, 2005, pp. 255-265.

[8] I. Satoh, "RFID-enabled carbon offsetting and trading," Pervasive and Mobile Computing, 2013, Vol. 9, No. 1, pp. 149-160.

[9] I. Satoh, "IT-enabled Personal-level Carbon Emission Allowance," in Proceedings of the 5th International Conference on Ambient Systems, Networks and Technologies (ANT 2014), the 5th International Conference on Sustainable Energy Information Technology (SEIT-2014), 2014, pp. 665-672.

Citizen -centric Smart City Planning for Africa: A Qualitative Case Study of Early Stage Co-creation of a Namibian Smart Community

Virpi Oksman,
VTT technology Centre of Finland,
Tekniikankatu 1, Tampere, Finland
e-mail: virpi.oksman@vtt.fi

Mika Raunio,
University of Tampere,
Kanslerinrinne 1, Tampere, Finland
e-mail: Mika.M.Raunio@staff.uta.fi

Abstract— This paper examines social and economic development of African urban areas using the Smart Community concept. Sub-Saharan African communities face an urgent need for affordable housing, new working and learning environments, and new technologies to support sustainable development. The paper provides insights to the main research questions: 1. How can citizen-centric engagement process for community development be enhanced in an African context? 2. What kinds of information and communication technology (ICT) tools can support such processes? and 3. What is required for citizen-centric Smart Community development? We conducted a focus group study in Keetmanshoop, the Karas region in Southern Namibia. The main lesson learned focus on the need to develop a reliable ICT infrastructure along with affordable housing and feasible services.

Keywords-Citizen-centric; Smart City; co-creation; virtual reality, Africa, developing economies.

I. INTRODUCTION

In Sub-Saharan Africa, there is an urgent need for affordable housing, new working and learning environment and new digital services to support societal and economic development. The African population will continue its radical shift from rural to urban areas; in 2010 urban dwellers made up nearly 40 percent of the total population, and the estimation for 2030 is 50% and for 2060 65% [1]. The urban population of Namibia has been increasing from 28% in 1991 to 33% in 2001 and to 42% in 2011. The evolution of the society requires public administrations to tackle many new challenges, including civic rights, gender equality, employment, mobility, digitalization, security, environment and many others. One of the main challenges in African governments is to develop more democratic and transparent societies without corruption. The widespread use of new technologies, such as social media and mobile services, has increased the demands for openness and transparency for public decision-making and administrations. There is a need to enhance the communication between citizens and government, and to increase public engagement and to help citizens stay informed about decisions.

Urbanization in Africa tends to differ from the experiences acquired from other parts of the world. In Africa, urbanization is "decoupled from overall structural transformation of the economies". According to a theory, urbanization is a process of transformation where economies evolve from rural agricultural economies towards industry- and service- based economies, and they simultaneously move from low-income to high-income societies [2]. However, in Africa urbanization seems to miss this link to development towards industrialization and higher income. Instead, urbanization in Africa frequently refers to "resettlement from the rural hinterlands, to rural market towns". In fact, over 70% of African populations live in towns with less than 100 000 inhabitants, in sparsely populated small towns and along the road networks. There are only a few mega cities in Africa [3].

However, Smart Cities are frequently linked to big cities and advanced technologies that improve the living conditions and foster economic growth in these highly populated and well-connected urban agglomerations. Slavova and Okwechime [3] emphasize the fact, that African urbanization provides some preconditions, which should be considered when the Smart City approach is used to foster the urban and economic development in Africa. They make a distinction between "hard" and "soft" qualities, or best-practices, as domains that Smart City approach provides for city planners and stakeholders, who may then select a combination that best fits for their city's needs. Hard domain includes, for example, physical infrastructure like water resources, which can be used more efficiently with more innovative management solutions. Soft domain includes social issues that may be ameliorated, for instance, by provision of housing and social services with integrating such services with ICT. Also fostering of economic development through innovation and entrepreneurship may be considered as a soft approach.

Slavova and Okwechime [3] also point out different strategies needed for different agglomerations; mega-cities (over 5 million), medium cities (from 5 to 0,5 million) and small cities (less than 0,5 million) and other urban (less than 0,3 million), that cannot be developed with similar agendas. To simplify, soft qualities – social and human oriented development – are likely to be emphasized in small towns and rural environments rather than technology and data driven solutions. Rather than "hard domains", that are typical to big cities (e.g., physical infrastructure, urban density and congestion) more generic challenges of poor regions (e.g., slums and informal settlements) and especially qualities of "soft domain" (e.g., low quality and segregated social services, unemployment) are key elements to focus on in case of small towns [3]. It should be noticed, that in Namibia small towns, rather than cities are typical urban agglomerations. Event the biggest city, Windhoek, has less than million inhabitants. In our case town Keetmanshoop, there is only 30 000 inhabitants approximately, although it is major urban agglomeration in southern Namibia, and locates close to South Africa, which is Namibia's main trading partner. Therefore, "soft and human" solutions of Smart City approach are especially important in this case. Keetmanshoop also hosts different social and ethnic groups that have had conflicts in the recent history, which may influence the socio-economic development in the context of urban development also in the future. Having these guidelines in mind, it is safe to conclude, that especially social and human aspects of Smart City approach are relevant for the development of communities in the case area. In addition, it is more appropriate to discuss Smart *Communities* than Smart Cities in this context, as maybe is the case in most areas in (Sub-Saharan) Africa. Finally, due to decoupling of socio-economic development and urbanization in Africa, it is even more important effort to apply approaches like "Smart City" in this context, in order to converge these processes in the immediate future.

Widely acknowledged as the administrative capital of southern Namibia, Keetmanshoop attracts significant interest from private and public investors. Investment opportunities range from real estate, retail, solar energy, to logistics and hospitality. Some of the most significant projects on the horizon include the University of Namibia Campus, with 420 upmarket residential plots and a 10 000 square meter retail centre. The Municipal Council values the importance of Private Public Partnerships aimed at delivering essential infrastructure and welcomes investors to tap into the opportunities.

However, the development and building projects may face many challenges starting from the decision-making about the land, to transparency of the communication processes, getting raw materials and qualified professionals to work for the building sites. Our aim in this study was to examine the possibilities of co-creation approach in the context of building new affordable housing in the Keetmaanshop area. Moreover, user needs for local service infrastructure, public and private service development and business possibilities are also studied. In Smart City planning, the open innovation approach and new technologies are increasingly used to support stakeholder communication in urban planning. Advanced virtual reality (VR) models and tools, such as augmented reality (AR) and mixed reality (MR) can be used to visualize future urban plans. These kinds of tools can significantly improve the understanding of what is being proposed and the potential impacts of different alternatives on landscape and living environment as it is shown earlier in quantitative studies with citizens as well [4]. Moreover, we were interested in to finding out how this kinds of tools would support the co-creation process in Africa. To understand the challenges of current housing situation, and citizens' needs for Smart Community development, we conducted five focus groups in Keetmanshoop, the Karas region in Southern Namibia.

This paper focuses on communities based development possibilities, to enhance socially inclusive bottom-up approach that harness the collective intelligence and creativity of communities. The paper is structured as follows: Section II describes the concept of Smart Community. Section III presents the VR and MR tools for urban planning. Section IV explicates the focus group study. In Section V, we draw conclusions and define next steps of the research.

II. SMART COMMUNITY OR SMART CITY?

In European and in other industrialized countries contexts, there has been an intensive development work, projects and research on the concept of Smart City. The Smart City concept is often approached from a technology-oriented, systemic perspective that provides new technological solutions, big data and innovations to make the living environments smarter through the application of digital technologies [5]. Less attention, however, is given to societal aspects of the Smart City for instance smart governance, smart people, sense of community and social learning [6]. In addition, what seems to be largely missing is empirical insight into the extent to which different smart city aspects can be applied in different geographical or in decisively different cultural contexts [7]. In addition, less is discussed how to involve citizens and other stakeholders for the development processes with new digital tools for sustainable, long-term results.

Why is the concept of Smart Communities relevant in the African societal contexts? Smart Cities go hand in hand with smart communities and one is dependent on the other. Smart Cities need also smart citizens – the citizens who live and work in these cities need to participate in adoption and usage of new solutions, at least. Smart Community concept allows socially, economically, technically and environmentally sustainable solution for urban living and advanced digital service-ecosystem for health, wellbeing, and equity of citizens (see Figure 1).

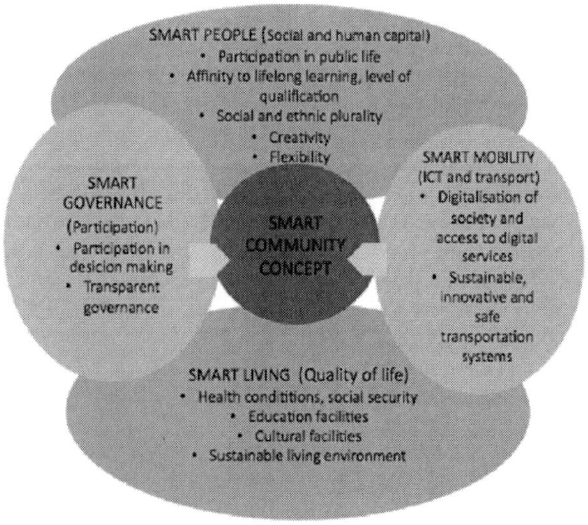

Figure 1. Elements of smart community as modified from [8][9].

In other words, Smart Community resembles Smart City approach that foster broad social, economic and environmental sustainability in urban development. However, Smart Community is application for smaller scale solutions and especially targeted for the less advanced regions, with more emphasis on social and economic sustainability ("smartness in people") than on technology and digital solutions ("smartness in technology"), as is often the case in Smart City concepts [5][6][7][8][9]. The Smart Community approach aims to introduce an organized and systematic approach to community development that provides better living conditions for local people. The specific qualities that may be considered as benefits of Smart Community solution include emphasizing local value addition in the construction process, environmental sustainability and cultural and social advantages and long-term sustainability.

Smart management and communication technologies give citizens the opportunity to shape both the culture and the structure of cities. A successful governance of the accelerating urbanization in Africa is a key process in terms of a positive economic and social development of the continent. One of the major systemic challenges based on the observation is that the growth of cities will foster the economic development and growth in the continent, but the low quality of infrastructure and urban planning hinders the positive socioeconomic impacts of the processes. For example, Namibian cities act as nodes through which development occurs and the rapid urbanization simultaneously poses risks that affect sustainable livelihoods of people [10].

Hence, citizen participation and social capital are essential elements of Smart Community. In Social scientific research, the term 'community' may refer to both to communities that are location-based, whose social ties rely mainly on geographical proximity (such as neighborhoods) or modern communities that are rather formed around interests and skills (such as professional communities) than around locality [11]. Social scientific research has also recognized the concept of 'imagined communities', understood as socially constructed community, imagined by the people who perceive themselves as a part of that group [12]. In addition, online and virtual communities have gained recently more and more attention. They have been defined as a combination of people, who have a shared purpose, and computer systems, to support and mediate social interaction and facilitate a sense of togetherness [13]. In this context, we are researching mostly local communities – although all kinds of modern communities, including imagined, online and virtual communities have impact on people's sense of community.

Citizen participation and social capital are essential elements of Smart Community. In Europe, governments have been launching ICT platforms to facilitate citizen participation for Smart City development. They allow different types of citizen participation, such as voting, rising public awareness and monitoring political processes. One of the main challenges of adopting advanced VR technologies, which are quite mature tested and capable in the Europe and in the industrialized world, in the African context, is the slowness of the internet connection. The average download speeds in Northern Europe are among the highest in the world (over 25 Megabits per second). In Namibia it is 7,5 -10 Mbps, which is higher than the average in African and Sub-Saharan African countries in general, but still low compared to the more digitalized areas of the world.

Moreover, co-creation and co-design of urban public services support resilience building and acceptance of public urban services that support sustainability [14]. Co-creation has impact on experienced quality of living environment. Co-design activities affect the experienced quality of a living environment, and diverse fields have recognized the relationship between the citizens' sense of the place, social cohesion and public health outcomes [15][16][17].

III. Virtual and Mixed Reality Tools for Co-Creation of Smart Communities

Recently VR and MR tools have been created to involve citizens and other stakeholders contributing to urban planning. Traditionally, urban planning processes are regulated by the public legal service sector. However, legal requirements typically base on a top-down distribution of information, even if the perception among different stakeholders of, for example, the characteristics of urban attractiveness and livability may vary significantly. To make cities more inclusive, planning processes should be developed towards exchanging of ideas. Such processes could use computer-aided design, including VR and MR modelling. Moreover, co-creation and co-design of urban public services support resilience building and acceptance of public urban services that support sustainability in the long run [14][15][16][17].

Currently, in Africa, urban planning proposals are communicated to stakeholders and the public to a varying extent and by different means. Often only, a limited amount of stakeholders is well informed and new technologies, such as virtual models, are not widely used. However, statistic images and technical reports may be inadequate if a meaningful participation and convincing common vision is desired [18].

MR models and applications have been increasingly piloted in various urban planning and renewal projects [19]. VR and MR technologies can provide users ubiquitous experience: need for information any time anywhere with their smart mobile devices. In addition to visualizing future city environments with VR and MR models, more recent extension of this technology allows citizens to comment and ask city planners questions considering the future plans. Mobile applications for instance, have been recently piloted for developing two-way communication between city governance and citizens. The piloted applications allow citizens and city officials to discuss local urban planning development issues [20].

A prototype of MR application supporting a range of devices for a collaborative multimodal interaction was developed by Wagner et al. [19] to enable a group of participants to create a vision of urban projects. The stakeholders and users involved in the urban planning project had various backgrounds ranging from local urban planning specialists to other stakeholders such as members of local commerce. MR visualizations proved useful in enriching the available representations and enhancing stakeholders' understanding of urban situations. 3D visualizations, videos and sounds helped to express and co-construct their ideas.

Smartphones for urban planning have been piloted with citizens [20]. An augmented reality (AR) prototype system on smartphones was experienced as a useful tool for visualising proposed architectural designs [21].

The mobile and MR and AR technology tools above described, have been applied in various parts of the world like in Europe and in New Zealand [19][21]. Consequently, we were interested in to finding out how these kinds of tools would support the co-creation process in Africa.

One possible way to communicate Smart Community planning in the future was by using a virtual reality solution that was developed in order to visualize the planned residential area in Namibia. The system was developed by engineering firm A-insinöörit using virtual models by architecture firm Aihio Architects (Figure 2 and Figure 3).

Figure 2. Virtual reality models from the future housing area planned in Keetmanshoop, Namibia.

Figure 3. A Virtual reality system with devices for demonstrating virtual reality solutions.

The aim of the virtual reality model is to visualize the future residential area and to enhance the co-creation process with different stakeholders. The virtual model also aids in visualizing and choosing different material for houses and overall planning of the area. The system uses devices for demonstrating VR solutions such as AR and MR head mounted glasses (HMD) and their peripherals to produce a fully immersive simulation of the area. Furthermore, to create virtual worlds from a real world environment, special capturing devices are needed, for instance drones equipped with camera. Fully immersive simulations are able to provide very realistic user experiences by delivering a wide field of view and high resolutions.

IV. A Case Study - Methods

We conducted a focus group study in Keetmanshoop in February, 2017. The aim of the focus groups was to discuss and share ideas about living, planning of the future houses and environment in Namibia and Keetmanshoop with different stakeholders. After conducting the focus groups, we were able to present the findings and discuss them with Keetmanshoop Municipal Council and the decision-makers. The focus groups were selected from different social groups including: young people, families, mobile professionals, social and health workers and traditional community leaders. The groups were selected to provide different insights for the new area under development. Five separate focus groups were conducted with the following groups in Keetmanshoop:

- Potential dwellers who are listed by the Keetmanshoop municipality and First Capital Housing Fund (8 persons)
- UNAM final year students (8 persons)
- UNAM faculty/Staff members (3 persons)
- Social and community development workers (4 persons)
- Community leaders representing different parishes (4 persons)

Figure 4. Five focus groups were conducted in Keetmanshop in Namibia.

Because of the slow internet connections in the whole area, we could not use any internet-based VR visualization methods. Instead, we used different visual material to facilitate discussing such as photos, post-its and drawings (Figure 5).

The focus group study was exploring the following topics:

- Living and finance- how the dwellers perceive housing prices in Keetmanshoop and Namibia, and how does it impact on the participant's future location?
- Housing styles and alternatives - new solutions and materials in housing
- Social and cultural sustainability of the neighborhood – safety, diversity and community building issues
- Needed public and private services for Smart Community

V. Research Findings

In general, the need for development of wiFi network, as well as the need for affordable housing and feasible services was most highlighted in young people's focus group. However, these themes came up in all other focus groups as well. House may be smaller and cheaper at first, and as prosperity and family grows, it may be extended by building new rooms to the house. At the moment housing markets are not very dynamic, and houses are seldom sold by the individuals, but mostly by investors or contractors who have new housing projects.

In the families focus group, it was interpreted as a positive way to create areas with more various income levels to make housing markets more dynamic. People are ready to accept also less typical solutions, also partly because for the many the situation or circumstances is that "you have to take what you got", due to growing price level and low availability of houses. One suggestion was that the government and relevant authorities should offer more affordable options and venture cheaper building materials as most Namibians cannot afford the housing prices at the moment. However, some people also expect more expensive and unique solutions than standard houses; more spacious, two-storey houses and using quality materials for walls, doors etc.

The families also expected more transparency about the housing situation. At the moment families do not know, and cannot check, what is their position in the municipality's waiting list for a new apartment or a house. It may also be unclear, how one proceeds on the list, and why someone receives an invitation to see the house and some others do not. Support for local companies and constructors is seen as a good thing, but not at the expense of the quality: quality of houses is not always good and cracks to walls may come fast. Regarding sustainable energy solutions, already now for example solar panels are widely used for energy, so sustainable (solar) energy sources are not distinctive factor as such, but rather usual solution.

The mobile professionals' focus groups ephasized the wide availability of different affordable services and quality housing. The mobile professionals, even though they had a job at the city were not planning to stay permanently at this stage. They emphasized the need for liveable service structures, including a wide range of public and private services. For instance libraries, schools, commercial services, day care with qualified people and good quality premises were seen as important. Many basic services, like car maintenance, are still missing or too expensive in the rural areas, which is keeping professionals living in two locations simultaneously.

The social workers and community leaders also pointed out the need for more healthy and safe recreational area choices like playgrounds, parks, gymn, libarary and sports clubs for kids and young people to keep youngsters out of bars.

VII. Conclusions and Future Work

The participatory urban planning processes and Smart City development are sensitive for different cultural and global contexts. The advanced virtual reality technologies may work well in the countries and areas with high WiFi speed, but these kind of technology-driven solutions may be less usable in rural regions with occasionally very slow internet access. Consequently, there is also a need for lightweight mobile solutions, which could function more securely in rural areas to involve more citizens in the co-creation process.

To enhance citizen-driven planning processes, more transparency and information sharing is need. Citizens in general were expecting more transparency to the urban planning and housing projects. In particular, simple online tools that would inform citizens about their position on the municipality's waiting list for new apartment or house and would notify about the progress of the building project, would improve the communication between government and citizens.

Different citizen groups such as young people, families and mobile professionals have different needs for Smart Community development. Typical standard house solution is not serving all groups and especially mobile professionals were emphasizing a wide variety of both public and private services. However, the most highlighted issue in the all groups was the need for affordable houses. At the moment housing markets are not very dynamic and cannot provide apartments for all.

Our qualitative study is limited to one rural, but developing community in Namibia and as such, the results cannot be generalized to all African or Sub-Saharan countries, as the socio-economic situations might be quite different. In the next stages of the research, we are going to focus on developing frugal innovations, i.e., adapting local technology and locally designed and co-created solutions for engaging citizens in planning or developing in their living environments and service-ecosystem in Namibia. Moreover, other important questions to research further are: how local people can be engaged to participate in planning, what kind of feedback channels do people need and how should be the communication and the interaction in between the governance and citizens in urban planning be developed.

ACKNOWLEDGMENT

This paper is part of SmartCom –project, which is funded by Business Finland, A-Insinöörit Ltd., Aihio Architects Ltd., Earth House Systems Ltd. and Sopimusvuori Ltd. We would like to thank SmartCom –project partners for their co-operation. In addition, we would like to thank Disney Andreas from University of Namibia for facilitating the focus groups with us.

REFERENCES

[1] African Development Bank. Annual report 2011. https://www.afdb.org/en/knowledge/publications/annual-report/annual-report-2011[retrieved 5.2. 2018]

[2] P. C. Annez and R.M. Buckley, "Urbanization and growth: Setting the context," In M. Spence, P. C. Annez & R. M. Buckley (Eds.), Urbanization and growth. Commission on growth and development (pp. 1-45). Washington, DC: The World Bank, 2009.

[3] M. Slavova and E. Okwechime,"African smart cities strategies for agenda 2063," *Africa Journal of Management*, vol. 2, no. 2, pp. 210-229, 2016.

[4] V. Oksman and M. Kulju, "Developing on-line illustrative and participatory tools for urban planning: towards open innovation and co-production through citizen engagement", International Journal of Service Technology Management, vol 23, no 5/6, pp. 2017, pp. 445-464.

[5] P. Neirotti, et al., "Current trends in Smart City initiatives: Some stylised facts." Cities, Vol. 38, pp. 25-36, 2014.

[6] L. de Wijs, P. Witte, and D. de Klerk, "Smart City Trends and Ambitions" AGILE 2017, Wageningen, May, 2017. ISBN 978-90-816960-7 - 4. https://agileonline.org/index.php/conference/proceedings/proceedings-2017 [retrieved 5.2. 2018]

[7] T. Nam and T. A. Pardo, "Conceptualizing Smart City with Dimensions of Technology, People, and Institutions" Proceedings of the 12th Annual International Digital Government Research Conference: Digital Government Innovation in Challenging Times. dg.o '11, 2011, pp. 282-291.

[8] R. Giffinger, C. Fertner, H. Kramar, R. Kalasek , N. Pichler-Milanovič, E. Meijers. "Smart cities, Ranking of European medium-sized cities", Vienna: University of Technology, 2007.

[9] R. G. Hollands, Will the real smart city please stand up? City, vol 12, no. 3, pp. 303-320, 2008, doi: 10.1080/13604810802479126.

[10] N. Indongo, S. Angombe, and N. Nickanor, "Urbanisation in Namibia: Views from semi-formal and informal settlements. University of Namibia", 2013.

[11] D. McMillan and D. M. Chavis, "Sense of community: A definition and theory", Journal of Community Theory, vol. 14, no. 1, pp. 6–23, 1986.

[12] B. Anderson, "Imagined Communities. Reflection of the Origin and Spread of Nationalism", Verso: London & New York, 2006.

[13] J. Preece and D. Maloney-Krichman, "Online Communities: Design, Theory, and Practice", Journal of Computer-Mediated Communication, vol. 10, no. 4, pp. 0, 2005.

[14] M. Steen, M. Manschot, and N. De Koning, "Benefits of co-design in service design projects." International Journal of Design, vol.5, 2011, pp. 53-60.

[15] D.F. Shanahan et al. Toward improved public health outcomes from urban nature. American Journal of Public Health, vol. 105, no. 3, pp. 470-7, 2015.

[16] H. Frumkin, "Healthy Places: Exploring the Evidence: American Journal of Public Health., vol 93, no. 9, pp. 1451-1456, Sept. 2003.

[17] A. Grahn and P. Stigsdotter, "The relation between perceived sensory dimensions of urban green space and stress restoration", Landscape and Urban Planning, vol. 94, pp. 264-275, 201

[18] J. D. Salter, C. Campbell., M. Journey, and S. R. J. Sheppard. The Digital Workshop: Exploring the Use of Interactive and Immersive Visualisation Tools in Participatory Planning. Journal of Environmental Management, vol 90, pp. 2090–2101, 2009.

[19] I. Wagner et al., "MR Tent: a place for constructing mixed realities in urban planning", Proceedings of the fourth international conference on Communities and technologies, (C&T '09) May 2009, pp. 185-194

[20] T. P. Ertiö, "Participatory Apps for Urban Planning—Space for Improvement", Planning Practice and Research, vol. 30, no 3, pp. 303-321, May 2015.

[21] M. Allen, "Smart-phone augmented reality for public participation in urban planning", Proceedings of the 23rd Australian Computer-Human Interaction Conference, (OzCHI '11) Nov. 2011, pp. 11-20.

A Methodology Based on Model-Driven Engineering for IoT Application Development

Claudia Maricela Sosa-Reyna, Edgar Tello-Leal, David Lara-Alabazares, Jonathan Alfonso Mata-Torres, Esmeralda Lopez-Garza
Reynosa-Rodhe Multidisciplinary Academic Unit - Faculty of Engineering and Science
Autonomous University of Tamaulipas
Victoria, Mexico
e-mail: clauqueen1@gmail.com, etello@uat.edu.mx, dlara@uat.edu.mx, mata.jona@gmail.com, elgarza@uat.edu.mx

***Abstract*—The Internet of Things can be understood as an infrastructure of the dynamic global network with a capacity of self-configuration, based on standard communication protocols, where things -physical and virtual- have an identity, physical attributes, and virtual personalities. In this paper, we propose a methodology based on Model-Driven Engineering with different levels of abstraction, points of view, and granularity, with the objective of guiding the development of software applications for Internet of Things. The methodology is supported by methods of model transformation, enabling the generation of the code of the software applications for Internet of Things. In addition, a Service-Oriented Architecture is presented for the deployment of software applications, composed of four layers that allow the identification of the components required for the implementation of the Internet of Things systems.**

Keywords-thing; IoT; MDE; SOA; model; transformation.

I. INTRODUCTION

Nowadays, the advances in research and development of the Information and Communications Technology (ICT) encourages to try to connect all things or objects to the world via the Internet, in order to provide an integrated system to improve their performance in the transmission of information, and offer new services over the Internet. This converts an object into a smart object, allowing to control any tangible object remotely, and has been called the Internet of Things (IoT) [1]. IoT consists of a global infrastructure for the information society, enabling advanced services by interconnecting (physical and virtual) things based on existing and evolving interoperable information and communication technologies [2].

In the IoT paradigm, a thing is an object of the physical world (physical thing) or the information world (virtual thing), which is capable of being identified and integrated into communication networks [2]. Hence, IoT represents a significant extension of the Internet with a large number of physical objects and devices that show pervasive sensing, detection, actuation, and computational capabilities. IoT is usually related to a physical thing or object, but a fundamental component in IoT is the software used to connect and manage things and as well as to analyze their collected data. This software can be found in different locations, such as embedded, or at the level of middleware, applications, logic in the composition of services, or management tools [3][4].

The advances achieved in automation and intelligent environments have reached important levels, and some contributions in this sense through IoT concepts include smart cities, smart homes, e-health, smart grids, intelligent transportation systems, and intelligent use of water, among others [5]-[9]. While these paradigms have their advantages, their development is complex; that is why new alternatives to facilitate generation processes and implementation of innovative applications are sought. Moreover, the principal characteristic of IoT systems is that heterogeneity between its components, in where things might be totally different among themselves in terms of both hardware and software. However, the very same software functionalities are expected to be deployable on different devices having only a limited set of core common features [10]. Therefore, having models that conceptualize the domain of a specific problem, and with which the elements that integrate it can be identified, classified and abstracted, represents the possibility of achieving efficient automated implementation, as well as support the complexity of the heterogeneous things.

In this respect, Model-Driven Engineering (MDE) is based on models that in an early stage in the development minimize the technological aspects, so that communication between users, analysts, and system developers, can be more efficient, allowing the selection of the technological platform until the end of the process. With the use of MDE, the automatic generation of the code as the product of a set of model transformations represents an increase in productivity, favoring consistency through automation. In the MDE approach, high-level abstraction models are transformed into lower-level models, where the relationship between both models results in a dependence that keeps the process that has been followed until a technological solution, helping to understand the consequences of the changes at any point in the development process [11]. When developing systems based on models, it is possible to achieve an easy adaptation to the changes, both technological and the business requirements that may appear in the development process, turning the models into reusable and enduring units. As part of the development process, where models are productive units from which automated implementations emanate, we find as core points: 1) the abstraction, represented by high-level modeling languages; 2) the automation, that allows to transform the models in computer programs; and 3) the standard, or complementary development tools; with the aim of obtaining formal models or software artifacts that can be understood by a computer [12].

Moreover, considering the ubiquity and particularity existing in intelligent environments in IoT systems, MDE allows the management of heterogeneous technologies through automatic transformation methods and generation of code for specific platforms. In MDE, the transformation of models can be vertical, where it refines abstract models in more specific models, or horizontal form, defining mappings between models of the same level of abstraction, and in this way to identify the best solution.

Furthermore, in the Service-Oriented Architecture (SOA) approach, a complex system is treated as a set of well-defined objects or subsystems [13]. These subsystems can be reused, maintaining their individual form. Hence, software and hardware components in an IoT architecture, implemented with SOA, can be efficiently reused and updated. Therefore, when SOA is applied in IoT, the generated design can provide extensibility, scalability, modularity, and interoperability between heterogeneous things, as well as the functionalities and capabilities that were encapsulated in a set of services.

In this paper, we propose a methodology supported by the MDE for solving the challenges in the IoT system developments. The methodology is composed of four phases with different levels of abstraction, viewpoint, and granularity. The phases of the methodology are supported by methods of transformation of models based on MDE. In addition, an architecture for IoT systems composed of four layers is presented, which is based on the SOA approach. This architecture allows the interoperability between heterogeneous devices to be guaranteed in multiple ways, establishing a bridge between the digital and physical world of IoT. Therefore, the architecture and methodology enable guides the process of development of software applications oriented to services, which make it possible to satisfy the business requirements of the IoT domain.

The reminder of the paper is organized as follows. In Section II there is a review of the related research which deals with the technology of Internet of Things and MDE and their integration. Section III introduces the architecture based on SOA. In Section IV, we propose the MDE methodology for Internet of Things, together with conclusions, in Section V.

II. Related Work

The development of technological solutions for the specification of software systems for IoT using the principles of MDD has been previously studied. The most relevant proposals that are related to the approach proposed in this research work are discussed in this Section. Nguyen et al. [14] proposed a Framework for Sensor Application Development (FRASAD) based on MDD approach, which aims at improving the re-usability, flexibility, and maintainability of sensor software. In the highest abstraction level of your architecture, a rule-based model and a Domain Specific Language (DSL) are used to describe the applications. It has been elaborated to uncouple the programming language and their execution model from the underlying OS and hardware. The DSL model has been extended for support to the different operating systems such as TinyOS or Contiki.

Pramudianto et al. [15] presented a MDD approach for the development of software components of the IoT domain, using three levels of abstraction. The Platform Specific Model (PSM) can be transformed into a Java code, which requires refinement before implementation. The code generated run as a standalone application that exposes the domain objects through different protocols and serialization formats. Similarly, Conzon et al. [16] proposed a tool using MDD for extending a platform to be used in factory automation and on techniques used for energy consumption optimization and CO2 reduction. This MDD tool allows developers to discover and compose distributed devices and services into mashups, enabling developers to model the integration of IoT components visually and programmatically, transforming the model into the software code.

In [17], Einarsson et al. presented a Domain-Specific Modelling Language (SmartHomeML) for smart home applications, incorporating a metamodel that enables the capture the architecture and specifications of smart home devices, as well as two transformation templates that generate code from instances of SmartHomeML for Alexa and SmartThings. This transformation was designed trough MDD approach, using a model-to-text transformation in a platform-specific model level to code (implementation artifact). Brambilla et al. [18] proposed a model-driven development based approach for the definition of user interface components and design patterns specific to the IoT domain. In addition, a proposed an extension of the standard Interaction Flow Modeling Language (IFML) in order to support the implementation of the user interfaces. The IFML extension designed focuses on mobile applications, enable for expressing the content, user interaction, and control behavior of the front-end of IoT applications.

In our work, we propose a methodology that explicitly describes the phases for the design of software applications for the IoT domain. In this proposal, the abstraction levels and granularity (of each source or target model required) of the phases and stages of the methodology are described in detail, as well as the model transformation methods (based on MDD) that allow giving support each of the phases of the methodology.

III. SOA-based Architecture for IoT Systems

The main requirement of IoT is that things in the network must be interconnected. The architecture of an IoT system must guarantee the operations of things, allowing a bridge between things (physical part) and the virtual world of IoT. The SOA-based architecture for the development of proposed IoT systems is composed of 4 layers, as shown in Figure 1.

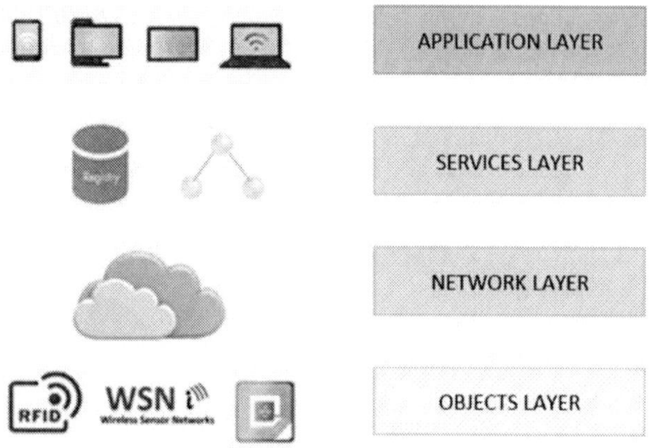

Figure 1. Architecture based on SOA for IoT systems.

A. *Object Layer*

The Object layer is composed of hardware objects available on the network that detect the state of things. In the object layer, the intelligent systems through labels or sensors, are able to automatically detect the environment and perform data exchange between devices. The objects in this layer must have a digital identity (universal identifier, UUID), allowing to trace the object in the digital domain, making it possible to meet IoT's expectation of being a physical interconnected network all over the world, where things are seamlessly connected and can be controlled remotely [13].

B. *Network Layer*

The Network layer consists of the infrastructure that supports wired, wireless or mobile connections between things, allowing to detect their environment, which enables to share data between connected things, enabling event management and intelligent IoT processing. The network layer enables to manage the communication in the IoT environment and to transmit messages between the objects and systems. In the SOA approach, services will be consumed by things that have been enabled in the network layer. The network layer is crucial in any IoT approach, considering QoS functionalities, efficient energy management in the network and in things, signal and data processing, security and privacy, among others.

C. *Service Layer*

In the Service layer, there are created and managed the services required by the users or software applications. The service layer is based on middleware technologies, which is fundamental for consuming services and the execution of IoT applications, where hardware and software platforms can be re-usable. Middleware plays a key role in supporting the development of such IoT enhanced applications and services. The IoT systems introduce significant new challenges for middleware stemming from the vast number of connected objects, the volume and variety of the data produced, the patterns of communication required, the heterogeneity of communicating components, and new challenges in terms of quality-of-service, privacy, and security [7]. It is one of the architecture's critical layers of operation, which operates in bidirectional mode. This layer operates as an interface between the object layer (at the bottom of the architecture), and the application layer (at the top of the architecture). It is responsible for functions such as device management, information management, data filtering, data aggregation, semantic analysis, and information discovery [19]. The services layer consists of: service discovery, service composition, APIs, and reliability management (see Figure 2), among others. The discovery of services allows to find the objects that can provide the required service and the necessary information in an efficient way, through the UUID in the registry of services or repository of services. The composition of services allows the interaction between connected things by combining the available services to perform a specific task, that is, when the services are created and stored in the service repository, they can be combine in services of higher level of complexity from the business logic.

D. *Application Layer*

The Application layer is responsible for delivering the applications to different IoT users. The application layer usually plays the role of providing services or applications that integrate or analyze the information received from the other three layers. The intent of the architecture is to support vertical applications. The development of applications in IoT has focused on the areas of health, agriculture, transportation, intelligent cities, home automation, complex systems for decision making, water use management, etc. [4][5][8][9].

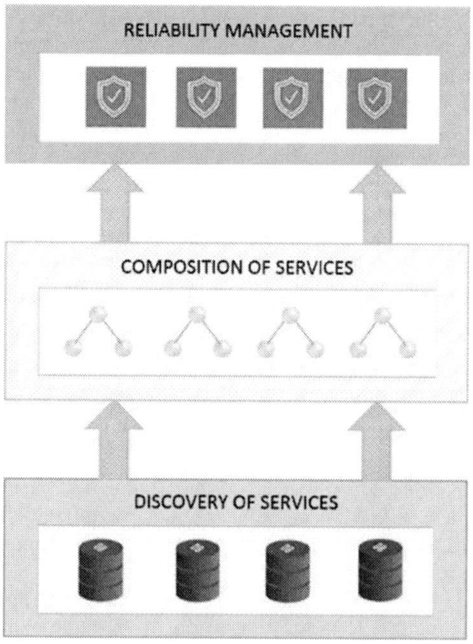

Figure 2. Scheme of the SOA service layer.

IV. MDE METHODOLOGY FOR IOT APPLICATIONS

The proposed methodology is oriented to the use of conceptual models in different points of view, levels of abstraction, and granularity. The output artifacts of the phases of this methodology are represented by models, generated by the application of the principles of MDE. The end result are software implementation artifacts, that is, the code of the applications or software systems for IoT. In Figure 3, the phases that make up this methodology are presented: 1) analysis of business requirements, 2) definition of the business logic, 3) design of the integrated services solution, and 4) generation of the technological solution.

A. *Phase 1. Analysis of business requirements.*

In this phase, the problem domain is analyzed and the business requirements are identified. This is done considering the functional and non-functional requirements of the system. In order to define the business requirements model, the UML language is used, capturing the flow of the software process through use case diagrams and activity diagrams, generating a model defined in a Platform Independent Model (PIM) level. A PIM is a platform-independent system view, that is, a model with a high level of abstraction independent of any technology or implementation language that exhibits a sufficient degree of platform independence to allow mapping to one or more platforms.

B. *Phase 2. Definition of the business logic.*

This phase focuses on the design of the business processes required to support the business logic and business requirements. Then, the pre-generated business requirements model is used as input to the phase, and is complemented by the definition of the business process logic, using the Business Process Model and Notation language (BPMN), which allows to generate a model of the business solution defined in a PIM level of the MDE, describing the behavior and interactions of the business process from a global viewpoint.

C. *Phase 3. Design of the integrated services solution.*

In this phase, a model of the IT architecture is defined, at a platform independent level to separate the business logic solution from the technical aspects of implementation (IT), which allows that this type of implementation can be generated on different target platforms. The IT architecture model is derived from the model of the business solution generated in the previous phase, the generated model remains unchanged on any platform. In this case, the IT architecture model is generated following the approach oriented to SOA services. The output of this stage is a model defined in a PIM level.

D. *Phase 4. Generation of the technological solution.*

In this phase, specific concepts of the implementation platform are used in order to convert this solution into an executable code of a particular software application. This phase is accomplished through the implementation of two stages: 1) design of the IT platform specific solution, and 2) generation of the specifications or code of the software system. The first stage consists of the definition of the specifications model based on a standard or specific technology (for example, TinyOS 2.0 or WSN Operating Systems), using as input to the phase, the IT architecture model, previously generated. The output of this stage is a model defined in a Platform-Specific Model (PSM) level. A PSM presents a view of the system from the perspective of a specific technological platform, that is, an associated solution model to a platform that includes the details of the PIM and describes how the implementation is performed on that platform. The technology solution model contains the information required for the specific platform (specific messages in the send or receive format for things or objects, transport protocols used, sensor UUID, sender or receiver). The second stage consists of a transformation of the PSM to text, which represents the code skeleton or executable code of an application, usually in XML-based specifications.

E. *Model transformation methods.*

The methodology is supported by methods based on the MDE approach, to reduce costs and development time, allowing automatic and semi-automated model transformations to generate the output models of each phase. A model transformation consists of a set of transformation rules, which define how an input model is mapped to one or more models or executable code. In order to support the necessary model transformations for the methodology, it is proposed the application of different model transformation methods.

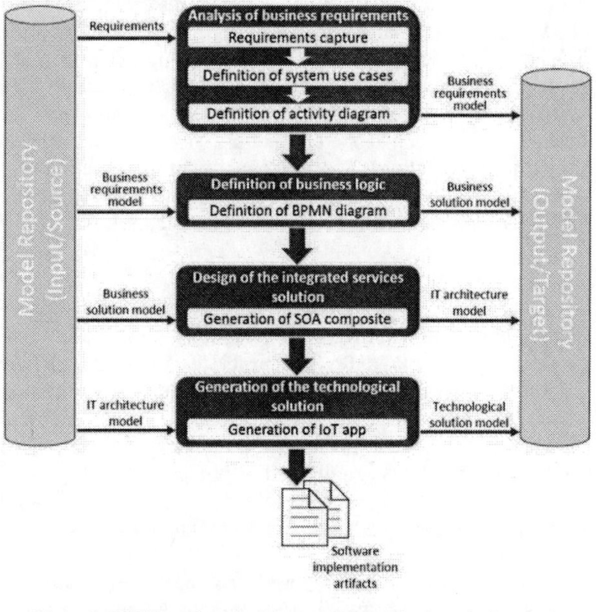

Figure 3. MDE based methodology to IoT applications deployment.

The proposed MDE methods to generate the technological solutions in IoT environments, through software applications oriented to services, consist of 4 transformations. Through the T1 transformation, a conceptual model of the business solution is generated based on a business requirements model, complemented with the business logic and the business process designed through a horizontal PIM-to-PIM transformation. This transformation is derived from the business solution model, using the concepts of the Service Oriented Architecture (SOA), maintaining an independence of the implementation platform. Figure 4 shows an example of a transformation rule (T2), where the BPMN language meta-model is used as input and the SOA architecture meta-model is used as a destination (Rule 1). The transformation methods and proposed rules were defined using the Eclipse Atlas Transformation Language (ATL).

```
rule participant2scope {
      from
            participant: MMbpmn2!Participant (
                  not
participant.processRef.oclIsUndefined()
            )
      to
            scope: MMUML4SOA!Receive (
                  lnk <- participant.name,
                  rvc <- participant.document
            )
}
```

Rule 1

```
rule scope2vehicle {
      from
            participant: MMUML4SOA!Recieve (
                  not
recieve.processRef.oclIsUndefined()
            )
      to
            vehicle: MMSmartVehicle!sensor (
                  sensorData <- receive.lnk,
                  command <- receive.rvc
            )
}
```

Rule 2

Figure 4. Example of transformation rules for method T2 (Rule 1) and T3 (Rule 2).

The technological solution is generated by two model-driven methods. The first method applies a model-to-model transformation T3, generating an output model based on the specific implementation platform that is selected, using a model of the IT architecture as input. The generated model is defined at a specific level of the PSM platform, using concepts from the IoT implementation platform. Figure 4 shows an example of a transformation rule (Rule 2) of the SOA meta-model (PIM level) to a meta-model at a PSM level. In the example, the data to be sent to a sensor of a software application of a smart vehicle simulator is generated. The second method is done by the direct model-to-text transformation T4, which consists of the generation of a document with the source code that represents the structure and behavior of the object when an event occurs.

V. Conclusions

In this paper, a methodology was presented for the development of software applications for IoT. The methodology is based on the principles of Model-Driven Engineering (MDE), where a set of model transformation methods were defined and specified with different viewpoints, abstraction levels, and granularity. The proposed methodology allows guiding the process of developing software applications oriented to services, from conceptual models to the code of a specific application and a selected technology platform.

The objective of the proposed approach is to reduce the time and costs in software development by implementing automatic and semi-automatic model transformations. In addition, an architecture to support the applications or software systems for IoT was proposed. The architecture describes, in a generic way, the different layers required for the deployment of software applications in IoT, using the concepts of Service-Oriented Architecture (SOA).

Acknowledgment

This work was supported by the National Council of Science and Technology (CONACYT) of Mexico under Grant 256922.

References

[1] C.-W. Tsai, C.-F. Lai, and A. V. Vasilakos, "Future internet of things: open issues and challenges," Wireless Networks, vol. 20, no. 8, pp. 2201–2217, 2014.

[2] ITU-T, "Overview of the internet of things," Telecommunication Standardization Sector of ITU, Specification ITU-T Y.2060, January 2013. [Online]. Available: http://handle.itu.int/11.1002/1000/11559

[3] L. Atzori, A. Iera, and G. Morabito, "The internet of things: A survey," Comput. Netw., vol. 54, no. 15, pp. 2787–2805, 2010.

[4] S. Stastny, B. A. Farshchian, and T. Vilarinho, "Designing an application store for the Internet of Things: Requirements and challenges," Proc. Ambient Intelligence: 12th European Conference (AmI 2015), Springer International Publishing, Nov 2015, pp. 313–327, doi:10.1007/978-3-319-26005-1_21

[5] C. Yin, Z. Xiong, H. Chen, J. Wang, D. Cooper, and B. David, "A literature survey on smart cities," Science China Information Sciences, vol. 58, no. 10, Oct 2015, pp. 1–18. [Online]. Available: https://doi.org/10.1007/s11432-015-5397-4

[6] E. Al Nuaimi, H. Al Neyadi, N. Mohamed, and J. Al-Jaroodi, "Applications of big data to smart cities," Journal of Internet Services and Applications, vol. 6, no. 1, Dec 2015, pp. 1-15. [Online]. Available: https://doi.org/10.1186/s13174-015-0041-5

[7] G. Blair, D. Schmidt, and C. Taconet, "Middleware for internet distribution in the context of cloud computing and the internet of things," Annals of Telecommunications, vol. 71, no. 3, pp. 87–92, 2016. [Online]. Available: https://doi.org/10.1007/s12243-016-0493-z

[8] J. Gubbi, R. Buyya, S. Marusic, and M. Palaniswami, "Internet of things (IoT): A vision, architectural elements, and future directions," Future Generation Computer Systems, vol. 29, no. 7, 2013, pp. 1645-1660. [Online].Available:https://doi.org/10.1016/j.future.2013.01.010

[9] B. d. T. Pereira, L. C. Melo, F. J. da Silva, L. E. Talavera, and M. Endler, "A comprehensive and scalable middleware for ambient assisted living based on cloud computing and internet of things," Concurrency and Computation: Practice and Experience, vol. 29, no. 11, 2017, pp. 1-19. [Online]. Available: http://dx.doi.org/10.1002/cpe.4043

[10] F. Ciccozzi, and R. Spalazzese, "MDE4IoT: Supporting the Internet of Things with Model-Driven Engineering," Proc. 10th International Symposium on Intelligent Distributed Computing (IDC 2016), Springer International Publishing, October 2016, pp. 67–76, doi: 10.1007/978-3-319-48829-5_7

[11] E. Tello-Leal, A. B. Rios-Alvarado, I. Lopez-Arevalo, O. Chiotti, and P. D. Villarreal, Methodology based on Model-Driven Development for the execution of collaborative processes through software agents, 1st ed. México, Ediciones UAT - Plaza y Valdes, 2016.

[12] C. Pons, R. Giandini, and G. Perez, Model-Driven Software Development, 1st ed. Argentina, Editorial Universidad Nacional La Plata - McGraw Hill, 2010.

[13] L. Shancang, X. L. Da, and Z. Shanshan, "The internet of things: a survey," Information Systems Frontiers, vol. 17, no. 2, pp. 243–259, 2015. [Online]. Available: http://dx.doi.org/10.1007/s10796-014-9492-7

[14] X. T. Nguyen, H. T. Tran, H. Baraki, and K. Geihs, "FRASAD: A Framework for Model-Driven IoT Application Development," Proc. IEEE 2nd World Forum on Internet of Things (WF-IoT 2015), 2015, pp. 387–392. Available: doi:10.1109/WF-IoT.2015.7389085

[15] F. Pramudianto, C. A. Kamienski, E. Souto, F. Borelli, L. L. Gomes, D. Sadok, and M. Jarke, "IoT Link: An Internet of Things prototyping toolkit," Proc. 2014 IEEE 11th Intl Conf on Ubiquitous Intelligence and Computing, and IEEE 11th Intl Conf on Autonomic and Trusted Computing, and IEEE 14th Intl Conf on Scalable Computing and Communications (UTC-ATC-ScalCom), 2014, pp. 1–9. [Online]. Available: doi:10.1109/UIC-ATC-ScalCom.2014.95

[16] D. Conzon, P. Brizzi, P. Kasinathan, C. Pastrone, F. Pramudianto, and P. Cultrona, "Industrial application development exploiting IoT vision and Model-Driven programming," Proc. 18th International Conference on Intelligence in Next Generation Networks (ICIN 2015), 2015, pp. 168–175. [Online]. Available: doi:10.1109/ICIN.2015.7073828

[17] A. F. Einarsson, P. Patreksson, M. Hamdaqa, and A. Hamou-Lhadj, "SmarthomeML: Towards a domain-specific modeling language for creating smart home applications," Proc. IEEE International Congress on Internet of Things (ICIOT 2017), June 2017, pp. 82–88. [Online]. Available: doi:10.1109/IEEE.ICIOT.2017.35

[18] M. Brambilla, E. Umuhoza, and R. Acerbis, "Model-Driven Development of user interfaces for IoT systems via domain-specific components and patterns," Journal of Internet Services and Applications, vol. 8, no. 1, pp. 1-21, 2017. [Online]. Available: https://doi.org/10.1186/s13174-017-0064-1

[19] D. Bandyopadhyay and J. Sen, "Internet of things: Applications and challenges in technology and standardization," Wireless Personal Communications, vol. 58, no. 1, pp. 49–69, 2011. [Online]. Available: https://doi.org/10.1007/s11277-011-0288-5

Denial of Service Attack in Wireless LAN

∗Tauseef Jamal, ‡∗Pedro Amaral, ±Asifullah Khan, ±Aneela Zameer, ±Kiramat Ullah, ±Shariq Aziz Butt
∗Instituto de Telecomunicações, Lisboa, Portugal.
‡Dept de Eng Electrotecnica, Faculdade de Ciencias e Tecnologia, Universidade Nova de Lisboa, Caparica, Portugal
±DCIS, Pakistan Institute of Engineering and Applied Sciences, Islamabad, Pakistan
tauseef.jamal@lx.it.pt, pfa@fct.unl.pt, [asif, aneelaz]@pieas.edu.pk, [shariq2314, kiramat1990l]@gmail.com

***Abstract*—IEEE 802.11 specifications set the standard for Physical and Medium Access Control (MAC) layer for implementing wireless Local Area Network (LAN). In the wireless network, nodes share media elements with each other. Nodes in wireless network access the media through physical layer using Clear Channel Assessment (CCA) plus Virtual Carrier Sense (VCS) at MAC layer. If VCS timer is not properly handled, there is the possibility of Denial of Service (DoS) attack. In this article, we discuss two scenarios. In the first scenario, DoS attack is launched by increasing the time duration of Clear To Send (CTS) frame. When the CTS frame is received by other nodes, they update their Network Allocation Vector (NAV) for extra time. In prevention step, nodes first detect the malicious duration in the CTS frame and then correct the NAV timer to mitigate the attack. This technique is known as RCD (Re-Evaluation of CTS Duration). In the second scenario, DoS attack is launched by flooding the CTS frame periodically. All other overhearing nodes update their NAV and remain in wait state. To handle such kind of attack, nodes never directly update their NAV after receiving CTS, but after checking the Transmitter Address (TA) and Receiver Address (RA). To increase back the performance of network, blacklisting of malicious node technique is used in both scenarios when a DoS attack is detected.**

Keywords- Virtual Carrier Sense; Medium Access Control; CTS Attack; DoS Attack.

I. INTRODUCTION

Wireless technology is one of the fastest growing industries nowadays. The main reason for this growth is the advantages that only wireless technology has. In wireless communication, there is no need of wires to transmit data from one device to another, which provides flexibility to the network. New devices can be easily added to the network. However, due to the broadcast nature and shared medium of wireless communications, there exist a variety of risks. These risks include packet loss due to distance or mobility, interference, collisions, delay, overhearing, eavesdropping, session hijacking and DoS attacks [1].

In DoS attacks [2], the attacker overloads the network bandwidth with unusual traffic, which makes resources unavailable for others, because other nodes will not be able to send their data after sensing the busy medium. DoS attackers normally exploit the NAV behavior by tempering some of the flags in control frames. In IEEE 802.11 standard, the nodes do not counter check all the flags in control frames, therefore, it is hard to detect such kind of attacks. In this paper, we discuss how DoS attack can be launched when NAV is updated for illegitimate time, by exploiting the duration field of CTS frame in one scenario and exploiting the RA field of CTS frame in the second scenario.

WLANs can be divided into two types: Infrastructure WLANs and Ad-Hoc WLANs. In infrastructure WLAN there is an Access Point (AP) which is surrounded by nodes; AP reserves the media for a node when it has data to send. If one node has data to send to another node, it must pass through AP. In contrast to infrastructure type, the Ad-Hoc WLANs are not centrally connected. In Ad-Hoc mode, the wireless devices are directly connected to each other, handling all communications in distributed fashion.

In Ad-Hoc networks, media is accessed by Distributed Coordinated Function (DCF) with VCS mechanism [3] which includes three-way handshake mechanism before sending data. If a node wants to send data, it sends a Request To Send (RTS) frame to destination. The RTS frame contains reservation duration that is required to complete the data transfer. After receiving an RTS frame by destination, it sends back a CTS frame containing the duration which node requested. According to 802.11 standards all another node when overhear either RTS or CTS must update their NAV and stay quiet until their NAV time reached to zero, NAV is a timer that can uniformly reduce to zero. After all setup, the node sends DATA and waits for ACK, that completes the process. The complete process is shown in Figure 1.

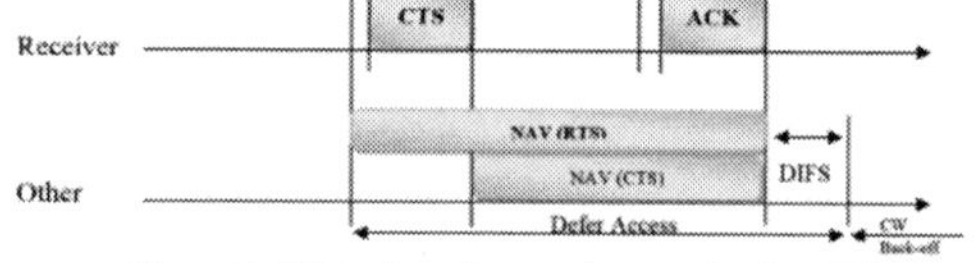

Figure 1. Virtual carrier sensing mechanism [3].

The rest of the paper is structured as follows: In Section 2 we describe related work, while Sections 3 and 4 detaile about DoS attack launching, detection and prevention of two scenarios. Section 5 shows the evaluations of both scenarios. Finally, we concluded the paper in Section 6.

II. RELATED WORK

Table I elaborates the related work about DoS attacks.

Table I. DOS ATTACK IN WLAN

Type of Attack	Description	Counter measurement
(ICMP echo) [4]	Fill a network bandwidth with ICMP echo request packets	Rearranging firewall configuration such that it blocks such packets which are not part of the network.
SYN Flood Attack	In SYN flood attacker requests to the target system to provide adequate server resources and network capabilities	Filtering, increasing backlog, reducing SYN-RECEIVED Timer and SYN cache techniques are used as a counter measurement. [5]
DDoS Attack	The main goal of the attacker is launching a large traffic and makes that flow direction towards victim system.	Configuring proper incident response plan before the DDoS attack in the network, checking traffic format and pattern regularly will help out to mitigate such type of attack.[6]
Land Attack (Local Area Network Denial)[6]	The attackers send malicious packets such that it has the same source and destination address.	By enabling both ingress and egress filters in the router to check the source and destination of packets will help out to mitigate the LAND attack.
Authentication request flood	Flood the state table by malicious requests, after the attack there is no space for acceptance from legitimate requests in the state table.	Tracking of client authentication process by wIPS. [7]
Association request flood	Flooding the associate table.	Log the authenticated user and implementation of the tracking system.[7]
RTS /CTS DoS Attack	Sending malicious RTS/CTS back to back.	Using RRD technique protect from such kind of attack. [8]

For better understanding of DoS attacks in WLANs authors in [9] and [10] discussed and analyzed some weaknesses in 802.11 protocols. The cryptographically protection is not effective because MAC spoofing is still vulnerable and DoS attacks are still possible [9]. While exploiting the authentication mechanism [10] leads to additional overhead.

In [11], the authors analyzed Ad-Hoc network, and its vulnerabilities to DoS attack. The malicious node sends control frames to a node which does not exist in the network; while other nodes find it as true communication in the network which leads to DoS attack. However, they did not consider CTS frame. This kind of DoS attack is more prominent when CTS is sent.

In [12], the authors proposed a solution for flood attack using Letter Envelop Protocol (LEP) with Traffic Pattern Filtering (TPF) protocol. They can be used by Central Manager (CM), but if CM is spoofed and maliciously used another mirror of CM, then it will not be effective.

In [12], the authors analyzed the attacks related to VCS. The main focus of the paper is RTS flooding. They analyzed the effects of RTS flood in different conditions. However, they never considered the hidden node problem in all scenarios.

In [13], the authors increased RTS duration and by re-evaluation of the RTS Duration (RRD) technique bring the system performance up. However, this is not efficient either because other nodes already updated their NAV for extra time. Even if RTS duration is found malicious by CTS receiver node, it will not help.

One of the problems with all above solutions is the use of explicit control messages, which increase the overhead as well as they are prone to collisions. Therefore, our solution is based on implicit behavior without any additional control or broadcast messages.

III. FIRST SCENARIO

A. Attack launching

In our first scenario, one node works as receiver. It starts malicious behavior by increasing CTS frame duration to reserve medium more than the time required. CTS duration is increased more than two 2*SIFS+DATA + ACK frames length. Figure 2 shows that other overhearing nodes update their NAV for more than the time required. This leads to DoS attack.

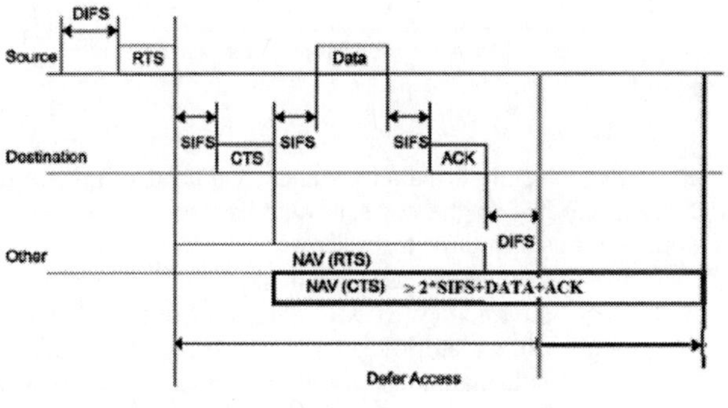

Figure 2. Launching DoS by increasing CTS duration.

B. Detection

We use revalidation technique to detect such kind of attack. In revalidation, there is a comparison between CTS frame duration which is received from receiver node and immediate RTS frame duration which are send by sender node, at lower layer by each node before updating NAV.

In RTS, the duration is set by the sender to keep in view the amount of data. The CTS duration is calculated by receiver node as:

$$\text{RTS\_Duration} - \text{SIFS} - \text{CTS}. \qquad (1)$$

According to IEEE 802.11 standard, when any frame is overheard by a node, it first checks if the frame is destined for it or not. If the frame does not belong to a node, such node just extracts the duration field from the frame and updates its NAV. However, in our proposed detection mechanism all overhearing nodes calculate the CTS duration according to (1), upon reception of RTS. When CTS frame arrives, the overhearing nodes extract the duration field from CTS frame, and compare it to the saved CTS frame (we call it expected CTC duration). Based on the comparison, it decides if the CTS frame is malicious or not. Figure 3 shows the flow diagram of the described mechanism.

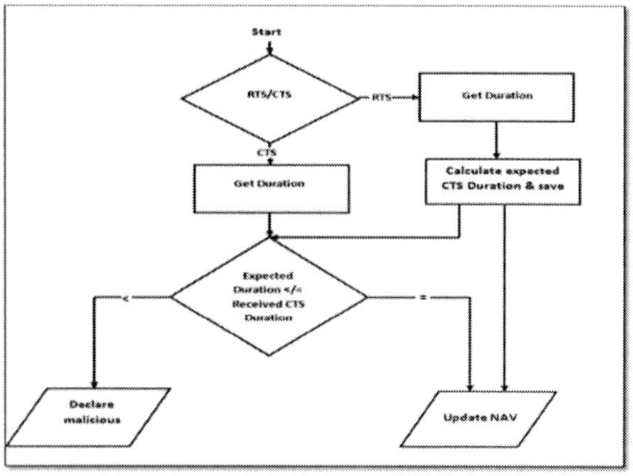

Figure 3. Detection mechanism for the first scenario.

C. Prevention

After detecting a malicious node, we need to update the NAV according to the correct value of duration field. Each node will perform three tasks shown in Figure 4.

- Calculates the malicious time interval by subtracting (CTS duration frame duration-immediate RTS). And save in a variable. In non-malicious case, this variable value must be zero.
- Adjust the actual time for NAV by subtracting the malicious time interval from malicious CTS duration.
- Update the NAV timer.

IV. SECOND SCENARIO

A. Attack launching

In our second scenario, a malicious node pretends to be receiver of itself, by replacing RA with its own MAC address (Figure 5) and sends malicious CTS periodically.

This way, the channel is occupied by the malicious node while other overhearing nodes update their NAV and remain in quiet state, leading to DoS attack [14].

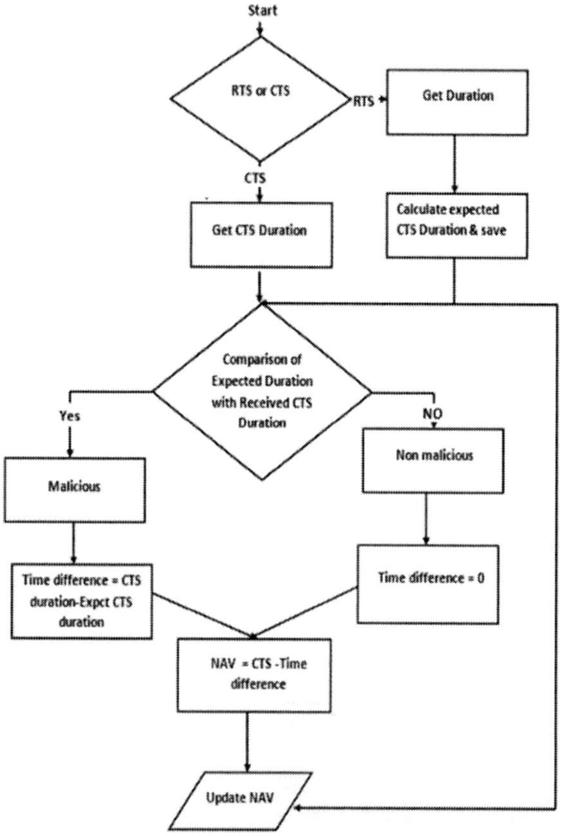

Figure 4. Detection and prevention for the first scenario.

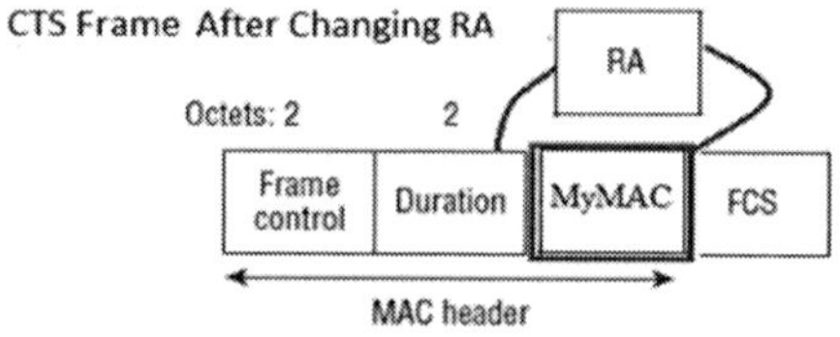

Figure 5. Replacing RA with MyMAC.

There are three kinds of nodes, sender, receiver and others nodes. In case of sender, when malicious CTS is received, it goes to CONTEND state and waits there until the medium is idle for sending the RTS again [15]. In receiver case, when a malicious CTS is received, it goes to QUIET state. The receiver finds that some other nodes are communicating so to avoid a collision it will stay in QUIET state. Other overhearing nodes, just update their NAV (as explained earlier), and most of the time they remain in the QUIET state. Therefore, attack in such a scenario is very critical and hard to detect.

B. Detection

This attack is critical because there is no check on receiver address of CTS frame. Other nodes do not know about CTS frame's Sender Address (SA). So, they can not find malicious CTS and would update NAV after receiving malicious CTS. This problem can be detected as follows:

- Since RTS frame includes the receiver address.
- Therefore, as RTS is received by other nodes, they retrieve the RA and save it.
- When CTS is arrived as a consequent of RTS, before updating the NAV, there would be a comparison at two steps:
  - Compare RA to MyMAC
  - Compare SA to RA.
- If SA is same RA, declare it malicious otherwise updated NAV.

Figure 6 describes the flow diagram of detection mechanism.

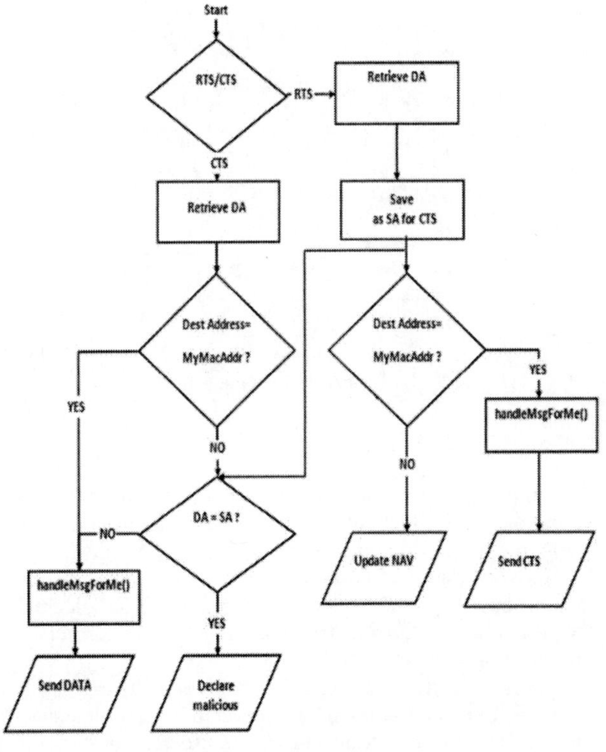

Figure 6. Detection of the second scenario.

C. Prevention

The main problem in this scenario is that malicious node will not release the medium. It will send that malicious CTS and other nodes must wait for the end of transmission. The longer the duration mentioned in malicious CTS, the more the network performance would go down. Therefore, in our proposed mechanism, each node maintains a list of MAC addresses. As soon the malicious CTS's originator is detected, its MAC is added to the list.

When a node is detected malicious, three steps are taken by each node: stop updating NAV, update the list and maintain the record of malicious MAC and send a broadcast alert message with malicious MAC to other nodes. So, any node may no longer involve in communication with such malicious node and ignore such CTS in the future. As a result, other nodes would have more chances to utilize the medium, increasing the overall capacity of the network.

V. EVALUATION

In our experimental setup, we used the OMNET++ framework with MIXIM simulator model on window 7 platform. In MIXIM wireless network IEEE 802.11 is implemented. For both scenarios the destination or receiver node is assigned MAC address of 0, while all other nodes are sender nodes. Node-0 sends CTS and behaves maliciously. The number of nodes varies from 3 to 15 nodes. We have performed three kinds of simulations for both scenarios, i.e., without malicious node (which is bench mark), with one malicious node and with our proposed prevention mechanism. We simulated each topology for 300s. We used throughput and latency as performance parameters. Other simulation parameters are listed in Table II.

Table II. SIMULATION PARAMETERS

Parameter	Values
cup-time-limit	300s
playgroundSizeX	500m
playgroundSizeY	500m
playgroundSizeZ	50m
carrier Frequency	2.4e+9Hz
Power	110.11mW
mobility.speed	0 mps
appl.burstSize	1frame
appl.trafficParam	50ms
appl.destAddr	0 node
appl.initializationTime	uniform(60000ms,60050ms)
mac.headerLength	272 bits
mac.queueLength	14 frames
acierate	2E+6bps# in bits/second
phy.useThermalNoise	true

A. First scenario results

Latency is the amount of time a message takes to traverse a system; we can observe that latency increases as many nodes increase in a network. We can see in Figure 7 that latency is increased due to the malicious node which means that nodes wait for extra time to send data. Here, our proposal brought the latency as close as possible to normal and decreased the latency up to 35% in case of one malicious node.

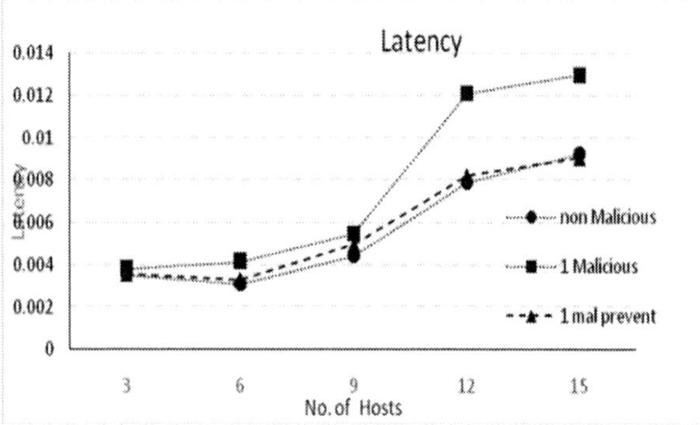

Figure 7. Latency for the first scenario.

Throughput is a measure of how many units of information a system can process in each amount of time. Throughput decreases as network density increases, in Figure 8; the throughput decreases with increase in number of hosts due to increase in latency. As the nodes update their NAV after receiving malicious CTS, the number of packets sent by a node would be less compared to the non-malicious case. Our proposal brought the throughput closer to normal and increased the throughput up to 35% in case of one malicious node.

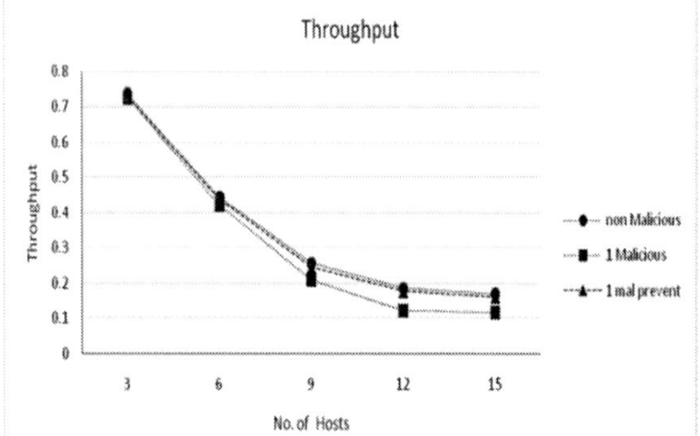

Figure 8. Throughput for the first scenario.

B. Second scenario results

In the second scenario, the DoS attack has the worst effect on network performance as compared to the first scenario. As shown in Figure 9, when receiving malicious CTS after the interval, here interval is 3 frames count in the network, sender node sends again RTS frame for sending data and other nodes just only update NAV. Other nodes only send their RTS frame when the first node RTS retries reaches its limit. That decreases throughput abruptly.

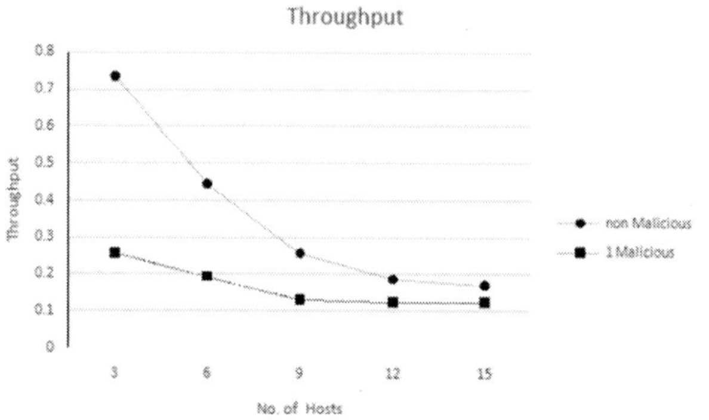

Figure 9. Throughput after malicious CTS for 2nd scenario.

After blacklisting the malicious node, other nodes ignore any kind of frame from the malicious node, the throughput is increased up to 41%, which is 65% increased to normal behavior. It still not reached to normal behavior because there is still a malicious CTS flow in the network. Also, there is slight overhead of broadcast alert, which decreases throughput c.f. Figure 10.

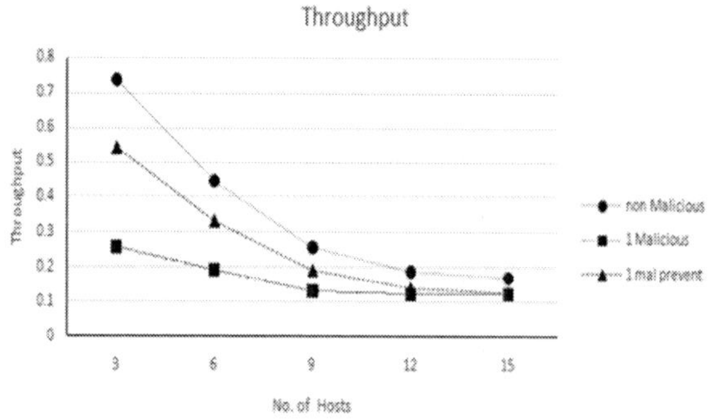

Figure 10. Throughput after prevention for 2nd scenario.

VI. Conclusions and Future Work

In the first scenario, the attacker increase the CTS frame duration field which reserves the media for a node longer than required and other nodes update NAV for the extra time. Nodes are not allowed to sense the media; therefore, we proposed a Re-Evaluate CTS Duration (RCD) technique to detect such behavior and then set back the correct value for NAV as a prevention.

In the second scenario, CTS frame exploits the RA field in CTS frame and sends a CTS frame to itself after a specific interval. In the detection phase, we use the comparison of destination and sender node addresses when CTS is received by any node. During the prevention mechanism, other nodes stop updating NAV and announce the MAC of the malicious node. After that, no other node would communicate with such node.

As a future work, we aim to extend the scenario towards dense network having 100s of highly mobile nodes randomly deployed, to test the proposal against increasing number of malicious nodes. Another extension would be learning the malicious behavior implicitly by other nodes and other nodes would ignore such node (implicitly). In this situation we would use relays to cooperate with [17], using the framework proposed in [18]. The aim is to implement and test in the real scenario.

ACKNOWLEDGMENT

This work is funded by FCT/MEC through national funds and when applicable co-funded by FEDER – PT2020 partnership agreement under the project UID/EEA/50008/2013.

REFERENCES

[1] SA Butt, T. Jamal, "Study of Black Hole Attack in AODV", in Proc of International Journal of Future Generation Communication and Networking, Vol.10, No.9 (2017), pp.37-48.

[2] T. Jamal, P. Mendes, and A. Zúquete, "Wireless Cooperative Relaying Based on Opportunistic Relay Selection," International Journal on Advances in Networks and Services, vol. 05, no. 2, pp. 116–127, Jun. 2012.

[3] T. Jamal and P. Mendes, "Relay Selection Approaches for Wireless Cooperative Networks," in Proc. of IEEE WiMob, Niagara Falls, Canada, Oct. 2010.

[4] B. John and S. Stefan. "802.11 Denial-of-Service Attacks: Real Vulnerabilities and Practical Solutions." Proceedings of the USENIX Security Symposium, August 2003.

[5] D.B.Roy, R.Chaki and N.Chaki, "A New Cluster-Based Wormhole Intrusion Detection Algorithm for Mobile Ad Hoc Neworks," International Journal of Network Security and Its Application (IJNSA), Vol. 1, No.1, April, 2009.

[6] H.Deng, W.Li and D.P.Agrawal, "Routing Security in Wireless Ad Hoc Networks," University of Cincinnati, IEEE Communication Magzine, Oct, 2002.

[7] C. Liu and J. Yu, "A Solution to WLAN Authentication and Association DoS Attacks," IAENG Int. J. Comput. Sci., vol. 34, no. 1, pp. 31–36, 2007.

[8] P. M. D. Nagarjun, V. A. Kumar, C. A. Kumar, and A. Ravi, "Simulation and analysis of RTS/CTS DoS attack variants in 802.11 networks," in 2013 International Conference on Pattern Recognition, Informatics and Mobile Engineering, 2013, pp. 258–263.

[9] K. Bicakci and B. Tavli, "Denial-of-Service attacks and countermeasures in IEEE 802.11 wireless networks," Comput. Stand. Interfaces, vol. 31, no. 5, pp. 931–941, Sep. 2009.

[10] J. Heo and C. S. Hong, "An Efficient and Secured Media Access Mechanism Using the Intelligent Coordinator in Low-Rate WPAN Environment," Springer, Berlin, Heidelberg, 2005, pp. 470–476.

[11] T. Jamal, P. Mendes, and A. Zúquete, "RelaySpot: A Framework for Opportunistic Cooperative Relaying," in Proc. of IARIA ACCESS, Luxembourg, Jun. 2011.

[12] A. L., V. B., S. S., and P. A., "A Solution to Prevent Resource Flooding Attacks in 802.11 WLAN," Springer, Berlin, Heidelberg, 2012, pp. 607–616.

[13] T. Jamal, M. Alam, and M. M. Umair, "Detection and prevention against RTS attacks in wireless LANs," in 2017 International Conference on Communication, Computing and Digital Systems (C-CODE), 2017, pp. 152–156.

[14] T. Jamal and P. Mendes, "802.11 Medium Access Control In MiXiM," Copelabs Technical Report, 2013.

[15] T. Jamal and P. Mendes, "Cooperative Relaying in Dynamic Wireless Networks under Interference Conditions (2014)", in: IEEE Communication Magazine, Special issue on User-centric Networking and Services.

[16] Y. Ohsita, S. Ata, and M. Murata, "Deployable overlay network for defense against distributed SYN flood attacks," IEICE Trans. Commun., vol. E91–B, no. 8, pp. 2618–2630, Aug. 2008.

[17] T. Jamal, P. Mendes, and A. Zúquete, "Interference-Aware Opportunistic Relay Selection," in Proc. of ACM CoNEXT, Tokyo, Japan, Dec. 2011.

[18] T. Jamal, P. Mendes, and A. Zúquete, "Opportunistic Relay Selection for Wireless Cooperative Network," in Proc. of IEEE IFIP NTMS, Istanbul, Turkey, May 2012.

Flow Table Congestion in Software Defined Networks

Tauseef Jamal∗, Pedro Amaral∗‡, Khurram Abbas
∗Instituto de Telecomunicações, Lisboa, Portugal
‡Dept de Eng Electrotecnica, Faculdade de Ciencias e Tecnologia, Universidade Nova de Lisboa, Caparica, Portugal
tauseef.jamal@lx.it.pt, pfa@fct.unl.pt, abbaskhurram98@gmail.com.

***Abstract*—Security is a major concern for today's networks and network applications. Denial of Service (DoS) is major threat to availability of service. DoS is easy to detect but hard to mitigate. There are several types of DoS attacks, such as flooding etc. Software Defined Networks (SDN) inherit security threats from traditional networks along with threats specific to them. Flow table congestion is an example of such problem specific to SDN networks. The attacker generates multiple packets as messages to the controller. Because of this, the switch's Ternary Content Addressable Memory (TCAM) is flooded with controller replies. TCAMs are very expensive and power hungry. To avoid this type of attack, different aggregation strategies have been proposed. These techniques save TCAMs at the cost of lost statistics in OpenFlow flow table. In this paper, we used an improved version of Optimal Routing Table Construction (ORTC) to perform flow aggregation similar to Fast Flow Table Aggregation (FFTA). Some disadvantages of FFTA include loss of flow table statistics and counts. Our proposed technique reduces the number of flows to solve Flow Table Congestion Problem along with maintaining the consistency of statistics.**

Keywords- congestion; flow table; optimal routing.

I. INTRODUCTION

Software Defined Networking (SDN) is an innovative paradigm for computer networking [1]. Traditional networks are hardware oriented, while SDN shifts the focus from hardware to software. It makes computer networks more maintainable by providing logically centralized control and separating them from the forwarding functionality. It offers network programmability, agility, central management, open standards and vendor neutral solutions.

On the other hand, this separation of network functionality opens a more targeted attack surface. Potential attackers can target control or data plane more accurately than ever before. In addition, if attackers can gain control of the control plane, the entire network is compromised. SDN inherits traditional network security issues along with issues specific to it. SDN centralized monitoring can be used to cope with security issues more efficiently [1].

One of these security issues is Denial of Service, which targets the availability of the system and disrupts the legitimate user to available system services. The attacker sends a huge amount of useless traffic or exploits some vulnerability on the target system. This causes the system to stop responding, crash or reboot. Sources of the DoS can be single or multiple. The scale of this attack varies i.e. it can employ a single system to thousands of systems, known as bots. These types of attacks are a real threat to systems which are supposed to be providing online services because these can result into loss of revenue, loss of customer's trust and loss of reputation.

This article revolves around the following problem.

A) How flow tables in OpenFlow can be used to avoid flow table saturation attack.

B) How a secure system can be designed around SDN control plane to avoid traditional attacks.

The rest of the paper is organized as follows. In Section II, related work is described; Section II models the problem statement and discusses the solution, while Section IV details the implementation.

II. LITERATURE ANALYSIS

A brief description of literature survey is given below.

A) Optimal Routing Table Construction

The backbone routers of the Internet are populated with routes by Border Gateway Protocol (BGP). Optimal Routing Table Construction (ORTC) calculates the minimal number of equivalent routes locally with modifying BGP [1]. First, the binary tree representation of IP routing table is constructed. Then, the resultant table is obtained by performing the following two generalized steps of netting in sequence on the original table.

1. Sub Netting
2. Super Netting

This causes a huge decrease in flows but ORTC is applied locally to every router because modifying BGP along with other protocol on every network device is a challenging task [1].

B) Fast Flow Table Aggregation

Flow tables of OpenFlow are TCAM hungry because they contain comparatively more fields in the header than traditional switches and routers. The flow table of OpenFlow v1.0.0 contains 12 matching fields for headers, whose size is more than 237 bits per flow entry. Newer versions of OpenFlow have increasing number of matching fields to cope with different dynamic requirements. On the other hand, TCAM's are very expensive and power hungry. Because of this OpenFlow, switches suffer from Flow Table Congestion Problem (FTCP).

Aggregation of flows can be used to reduce the demand of TCAM's by OpenFlow switches. Flow aggregation is an economical solution because it is software based. It best matches the nature of SDN. FFTA provides an improved technique for aggregation of flows. This technique consists of three steps [2].

1. Rule list is partitioned into permutable prefixes
2. Modified aggregation of prefixes
3. Merging of bits iteratively

This aggregation is very efficient, but there is a problem with this approach. It mixes up the entries which results in coarser grain statistics. It requires some statistical estimates to fine grain the statistics so that original flow counts and other parameters can be obtained from the aggregated flow [3].

C) Flow Table Reduction Scheme

In traditional networks switches perform actions according to rigid protocols. SDN overcomes this inflexibility by separating the control function from packet transmission. Using SDN, the dynamic policies can be easily implemented. On the other hand, this dynamic nature can cause redundant entries in flow tables. Flow tables are very important to SDN. However, due to limited size of TCAM, this redundancy leads to the problem of congestion of flow table. Some solutions are proposed to divide the flows into mice flows and giant flows. FRTS puts three constraints which every flow table reduction scheme should follow for proper functioning of OpenFlow enabled networks. These constraints are

Consistency: Same actions should be allotted to the flows after the reduction.

Absoluteness: Rules that are manually added should match and execute on priority.

Accuracy: The statistics should be accurate at any interval of time.

III. PROBLEM MODELLING

Attack trees [4] are conceptual diagrams well known for security assessment of a system. These show how an asset can be attacked. There exist two generic types of security modeling for systems.

- System oriented
- Attacker oriented

The former system models itself and performs security analysis on the system. The later one models the attack on the system with a focus on attacker objectives. An attack tree contains a single root which represents the overall objective of the attacker. This objective is iteratively decomposed into finer grained and quantitative objectives, which form the child and leaves of the attack tree.

The problem is modeled using attack tree with denial of service as a root node. Denial of service can be performed in SDN by attacking controller, switch or any of the hosts. To conduct a denial of service, the attacker should flood or exploit any one of these components. This type of relation is called "OR" relation because the attacker can achieve its parent objective by performing any one of child objectives.

Figure 1 shows first level of attack tree. It shows that denial of service can be achieved by attacking any one of the child components i.e. OpenFlow switch, controller or host.

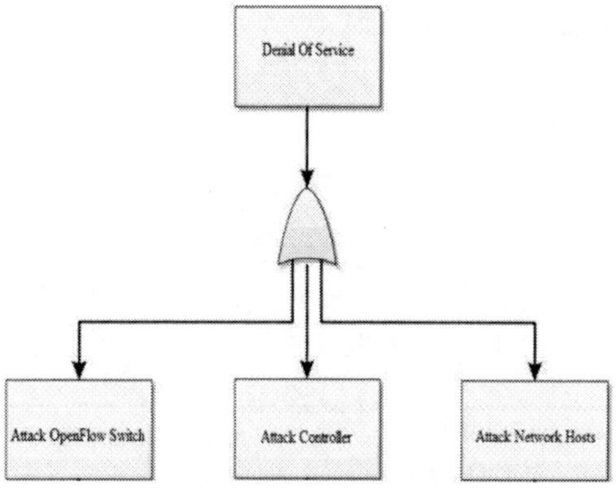

Figure 1. Level one attack tree for DoS.

A simplified attack tree for attack on controller is shown in Figure 2. This attack tree models the objective of the attacker having intent of attacking SDN controller. SDN controller can be exposed to DoS by flooding it or by performing logical or vulnerability attack on it. Vulnerability DoS requires three activities i.e. finger printing of OS, finding vulnerability of that OS and writing exploit along with payload. These all activities must be carried out to perform logical DoS on controller. On the other hand, flooding DoS can be performed by carrying out any one of the leaf activities, as shown in Figure 2.

The attack tree in Figure 3 models the actual threat against which we have proposed a solution. Flow tables store flow entries in TCAMs. TCAM is now a de facto industry standard [5][6]. TCAMs are very expensive and have limited amount of memory. Any attacker can generate a large amount of Packet_In messages to controller. In the response of those messages the switch is flooded with policy replies against messages from controller. However, due to TCAM's limited memory, new rules are not installed. Legal new packets suffer from such attack because policy against them cannot become part of flow table. To avoid this type of attack, an efficient and consistent mechanism of flow aggregation is required. On the other hand, aggregation of flows results in modification and generalization of counters. Statistics are mixed up due to aggregation.

A. Proposed Solution

An improved version of Optimal Routing Table Construction is used to minimize the flow entries in the flow table. Moreover, to ensure consistency of statistics improved ORTC is applied to core switches, which results in removal of redundant entries without modifying the statistics. Details of these techniques are provided below. First of all, we will discuss ORTC. After that, we will use Bit Weaving [7] approach to create a binary tree representation of non-prefix OpenFlow entries because ORTC works only at prefixes. After that, we will discuss where this technique should be applied along with considering the consistency of statistics of OpenFlow flow table.

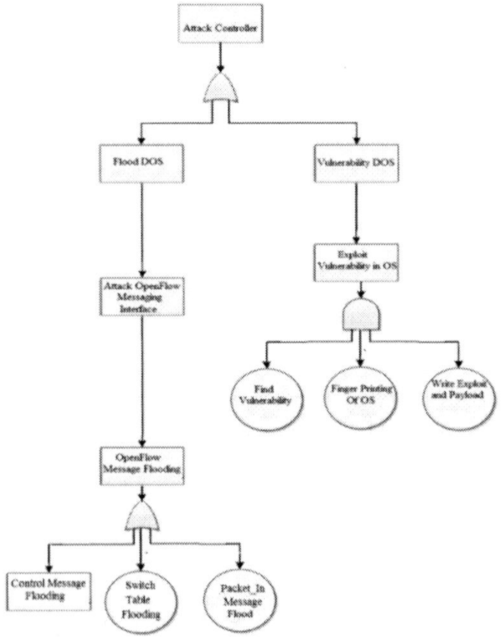

Figure 2. Attack tree for attack on controller.

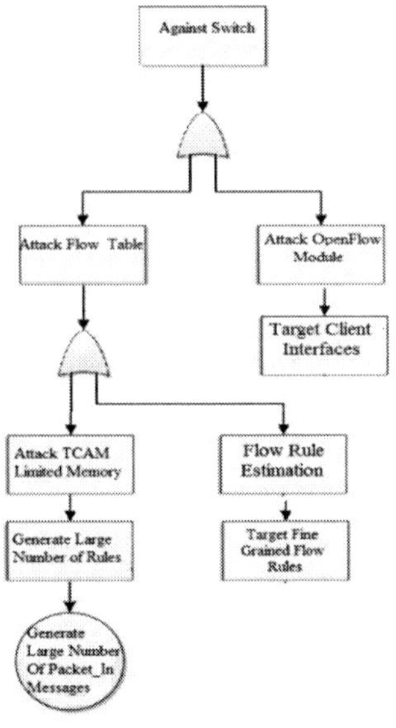

Figure 3. Attack tree for Flow Table Congestion Attack on OpenFlow switch.

a) Optimal Routing Table Construction

ORTC [1] is an optimal solution to minimize IP routing entries or prefixes. It contains 3 steps to get optimal reduced tree.

Step 1: In the first step, a tree representation of table in binary format is normalized by setting zero or two children for every node. This is done by initializing the next hop for newly created leaf node by the next hop of nearest ancestor. After the first step, Table I is converted into Figure 5.

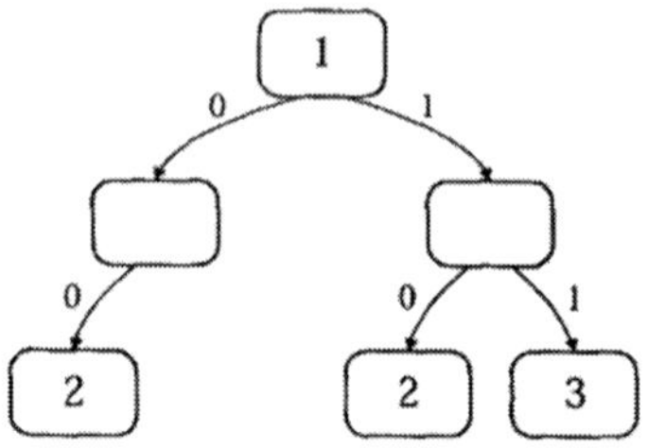

Figure 4. Normalized tree [1].

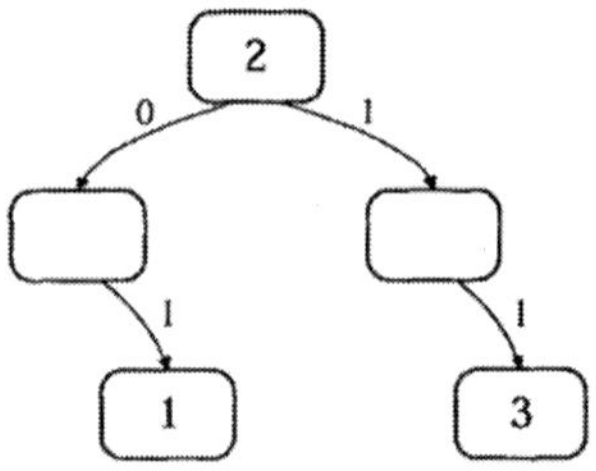

Figure 5. Results of ORTC application [1].

Table I. EXAMPLE ROUTING TABLE

Destination IPs (Binary	Action
*	1
00*	2
10*	2
11*	3

Step 2: The second step of ORTC performs calculation for next hop which are prevalent for every level of the given table. The following operation symbolically defined by "#", shown in Figure 6, is used to define next hops up the tree.

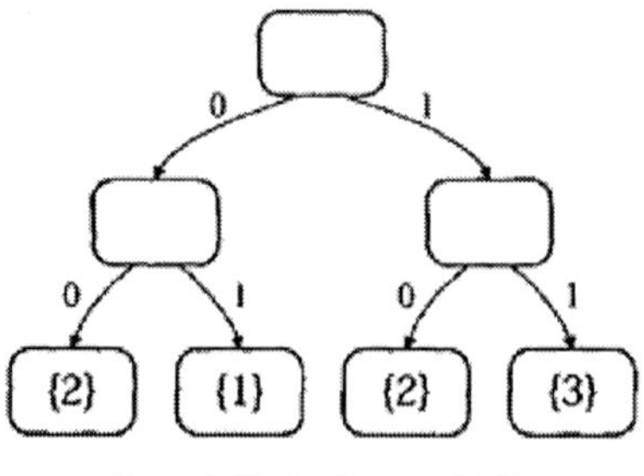

Figure 6. Table after step 1 [1].

Step 3: This step uses sub netting to remove redundant entries from the tree by selecting next hops. Pre order traversal can be used. Also, one can traverse by level down the root. If the nearest ancestor has a next hop, than it will be inherited by the node. The state of table during step 3 is shown in Figure 7, while Figure 4 shows the resultant binary tree representation. The equivalent table for routes is shown in Table II.

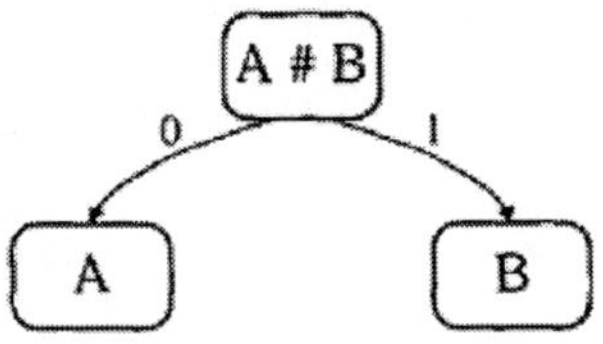

$$A\#B = \begin{cases} A \cap B & \text{if } A \cap B \neq \emptyset \\ A \cup B & \text{if } A \cap B = \emptyset \end{cases}$$

Figure 7. Prevalent hop calculation.

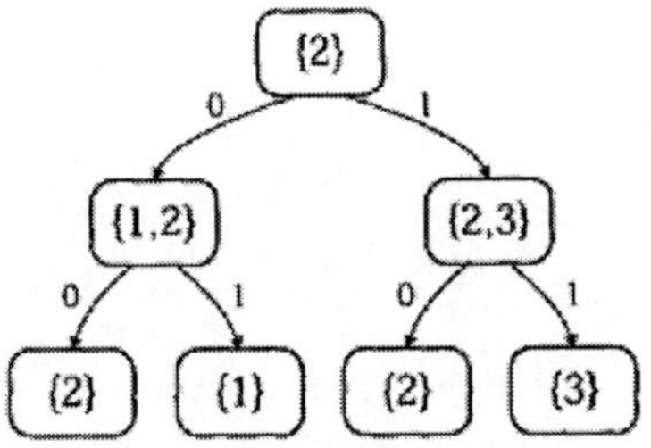

Figure 8. Table after step 2 [1].

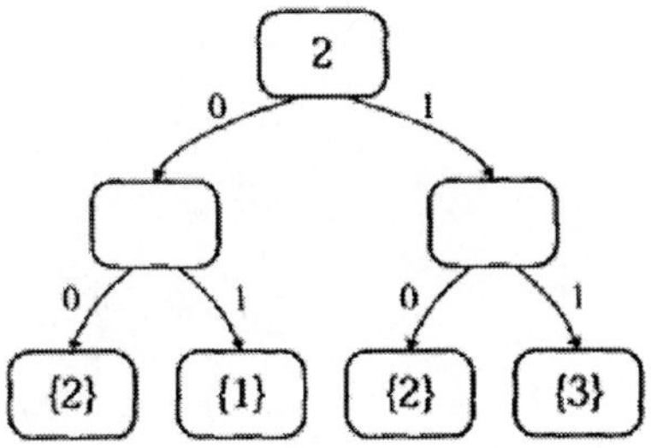

Figure 9. Table during step 3.

TABLE II. RESULTANT TABLE AFTER ORTC

Destination IPs (Binary	Action
*	2
01*	1
11*	3

b) Bit Weaving

ORTC is prefix based approach. So, it in not directly applicable to OpenFlow based flows because they can include wild card anywhere. Therefore, we need to get a binary tree representation of OpenFlow based flows by applying bit weaving initial permutation. The output of this permutation can be now directly utilized by ORTC engine.

c) Avoiding loss of statistics in OpenFlow Table

Consider the topology shown in Figure 8. In this topology S1 is the first level core switch. Similarly, S5 and S2 are second level core switches. While S3, S4, S6 and S7 are end switches. Consider Host 1 with IP 10.0.0.1. Different statistics and counts related to Host 1 may be available on every switch. But actual aggregated statistics of Host 1 in this case will be available at switch S3. On all other switches the statistics regarding Host 1 are redundant entries. Same is the case with all other hosts. Generally, we can say that end switches contain total statistics related to the connected host, while when we move from end switches to core switches, the statistics found here are redundant.

By comparing statistics for Host 1 at different switches, we can conclude that total statistics regarding Host 1 are available at end switch connected to it i.e. switch S1. While core switches contain only redundant statistics regarding to different hosts in network. Hence, it is safe to apply flow aggregation on core switches without the fear of losing statistics. Core switches also contain more flows than end switches in real life cases.

B. Implementations

There exist two types of development techniques for SDN application and policy enforcement.

Reactive Approach:

When a new packet arrives at OpenFlow switch, its header is matched against flow table entries. Packet is sent to controller if no match occurs in flow table. In reaction to that controller installs appropriate policy in flow table against that packet. This approach is called reactive approach, which is event based.

Proactive Approach:

In this approach all necessary policies are installed proactively. REST API's are widely used for this approach.

We used both approaches in our solution appropriately. For rate limiting and filtering reactive approach was used. To install reduced flows and remove the original flows from core switches proactive approach was used [8].

C. Data Collection

We classified data into two types.

a) Input Data:

There were two types of input data.

1. Flow rules for OpenFlow table were generated by using a wrapper around ClassBench [9] tool. This wrapper used same seed files generated and used by ClassBench.

2. To overflow switch TCAM storage with flow rules huge amount of *Packet_In* messages needed to generate. These messages were generated by Scapy [10]. Scapy is used to craft custom packets.

b) Output Data:

Output data was collected from three sources.

- CLI of different tools such as Mininet.
- Data written by custom utilities in log files.
- Web interface of SFlow tool was also used to collect some data.

IV. EVALUATION

In this section, statistics and results are presented against attacks carried out in the SDN environment, using attack trees. There were two types of attacks through which an attacker can achieve the objective of DoS in SDN. The first type of attack is a traditional attack which SDN inherits from traditional networks i.e., attack against host. While the second attack is specific to SDN network i.e., attack against switch. The evaluation presents the later type of attack.

A. Attack Against Switch

To avoid this type of attack, a solution is proposed in design and methodology. We used switch as learning switch to conduct the desired behavior. Script for POX learning switch [11] is available as learningswitch.py while for Opendaylight learning switch [27] is implemented using Service Abstraction Layer SAL with the name of MD-SAL Layer 2 switch. CBench is a tool used for benchmarking of controller. It measures throughput and latency of different SDN controllers. It connects to controller and simulates millions of devices sending messages to the controller. Throughput of Opendaylight, Floodlight and POX [12][13] are shown in Figure 10. The figure shows throughput of controllers in terms of flows per second for a given number of switches. These statistics are collected from a machine with Ubuntu 14.04 LTS and single core with 4 gb ram.

If considerable number of packets are generated on some given switch interface using scapy than packet_in messages will be generated and because of controller's response switch memory will be exhausted. After that, new incoming legitimate packets will be dropped at that switch, because rules against these packets will not be installed. Also, when several times a switch fails to install a flow, controller starts to ignore the packet in messages from that controller. This causes packet loss too. Figure 11 shows packet loss after flow table congestion for different controllers with link bandwidth set to 100 Mbps.

To cope with this type of problem, we used flow aggregation. Figure 12 shows the results of reduced set of rules along with original rule sets against number of switches and hosts. This shows that for core switches, where aggregation does not disturb statistics in our scenario, we were successfully able to reduce rule from 23% to 41%.

This technique also causes reduced bandwidth consumption between controller and switch, because now switch communicates with the controller less frequently in case of Packet_In messages.

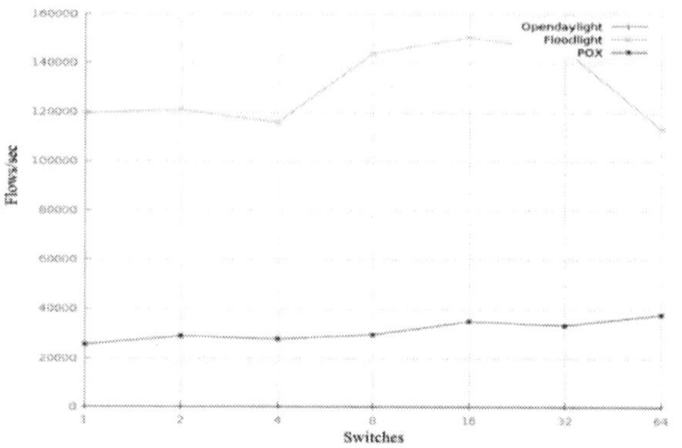

Figure 10. Throughput analysis.

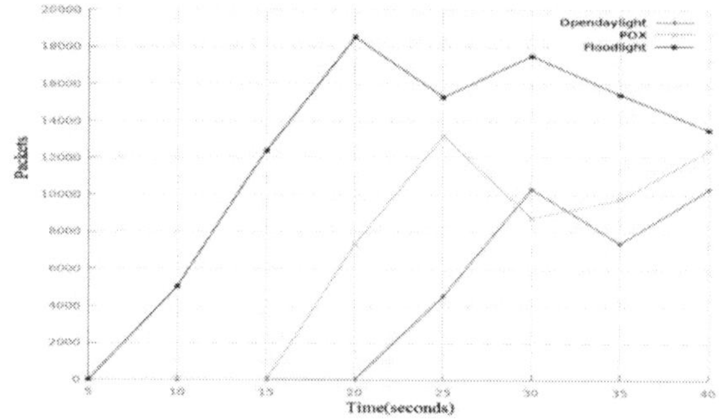

Figure 11. Packets loss analysis.

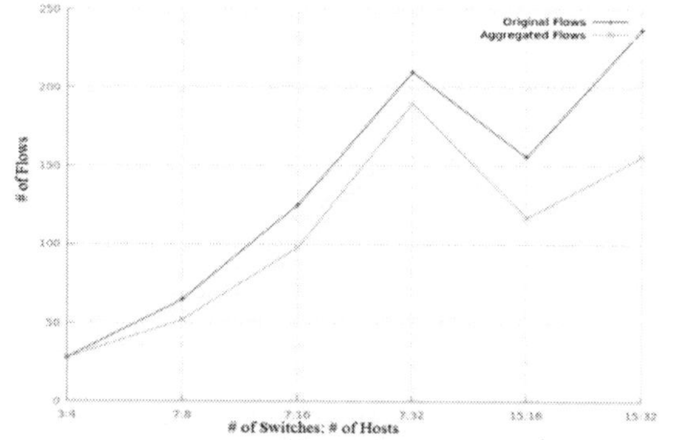

Figure 12. Reduced flows analysis.

V. CONCLUSIONS

Flow table congestion is a problem specific to SDN. Optimal routing table construction was used with enhancement to prevent this type of attack. Existing aggregation techniques also prevent flow table congestion, but these also cause in loss of counts and statistics. A simple strategy was used to identify redundant statistics. Next, aggregation was applied on those identified flow tables to avoid loss of statistics in OpenFlow table successfully. This caused about 23% to 40% percent compression in different cases.

A simple idea was also proposed to reconstruct redundant statistics for our sample topology. But that idea needs to be generalized with the use of different degree of equation along with statistical estimation. This technique can also be matured to be applied even on original flows and their reconstruction, so that aggregation can also be useful for edge switches. As a future work we aim to apply cooperative mechanism [14][15][16] to identify early congestion to avoid inefficiency in routers.

ACKNOWLEDGMENT

This work is funded by FCT/MEC through national funds and when applicable co-funded by FEDER – PT2020 partnership agreement under the project UID/EEA/50008/2013.

REFERENCES

[1] Richard P. Draves, Christopher King, Srinivasan Venkatachary and Brian N. Zill, " Constructing Optimal IP Routing Tables " 1998.

[2] Shouxi Luo "Fast incremental flow table aggregation in SDN" Aug. 2014.

[3] B. Leng, L. Huang and Y. Zhang, "A Mechanism for Reducing Flow Tables in Software Defined Network " 2015.

[4] V. Saini and V. Paruchuri, "Threat modeling using attack trees" J.Comput. Sci. Coll., 23(4):124{131, April 2008.

[5] K. Lakshminarayanan, A. Rangarajan, and S. Venkatachary, "Algorithms for advanced packet classification with ternary CAMs," in Proc.ACM SIGCOMM, Aug. 2005, pp. 193–204.

[6] "Content addressable memory," Integrated Device Technology, Inc.,

[7] Chad R. Meiners, Alex X. Liu, and Eric Torng "Bit Weaving: A Non-Prefix Approach to Compressing Packet Classifiers in TCAMs" April 2012.

[8] T. Jamal and P. Mendes, "Cooperative relaying in user-centric networking under interference conditions", Communications Magazine IEEE, vol. 52, pp. 18-24, 2014, ISSN 0163-6804.

[9] T. Jamal, P. Mendes, and A. Zúquete, "Wireless Cooperative Relaying Based on Opportunistic Relay Selection," International Journal on Advances in Networks and Services, vol. 05, no. 2, pp. 116–127, Jun. 2012.

[10] S Kaur and J Singh, "Network Programmability Using POX Controller" 2014.

[11] T. Jamal, M Alam and M Umair, "Detection and Prevention against RTS Attacks in Wireless LANs" in Proc of IEEE C-CODE, Islamabad, Pakistan 2017.

[12] Jeremy M. Dover "A denial of service attack against the SDN controller" 2013.

[13] Open Floodlight The OpenDaylight Platform | OpenDaylight https://www.opendaylight.org, Accessed on 7 October 2015.

[14] T. Jamal, P. Mendes, A. Zuquete, "Analysis of hybrid relaying in cooperative WLAN" In proc. of IEEE/IFIP Wireless Days 2013.

[15] T. Jamal and P. Mendes, "Relay Selection Approaches for Wireless Cooperative Networks," in Proc. of IEEE WiMob, Niagara Falls, Canada, Oct. 2010.

[16] T. Jamal, P. Mendes, and A. Zúquete, "RelaySpot: A Framework for Opportunistic Cooperative Relaying," in Proc. of IARIA ACCESS, Luxembourg, Jun. 2011.

Secure Communication System for Emergency Services in Network Congestion Scenarios

Alexandra Rivero-García, Iván Santos-González, Candelaria Hernández Goya, Pino Caballero-Gil

Department of Computer Engineering
University of La Laguna, Tenerife, Spain
Email: {ariverog, jsantosg, mchgoya, pcaballe}@ull.edu.es

***Abstract*—Every day different events, with different risk levels, take place in cities. Emergency services are responsible for the safety of citizens and communication between emergency staff is one of the main requirements for their correct coordination and operation. A problem arises when large numbers of people are located in a particular area, which could produce saturation in traditional network infrastructures. This paper presents a low-cost model of communication to be used in this scenario. The communication system described includes an ID-Based Signcryption scheme (IBSC) that works considering the location and the public identification of emergency service workers in order to provide integrity, confidentiality, authentication and non-repudiation in a single step and in an efficient way.**

***Index Terms*—Identity Based Signcryption (IBSC); mHealth; Mobile devices; Android; Communications**

I. Introduction

This paper presents a low-cost model for communication in scenarios where network congestion is produced by massive access of users involved in emergency situations. This is a predictive scheme based on the establishment of a second communication channel that does not rely on the cloud.

The objective is to provide a suitable way of communication for emergency services (police, firefighters, medical staff, etc.) in case of events where specific alerts or activities requiring their participation (flood risk, protest march, a concert, a fire, etc.) take place. Usually, the first step is the assignment of different emergency service workers to specific areas to preserve the civil security. Figure 1 presents as an example the geolocation of three simultaneous events: a cultural event with large flow of people in green, a protest march in orange and an area with high risk of flood in blue. When an event is declared, different types of emergency service workers must be assigned to that zone. In the proposed system, the assignation of service workers is also used to generate and pre-share information among them. That is why a generic event chat, in which workers can participate via mobile phone, is included. In the event that congestion is detected in the network, the emergency mode is declared. In this specific mode, the communications will be made directly, in a peer-to-peer mode through their smartphones and without additional tools.

A second goal in this paper, is to guarantee the security of the shared data, thus an ID-Based Signcryption scheme (IBSC) based on the location and the public identifications of emergency service workers is used. With this cryptosystem all the shared messages will be signed and encrypted.

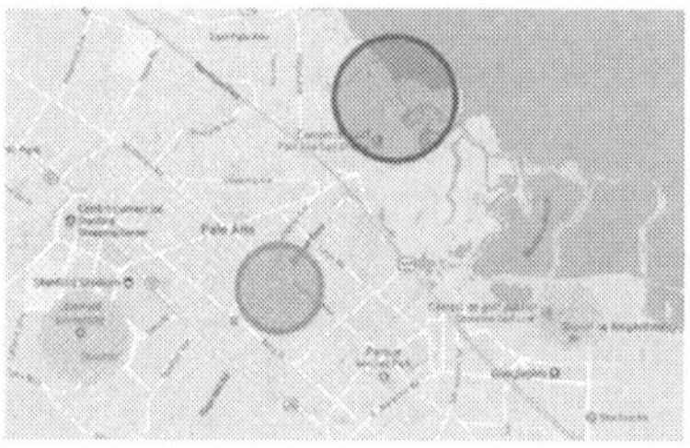

Fig. 1. Geolocation of events.

The majority of the communications that are currently developed within the emergency sections are carried out by radio frequency. In the proposal, communication is done through two different technologies using smartphones: Bluetooth Low Energy (BLE) [1] and via Wi-Fi Direct [2]. The features described below will be taken into account to choose the alternative. When possible the channel created by Wi-Fi Direct, due to its higher rate of speed and its greater range, will be used. Bluetooth Low Energy has a transmission rate of 25 Mbps and Wi-Fi Direct has a transmission rate of 250 Mbps. The maximum range of Bluetooth Low Energy Communication is 60 meters, while Wi-Fi Direct has a range of 200 meters. In the same range of Wi-Fi, Wi-Fi Aware improves the performance of Wi-Fi Direct. Wi-Fi Aware [3] is only available for the latest version of Android [4] and as a preview mode.

The structure of the article is described below. Section II includes a short review of publications that justify the novelty and adequacy of the proposed system. Section III deals, on the one hand, with the fundamentals of Identity-Based Cryptography since the proposal uses it to guarantee confidentiality, integrity and authenticity of the transferred information, and on the other hand deals with a presentation of a system overview. Section IV deals with the details of the communication scheme and its formal description. Some of the more common attacks in communication models are analyzed in V. Section VI ends the paper summarizing the main conclusions and contributions of the proposal.

II. Related work

Generally, communications currently deployed/used for emergency are carried out by radio frequency. It is a poor solution, because workers only can share audio in a specific frequency, effective grouping and sharing media data are not allowed. Multiple solutions based on Wi-Fi Direct and smartphones has been proposed like in [5] where there is an explanation of the potential of Wi-Fi Direct in the implementation of mobile P2P systems. This work includes some examples of the use of Wi-Fi Direct to share text messages, to disseminate information, etc. They use a middle-ware for P2P networking to distribute hash tables to search for peers. In [6], authors explain the possibility of generating opportunistic networks over Wi-Fi Direct by studying the latency at the link layer. It is an extension of [7], where multiple groups were generated. This work presents real measurements that confirm the Wi-Fi Direct's suitability for peer-to-peer systems.

There is something in common in all these systems, no security elements are proposed. Our approach differs from others in that it takes into account the distribution, assignation and location of human resources in multiple events. Furthermore, information security is addresed throughout the development of the proposed system. In [8], the authors propose the use of Wi-Fi Direct as an alternative communication system for emergency situations, but not for communication among emergency services. The main objective of the application developed there is to share the geolocation of people when they are isolated, without signal and in difficulties.

III. Proposed system

In this section, some tools are described to understand how the proposed system works. On the one hand, a cryptographic primitive is presented, which is used in the communication system and is based on identities. On the other hand, some mathematical tools are described to understand the security of the cryptographic scheme used.

A. Preliminaries

Identity based signcryption. In Identity Based Cryptosystems, the main objective is the use any string as a valid public key. These schemes often use as identifiers: email address, social security numbers, personal identifiers, etc. This kind of cryptosystem avoid problems related to certificates in public key infrastructure. Based on this idea some modifications appeared such us the Identity Based Signcryption where the main objective is to obtain a composition of an encryption scheme with a signature scheme.

Bilinear Groups. Two cycling groups $(\mathbb{G}, +)$ and $(\mathbb{G}_\mathbb{T}, \cdot)$ of the same prime order q are considered. P is a generator of $\mathbb{G}$ and there is a bilinear map paring $\hat{e} : \mathbb{G} \times \mathbb{G} \rightarrow \mathbb{G}_\mathbb{T}$ which satisfies following conditions: *Bilinear*, $\forall P, Q \in \mathbb{G}$ and $\forall a, b \in \mathbb{Z}$, $\hat{e}(aP, bQ) = \hat{e}(P, Q)^{ab}$. *Non-degenerate*, $\exists P_1, P_2 \in \mathbb{G}$ that $\hat{e}(P_1, P_2) \neq 1$. This means if P is generator of $\mathbb{G}$, then $\hat{e}(P, P)$ is a generator of $\mathbb{G}_\mathbb{T}$. *Computability*, there exists an algorithm to compute $\hat{e}(P, Q), \forall P, Q \in \mathbb{G}$ [9].

Elliptic Curve Discrete Logarithm Problem. Considering the cyclic group $\{\sigma, G, 2G, 3G, ...\}$ for any point G on a an elliptic curve. k is an integer where the operation kG is called a scalar multiplication. The Elliptic Curve Discrete Logarithm Problem is based on finding k given points kG and G.

B. Overview of the system

This paper presents an alternative communications system for emergency services through mobile phones in different scenarios. In order to prevent network congestion, users have to share some public information when the emergency mode is activated. This information is user's ID and it is shared through BLE using beacon mode (see Figure 2) to identify each participant. Every person has a list of identifiers (IDs) corresponding to nearby people. When an emergency service worker finds a peer sharing an ID, he/she stores this identification. Later on, IDs may be used to peer-to-peer communications.

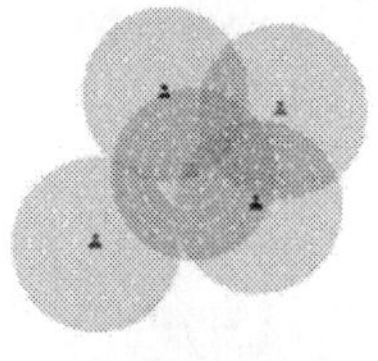

Fig. 2. Sharing identifiers through beacon mode.

The system supports two different communication modes: peer-to-peer and broadcast. In the first mode, two people can exchange information directly and bilaterally. In the broadcast mode, everyone in the affected area may receive the notification and by simply clicking on it, they can chat to help his/her colleague. Emergency staff can share text, images, audio and even videos. Security of the shared data is crucial in the proposed system. Thus, in both communication modes an ID-Based Signcryption scheme (IBSC) is used. In order to participate in the communications, each emergency service worker assigned to an area/event must also have some information. Firstly, from the central system, events are generated. Afterwards, the controller must assign different types of staff to that zone. Specific information that allows staff participation into the chat system is also provided, (see Figure 3).

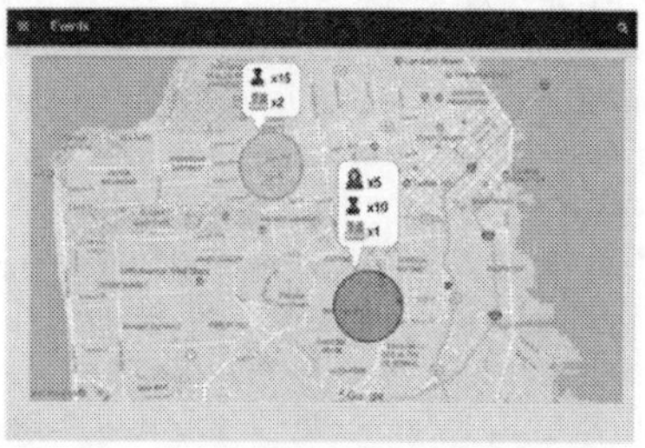

Fig. 3. Central system web application.

A unique identifier randomly generated is assigned to each event as well as the information for its geolocation. This geolocation is generated based on the focus of the event, and to prevent the generation of multiple events a range of some mills refer the same event. When a member of the emergency staff is assigned to an event, the system generates specific credentials and the keys to share data. Users may get their own location, peers's location and the area of the event from the mobile application, (see Figure 4).

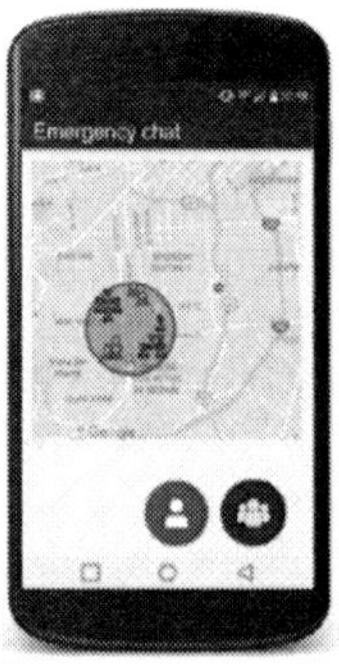

Fig. 4. Mobile application.

IV. EMERGENCY COMMUNICATION SCHEME

As mentioned in the previous section, an ID-Based Signature scheme is used. This approach offers the advantage of simplifying management by not having to define a public key infrastructure. This kind of scheme was chosen due to its low computational complexity, efficiency in terms of memory and its usability. Emergency service staff can share information with only one person in peer-to-peer mode through an ID-Based Signcryption and with multiple users in broadcast mode through an ID-Based Multi-Receiver Signcryption Scheme. In the proposed scheme, the central server supports the Private Key Generator (PKG). It is a crucial part of the proposal, because it is the service in charge of generating emergency staff private keys. The signcryption scheme used is a combination between the ID-Based Signcryption Scheme proposed in [10] and an ID-Based Signcryption Scheme for Multiple Receivers [11]. Below, some mathematical basic elements and notation used in the system description are presented. Several hash functions are also needed: $H_1 : \{0,1\}^* \to G^*, H_2 : \{0,1\}^* \to \mathbb{Z}_q^*, H_3 : \mathbb{Z}_q^* \to \{0,1\}^n, H_4 : \{0,1\}^n \to \{0,1\}^{|m|}, H_5 : G \times G \times \{0,1\}^n \times Z_q^* \times Z_q^* \times ... \times Z_q^* \to Z_q^*$, where n is the size of the message. $x \xleftarrow{r} S$ stands for an element x randomly selected from a set S, $x \leftarrow y$ denotes the assignation of the value y to x and $||$ is used for concatenation. The steps needed for the signcryption scheme are the following:

SETUP: In this first step, server initializes the parameters in order to generate its own keys: master public key (mpk) and master secret key (msk). To achieve it, some private data is necessary: $k \in \mathbb{Z}$ to generate a prime q based on it, two groups $\mathbb{G}$ and $\mathbb{G}_T$ of order q and a bilinear pairing map $\hat{e} : \mathbb{G} \times \mathbb{G} \to \mathbb{G}_T$ are selected. Next, $P \in \mathbb{G}$ is randomly selected and all the hash functions are also defined. Finally, server keys are generated $msk \xleftarrow{r} \mathbb{Z}_q^*$ and $mpk \leftarrow msk \cdot P$.

MASTER EXTRACT: In this step, the staff identification is carried out. Public key $Q_{ID} \in G$ is generated through a hash function applied on the ID, $Q_{ID} \leftarrow H_1(ID)$. Private key S_{ID}, used for communications with the server $S_{ID} \in G$, is calculated taking into account the msk, $S_{ID} \leftarrow msk \cdot Q_{ID}$. Note that key exchange between server and the staff is done using the stream cipher SNOW3G under the session key obtained through an Elliptic Curve Diffie-Hellman (ECDH).

EVENT EXTRACT: This step is required when a user is assigned to a new event. Each of the events generated has an unique identifier, $ID_e \xleftarrow{r} \mathbb{Z}_q^*$ and some location coordinates, lat and lon. In this step, the public key to this event $Q_{IDe} \in G$ is generated as: $Q_{IDe} \leftarrow H_1(ID||ID_e||lat||lon)$. Then, the secret key to this event $S_{IDe} \leftarrow msk \cdot Q_{IDe}$.

EVENT SINGLE SIGNCRYPTION: All the messages $m \in \{0,1\}^n$ will be encrypted and signed. The receiver's public key is generated taking into account his/her identification and the pre-shared data (ID_e, lat and lon): $Q_{IDe_b} \leftarrow H_1(ID_b||ID_e||lat||lon)$. Then, some operations are developed giving as result σ (a t-uple of three components: c, T, U). T is generated as $x \xleftarrow{r} \mathbb{Z}_q^*$ and $T \leftarrow x \cdot P$. Then the signature using sender's private key (S_{IDe_a}) is in U. It is obtained as follows $r \leftarrow H_2(T||m)$, $W \leftarrow x \cdot mpk$ and $U \leftarrow r \cdot S_{IDe_a} + W$. Finally the encrypted message is in c, and it is generated as shown below $y \leftarrow \hat{e}(W, Q_{IDe_b})$, $k \leftarrow H_3(y)$, $c \leftarrow k \oplus m$.

EVENT BROADCAST SIGNCRYPTION: In the broadcast mode there are n receivers, so the sender is identified by IDe_a and the receivers by $IDe_1, IDe_2, ..., IDe_n$. All the broadcast messages $m \in \{0,1\}^n$ will be encrypted and signed. The sender's public key is generated as bellows: $Q_{IDe_a} \leftarrow H_1(ID_a||ID_e||lat||lon)$. Then some operations are developed giving as result σ (a t-uple of components: $c, T, U, V, W, X, a_0, ...a_n - 1$), then the sender selects some random numbers $r \xleftarrow{r} \mathbb{Z}_q^*$, $r' \xleftarrow{r} \mathbb{Z}_q^*$, $s \xleftarrow{r} \mathbb{Z}_q^*$ and $p \xleftarrow{r} \mathbb{Z}_q^*$ and then, it operates $T \leftarrow r \cdot Q_{IDe_a}$, $U \leftarrow r \cdot P$, $X \leftarrow r' \cdot T$, $J \leftarrow r' \cdot mpk$. The receivers' public keys are generated taking into account all the identifications $ID_1, ID_2, ..., ID_n$, as follows: $f(x) = \prod_{i=0}^{n}(x - v_i) + p(modq) = a_0 + a_1x + ... + a_{n-1}x^{n-1} + x^n$ with $Qe_i \leftarrow H_1(ID_i||ID_e||lat||lon)$, $y_i \leftarrow \hat{e}(Q_i, J)$ and $v_i \leftarrow H_2(y_i)$. Then it calculates $V \leftarrow s \cdot H(p)$, the key k as $k \leftarrow H(s)$ and the encrypted message c as $c \leftarrow k \oplus m$. Finally an authenticator h is generated as $h \leftarrow H_5(c, X, U, V, a_0, a_1, ..., a_{n-1})$ and $W \leftarrow (r' + h)r \cdot S_{ID_a}$.

EVENT SINGLE UNSIGNCRYPTION: First of all the sender's public key is generated taking into account IDe_a and the pre-shared information as $Q_{ID_a} \leftarrow H_1(IDe_a||ID_e||lat||lon_e)$. Then σ is parse as (c, T, U). If everything is right, the message $m \in \{0,1\}^n$ is returned. Otherwise, if there are some problems in the signature or in the encryption of m, $\perp$ is returned. The verification is : $\hat{e}(U, P) == \hat{e}(Q_{IDe_a}, mpk)^r \cdot \hat{e}(T, mpk)$ Thus, the user calculates $y \leftarrow \hat{e}(S_{IDe_b}, T)$, $k \leftarrow y$, $m \leftarrow k \oplus c$ and $r \leftarrow H_2(T||m)$.

MULTIPLE RECEIVER UNSIGNCRYPTION: In this step, two verifications are carried out but first of all

σ is parse as $c, T, U, V, W, X, a_0, ...a_n - 1$ and $h \leftarrow H_5(c, X, U, V, a_0, a_1, ..., a_{n-1})$. The first verification is the public verification to check that the ciphertext is valid: $\hat{e}(W, P) == \hat{e}(X + hT, mpk)$ Otherwise, the ciphertext has been damaged or it is invalid and $\perp$ is returned. The second verification is: $\hat{e}(W, Qe_i) == \hat{e}(X + hT, S_{IDe_i})$ It is to check if ID_i is one of the receivers chosen by the sender and the ciphertext is valid. Otherwise, the receiver shall quit the decryption process and $\perp$ is returned. To generate the message some operations are generated: $y_i \leftarrow \hat{e}(S_{IDe_b}, U)$, $v_i \leftarrow H_2(y_i)$, $p \leftarrow f(v_i)$, $s \leftarrow V \oplus H_3(p)$, $k \leftarrow H_4(s)$ and $m \leftarrow k \oplus c$.

V. Prototype Analysis

A system prototype has been developed. It includes a web application and a mobile application to improve communication between emergency services in extreme situations. Security is one of the priorities that is why the system provides protection against different attacks. On the one hand, Denial of Service (DoS) attacks related to make multiple requests are restricted because only requests associated with a number of legitimate members of emergency services take effect. On the other hand, the typically "Man in the Middle" attack which conveys a successful authentication to the server with a legitimate identifier is very improbable, because once the corresponding user private key is assigned to the server further requests of this kind will be not attended. Impersonation will be easily detectable since the number of members who can make requests to the server is limited to those who are working at the time of the request.

An analysis of efficiency related to the technologies coverage, their range and their transmission efficiency was developed. A beta prototype has been also implemented with Wi-Fi Aware but in the preview mode of the technology. An Android application has been developed to share information between users. The implementation of the security has been developed with the generation of some random events on a map and with the assignation of users to events manually.

Note that the proposed prototype does not need a communication with the PKG, but just for the initialization where the generation of keys is performed in the Event Extract step. Afterwards, users can share messages with their own keys and with the pre-shared information related to the event. This eliminates the problem of saturated communication networks because an alternative scheme has been displayed with direct communications that do not need a central server.

VI. Conclusions and Future Work

In this paper a low-cost communication model has been presented as an alternative communication system for situations where network congestion was detected. The tool has been proposed like a combination of a web application, that manages all the emergency services and events, and a mobile application with an ubiquitous Wi-Fi Direct chat. Communication security was based on the use of a public key cryptosystem and BLE in beacon mode. Emergency services were able to know, with the mobile application, where the event was located and where they must deployed, as well as peers location. The system generated automatically the pre-shared data depending on the event to which the worker has been assigned; the main objective was that emergency workers was able to share information among them when different events saturate the network. The prototype has been developed like an emergency support tool to contact peers through a chat. An ID-Based Signcryption has been used to protect integrity, confidentiality, authentication and non-repudiation in the communications. Specifically, emergency service shared information with only one person in peer-to-peer mode and with multiple users in broadcast mode.

As future work, more functionalities will be added to the server, such as statistics, private chats based on roles, etc. The improvement of communication technologies is a must. A beta prototype has been implemented with Wi-Fi Aware that is available only in Android 8 and in the preview mode of the technology. The addition of LTE-Direct depends on the Native Development Kit (NDK), because right now this code is private.

Acknowledgment

Research supported by TESIS2015010102, TESIS-2015010106 and by the Spanish Ministry of Economy and Competitiveness, the European FEDER Fund, and the CajaCanarias Foundation, under Projects TEC2014-54110-R, RTC-2014-1648-8, MTM2015-69138-REDT and DIG02-INSITU.

References

[1] N. K. Gupta, *Inside Bluetooth low energy*. Artech House, 2016.

[2] W. Shen, B. Yin, X. Cao, L. X. Cai, and Y. Cheng, "Secure device-to-device communications over wifi direct," *IEEE Network*, vol. 30, no. 5, pp. 4–9, 2016.

[3] B. N. Schilit, A. LaMarca, G. Borriello, W. G. Griswold, D. McDonald, E. Lazowska, A. Balachandran, J. Hong, and V. Iverson, "Challenge: Ubiquitous location-aware computing and the place lab initiative," in *Proceedings of the 1st ACM international workshop on Wireless mobile applications and services on WLAN hotspots*. ACM, 2003, pp. 29–35.

[4] O. Android, "Android," *Retrieved February*, vol. 24, p. 2011, 2011.

[5] R. Motta and J. Pasquale, "Wireless p2p: Problem or opportunity?" in *Proceedings of the Second IARIA Conference on Advances in P2P Systems*, 2010, pp. 32–37.

[6] M. Conti, F. Delmastro, G. Minutiello, and R. Paris, "Experimenting opportunistic networks with wifi direct," in *Wireless Days (WD), 2013 IFIP*. IEEE, 2013, pp. 1–6.

[7] D. Camps-Mur, A. Garcia-Saavedra, and P. Serrano, "Device-to-device communications with wi-fi direct: overview and experimentation," *IEEE wireless communications*, vol. 20, no. 3, pp. 96–104, 2013.

[8] I. Santos-González, A. Rivero-García, P. Caballero-Gil, and C. Hernández-Goya, "Alternative communication system for emergency situations." in *WEBIST (2)*, 2014, pp. 397–402.

[9] J. Groth and A. Sahai, "Efficient non-interactive proof systems for bilinear groups," *Advances in Cryptology–EUROCRYPT 2008*, pp. 415–432, 2008.

[10] J. Malone-Lee, "Identity-based signcryption." *IACR Cryptology ePrint Archive*, vol. 2002, p. 98, 2002.

[11] S. S. D. Selvi, S. S. Vivek, R. Srinivasan, and P. R. Chandrasekaran, "An efficient identity-based signcryption scheme for multiple receivers," Cryptology ePrint Archive, Report 2008/341, 2008, https://eprint.iacr.org/2008/341.

Secure Indoor Positioning System based on Inertial Measurements for Low Cost Devices

Iván Santos-González, Alexandra Rivero-García, Pino Caballero-Gil, Jezabel Molina-Gil

Department of Computer Engineering
University of La Laguna, Tenerife, Spain
Email: {jsantosg, ariverog, pcaballe, jmmolina}@ull.edu.es

***Abstract*—This work describes an alternative solution for the problem of indoor location in places where the use of GPS devices is either impossible or not precise enough. The new proposal is based on different methods that provide useful information about location in this type of places. In particular, the use of Near Field Communication (NFC) technology in combination with an Inertial Measurement Unit through mobile phones or smartphones allows solving the problem of indoor location without incrementing costs. In particular, an Android application has been implemented to show the applicability of the proposed solution, which adds a layer of security that it is very important to protect the positioning information and avoid the possibility of traceability of the users of the system. To do this, the FourQ elliptic curve has been selected to generate a shared key using the elliptic curve Diffie-Hellman protocol. Then, the generated key is used to encrypt all communications through the use of the SNOW 3G stream cipher. The developed system offers promising results.**

Keywords*–*Security; Positioning; IMU; Elliptic Curves; Low Cost.

I. INTRODUCTION

One of the places where location is not working well nowadays is indoors. It is well known that outdoors the use of GPS positioning system provides an accurate location, but its use indoor is not possible. The need of an indoor location system is essential in huge indoor places like malls or airports. The traditional way to solve this problem has been to place static maps in different points of the building indicating where you are inside the building map. The main disadvantage of this kind of information points is that they are not accessible in all building spaces.

It is known that smartphones are becoming more and more essential in our daily lives because we do not use the smartphone only to make phone calls or to send Short Message Service (SMS) messages, but also to do other tasks such as taking pictures, recording videos, reading mails, locating with Global Positioning System (GPS) or surfing the Internet. Due to this, different indoor location solutions based on smartphones have been proposed in the last years.

The proposal presented here is based on the use of two technologies: Near Field Communication (NFC) technology [1], which provides a short-range positioning, and an Inertial Measurement Unit (IMU) [2] settled on the user foot, which provides inertial changes to track the user's movement. The use of these technologies allows us to provide real-time position in a smartphone using an indoor map of the building. An aspect that is very important in this kind of systems and that is not usually studied is its security, and in particular, the untraceability of the users. To avoid this, the presented proposal adds the use of an elliptic curve Diffie-Hellman protocol [3] using the FourQ elliptic curve to generate a shared key and the Snow 3G stream cipher algorithm [4] to encrypt all communications between the IMU and the smartphone.

This work is structured as follows. Section 2 describes some preliminaries. The proposed system is defined in Section 3. Section 4 introduces some features of the system security. Finally, some conclusions and open issues close this paper.

II. PRELIMINARIES

During the last years, different proposals have been presented in the field of use of IMUs to track the movement and/or position of users in different situations. There are different IMU types, but traditionally, the ones used to track the movement and/or position have been the 6 Degrees of Freedom (DoF) or 9 DoF IMUs. A 6 DoF IMU usually has a 3 DoF accelerometer and a 3 DoF gyroscope. The accelerometer is used to measure the acceleration on IMU movements in the x, y and z coordinate systems, that can be easily transformed into speed through the first time integral of the acceleration, and to position through the second time integral of the acceleration. Thus, it can be used to measure changes in the speed and position respectively. A problem that usually appears when obtaining speed and position through the use of the integral is that if the intrinsic constant error is not removed from the original measurement, the acceleration, it becomes a lineal error in the speed and in a quadratic error in the position, fact that would do the system unusable. The gyroscope measures the orientation in the x, y and z coordinate systems. A 9 DoF IMU has the 3 DoF accelerometer and gyroscope and adds a 3 DoF magnetometer, a sensor that measures the magnetic field and that is usually used to get the global orientation due to the earth magnetic field. A complete guide of the most common error sources of the use of IMU for positioning systems and its effects on the navigation performance can be found in [5].

This kind of systems is widely used to track the movements in the space, so different proposals have been presented during the last years. A method that is usually used and that is based on the measurements of these aforementioned sensors is the Dead-Reckoning. This method consists on the use of different algorithms based on easy trigonometric equations to get the actual position of an object or person, through operations based on the course and navigation speed. There are multiple algorithms that implement the Dead-Reckoning [6]. In that paper, a comparative study of different Pedestrian Dead-Reckoning algorithms is presented. A Pedestrian Dead-Reckoning algorithm is basically an algorithm that estimates the movement of a person by detecting steps, estimating stride lengths and the directions of motion. The results obtained in that work shows how this technique offers promising results with an average rate on the stride length estimation errors of about 1% and an estimation below 5% in the total travelled distance. Another method that is usually applied to improve the performance and to reduce the drift error on the sensors measurements is the use of static and adaptative filters, and one of the most used filters is the Kalman filter [7].

III. PROPOSED SYSTEM

The developed system consists on an Android application that shows in an indoor map the current position of the user. This building indoor map must be previously provided by the building staff with its correct scale to be added to the system. The system uses two different technologies to perform this feature.

On the one hand, the NFC technology is used at the entrance and some specific points of the indoor places to set an initial position of the user in the map. The NFC technology was chosen for this purpose because it is a short range communication technology with no error in the initial position estimation. The selection of this technology instead of another cheaper like QR codes is because the NFC technology is easier to protect than the QR codes as shown in Section IV.

On the other hand, the use of an IMU located on the user foot supposes an static reference point. The use of an IMU located on the user foot is a more accurate way of collecting data than the smartphone because it is static and produces less noise than the use of smartphone sensors. The IMU is used to collect data about the accelerometer, gyroscope and magnetometer sensors, which are sent to the user smartphone through the use of Bluetooth Low Energy (BLE) [8] technology. The use of the IMU unit instead of the user smartphone is due to the smartphone movements could add some noise to the measurements and the measurements obtained through the IMU sensors are more precise than the smartphone measurements. In the user smartphone, the sensor data are processed through the use of the Madgwick algorithm. This algorithm provides an accurate orientation of the user in a quaternion form [9], which provides an absolute orientation from a relative one. Then, the quaternion is used to orientate the position in the indoor map.

Finally, a step length estimation has been used to perform an exhaustive study of different methods. As initial method, we decided to use a simple way to calculate the step length in centimetres, l, which can be shown in the equation 1, where h represents the height in centimetres of the user and k is a constant that is 0.415 for men and 0.413 for women [10].

$$l = hk \tag{1}$$

In future versions of the system, more efficient, precise and complex step length estimation methods will be implemented. Moreover, a comparative study of the accuracy of the different methods will be performed too. Some screenshots of the developed prototype can be shown in Figure 1.

The general system performance can be shown in Figure 2. The steps that a user of the system takes during its use are:

1) The initial step of the system consists of putting the user's height the first time that he/she uses the application to calculate the step length.

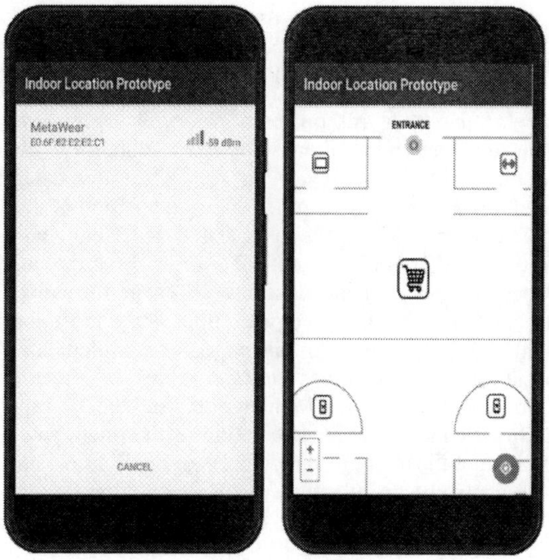

Figure 1. Prototype Aplication Screenshots

2) The user scans the NFC tag situated at the entrance. The NFC tag contains some identification numbers that represents the building, the entrance and the floor. The possibility of put more NFC tags around the building is open for some cases where the user forgot to do it at the entrance. This information is important to situate the user in the right place inside the building and floor.
3) Once the NFC tag has been read, the user can see her/his initial position over the floor map.
4) At this moment, the IMU unit starts to collect data and send them to the user smartphone, which is responsible for operating with it. The Madgwick algorithm is used to get the orientation in real time. With the quaternion obtained by algorithm and the step length, the user position for each step is shown in the smartphone.

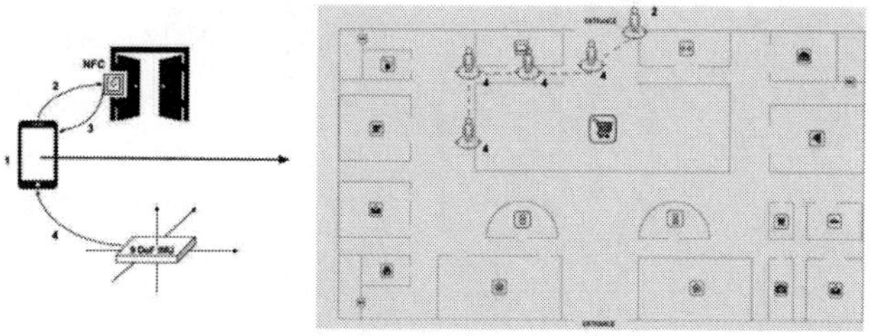

Figure 2. General System Performance

A. IMU Positioning System

The main part of the indoor positioning system is the part related to the IMU collected data and its treatment. In our positioning system a Metawear CPRO IMU that collect measures of the 3 sensors, accelerometer, gyroscope and magnetometer, obtaining g, $degrees/seconds$ and $Tesla$ units respectively, has been used. The complete specifications of the IMU unit can be shown in [11]. This IMU unit transmit the data through

BLE. The collected data is transmitted in real time to the smartphone where the treatment of the different variables is performed, including the conversion of accelerometer units, g, to m/s^2, and the gyroscope units, $degrees/seconds$, to rad/s. Then, the Madgwick filter is applied to obtain the quaternion that represents the pitch yaw and roll. With these data, the step detection and the step length, the user's position is shown over the map every time he/she takes a step. Different studies about the use of filters in IMU units data to improve the quality and reduce the noise in the data have been performed [12] [13] [14], showing that the Madgwick filter is the most appropriate in this kind of systems. In this paper, as complementary work, we decided to implement tests of three of the most used filters, a Kalman filter, a Mahony filter and the aforementioned Madgwick filter. The representation of the pitch, yaw and roll obtained in the tests are shown in Figure 3, Figure 4 and Figure 5, respectively. In all plots, the Kalman filter is represented in green color, the Mahony filter in blue and the Madgwick one in orange. During the different tests, the Magdwick filter shows a better accuracy by comparing the real position with the position shown in the Android application.

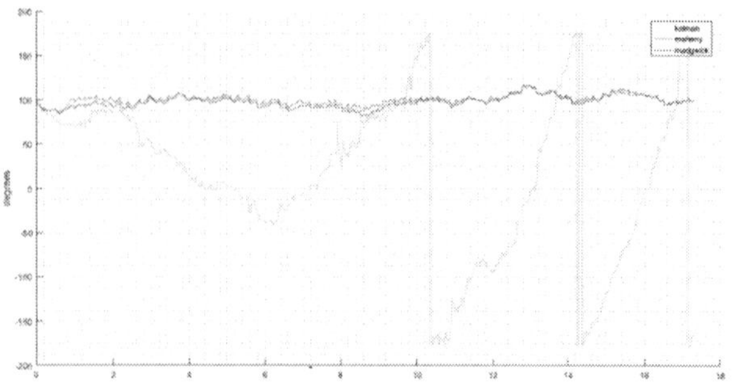

Figure 3. Filters Yaw

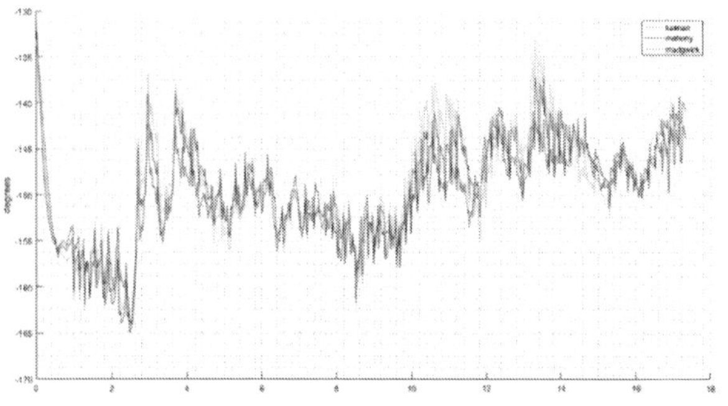

Figure 4. Filters Pitch

IV. SYSTEM SECURITY

In location systems, security is a very important aspect. A vulnerable application can involve a privacy problem, and in particular, traceability. The traceability of a user can imply a huge problem for the users of an application because an attacker could know where a user is in every moment and so perform derived attacks. For example, if the attacker knows that we are not at home, he/she could steal the house, or sell

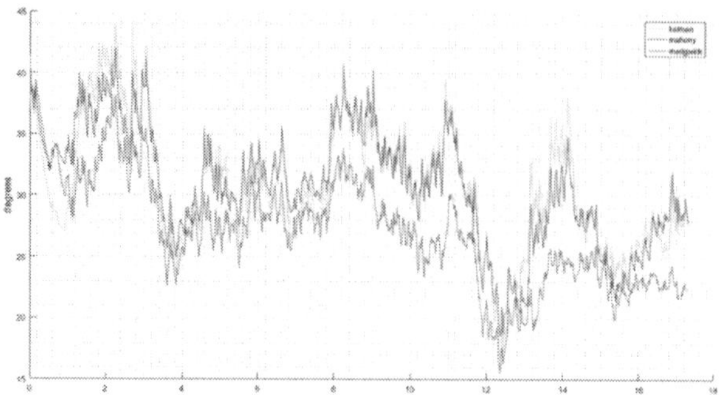

Figure 5. Filters roll

our data to different companies to allow that they send us, for example, food publicity if the user is in the kitchen, or shampoo publicity if the user is in the toilet, etc.

To protect the system, we decided to use two different methods. On the one hand, we used the Snow 3G stream cipher algorithm to encrypt all communications and an elliptic curve Diffie-Hellman (ECDH) protocol using the elliptic curve FourQ to generate a shared key. On the other hand, we decided to change the secret key every time the application is restarted to use it like a session protocol.

The trust model of the proposed system is based on using the FourQ elliptic curve through the ECDH protocol to generate a shared key each time a session starts. Then, this key is used to encrypt the communications between the IMU and the smartphone using the SNOW 3G stream cipher algorithm. The use of these two methods, ECDH and SNOW 3G, has been commonly used in different papers and its security is widely tested [15] [16].

A. *Snow 3G*

SNOW 3G is the stream cipher algorithm designated in 2006 as basis for the integrity protection and encryption of the UMTS technology. Thanks to the fact that the algorithm satisfies all the requirements imposed by the 3rd Generation Partnership Project (3GPP) with respect to time and memory resources, it was selected for the UMTS Encryption Algorithm 2 (UEA2) and UMTS Integrity Algorithm 2 (UIA2) [17] [18].

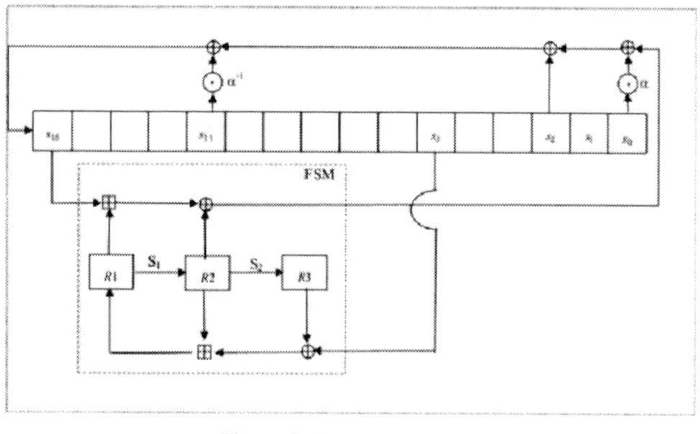

Figure 6. SNOW 3G scheme

The SNOW 3G algorithm derives from the SNOW 2 algorithm, and uses 128-bit keys and an initialization vector in order to generate in each iteration 32 bits of keystream. On the one hand, the LFSR used in this algorithm has 16 stages denoted s0, s1, s2... s15 with 32 bits each one. On the other hand, the used Finite State Machine (FSM) is based on three 32-bit records denoted R1, R2 and R3 and uses two Substitution-boxes called S1 and S2. The combination operation uses a XOR and an addition module 2^{32}, as we can see in Figure 6.

SNOW 3G has two execution modes: the initialization mode and the keystream mode. First, the initialization mode is executed without producing any keystream. Then, the keystream mode is executed. In particular, the number of iterations of such a mode depends on the number of 32-bit words that we want to generate.

B. FourQ ECDH

The use of elliptic curves in cryptography has been widely discussed during the last years and the advantages that they have with respect to the traditional cryptography both in key length and computational requirements are well known. The FourQ is a new elliptic curve developed by Microsoft Research [19], which accomplishes the NIST requirements for the selection of new generation elliptic curves. These requirements are that new curves must, at least, maintain the security level of the previous ones and be highly efficient in software and hardware implementations. This curve produces promising results, as shown in different studies presented by Microsoft Research, and offers improvements in the computing times in the tests done in traditional computers. To know if the improvements shown in the Microsoft Research tests are possible too in portable devices, where the processor architecture is totally different, because computers usually use an x32 or x64 architecture while the smartphones and portable devices usually use the arm architecture, we decided to port the implementation done by Microsoft Research to Java language to use it in Android devices. To do this, a java library was made and the FourQ computing time executing an elliptic curve Diffie-Hellman protocol was compared between FourQ, the NIST P-256 curve [20] and the Curve25519 curve [21]. The results of this comparison can be seen in Table I.

TABLE I. ELLIPTIC CURVES DIFFIE-HELLMAN EXECUTION TIME COMPARISON

Curve	Time
Curve25519	721 ms
Curve NIST P-256	1876 ms
Curve FourQ	417 ms

The computing times shown in Table I show that the FourQ elliptic curve offers interesting improvements in portable devices too. In particular, this curve is 2 times faster than the new generation Curve25519 curve and around 4-5 times faster than the NIST P-256 curve. The use of this curve can be an important advance in the IoT security due to the lower key length and higher efficiency, facts that are specially important in this kind of devices with low computing and storage capacities.

V. CONCLUSIONS

This work presents a new indoor location and positioning system that offers promising results. The combination of different technologies allow us to obtain the location indoors with a high level of precision. The use of a low cost IMU makes that the system could be used by a lot of people in a near future. During the simulations, an Android application prototype has been developed to collect the IMU information, proceed with the different calculations and show the path over the indoor map. The security of this kind of systems is essential, so different protocols and security algorithms have been implemented to avoid possible user's traceability by a malicious attacker. This is a work in progress, so several lines are still open. The first of them is the study of other sensor fusion algorithms that could fit the developed system better. Another improvement could be the use of sensors of the previously attached smartphone instead of the IMU to perform the positioning. On the other hand, security tests and controlled attacks to improve the system security are also necessary.

ACKNOWLEDGMENT

Research supported by TESIS2015010102, TESIS-2015010106 and by the Spanish Ministry of Economy and Competitiveness, the European FEDER Fund, and the CajaCanarias Foundation, under Projects TEC2014-54110-R, RTC-2014-1648-8, MTM2015-69138-REDT and DIG02-INSITU.

REFERENCES

[1] V. Coskun, K. Ok, and B. Ozdenizci, Near field communication (NFC): From theory to practice. John Wiley & Sons, 2011.

[2] M. M. Morrison, "Inertial measurement unit," Dec. 8 1987, uS Patent 4,711,125.

[3] N. Koblitz, "Elliptic curve cryptosystems," Mathematics of computation, vol. 48, no. 177, 1987, pp. 203–209.

[4] A. Kircanski and A. M. Youssef, "On the sliding property of snow 3g and snow 2.0," IET Information Security, vol. 5, no. 4, 2011, pp. 199–206.

[5] W. Flenniken, J. Wall, and D. Bevly, "Characterization of various imu error sources and the effect on navigation performance," in Ion Gnss, 2005, pp. 967–978.

[6] A. R. Jimenez, F. Seco, C. Prieto, and J. Guevara, "A comparison of pedestrian dead-reckoning algorithms using a low-cost mems imu," in Intelligent Signal Processing, 2009. WISP 2009. IEEE International Symposium on. IEEE, 2009, pp. 37–42.

[7] R. Van Der Merwe and E. A. Wan, "The square-root unscented kalman filter for state and parameter-estimation," in Acoustics, Speech, and Signal Processing, 2001. Proceedings.(ICASSP'01). 2001 IEEE International Conference on, vol. 6. IEEE, 2001, pp. 3461–3464.

[8] C. Gomez, J. Oller, and J. Paradells, "Overview and evaluation of bluetooth low energy: An emerging low-power wireless technology," Sensors, vol. 12, no. 9, 2012, pp. 11734–11753.

[9] B. K. Horn, "Closed-form solution of absolute orientation using unit quaternions," JOSA A, vol. 4, no. 4, 1987, pp. 629–642.

[10] I. Bylemans, M. Weyn, and M. Klepal, "Mobile phone-based displacement estimation for opportunistic localisation systems," in Mobile Ubiquitous Computing, Systems, Services and Technologies, 2009. UBICOMM'09. Third International Conference on. IEEE, 2009, pp. 113–118.

[11] MambientLab, "Metawear specifications," https://mbientlab.com/docs/MetaWearCPSv0.5.pdf, accessed: 08/01/2017.

[12] S. O. Madgwick, A. J. Harrison, and R. Vaidyanathan, "Estimation of imu and marg orientation using a gradient descent algorithm," in Rehabilitation Robotics (ICORR), 2011 IEEE International Conference on. IEEE, 2011, pp. 1–7.

[13] S. Madgwick, "An efficient orientation filter for inertial and inertial/magnetic sensor arrays," Report x-io and University of Bristol (UK), vol. 25, 2010, pp. 113–118.

[14] F. Alam, Z. ZhaiHe, and H. Jia, "A comparative analysis of orientation estimation filters using mems based imu," in Proceedings of the International Conference on Research in Science, Engineering and Technology, Dubai, UAE, 2014, pp. 21–22.

[15] S. Kumar, M. Girimondo, A. Weimerskirch, C. Paar, A. Patel, and A. S. Wander, "Embedded end-to-end wireless security with ecdh key exchange," in Circuits and Systems, 2003 IEEE 46th Midwest Symposium on, vol. 2. IEEE, 2003, pp. 786–789.

[16] J. Molina-Gil, P. Caballero-Gil, C. Caballero-Gil, and A. Fúster-Sabater, "Analysis and implementation of the snow 3g generator used in 4g/lte systems," in International Joint Conference SOCO'13-CISIS'13-ICEUTE'13. Springer, 2014, pp. 499–508.

[17] P. Kitsos, G. Selimis, and O. Koufopavlou, "High performance asic implementation of the snow 3g stream cipher," IFIP/IEEE VLSI-SOC, 2008, pp. 13–15.

[18] G. Orhanou, S. El Hajji, and Y. Bentaleb, "Snow 3g stream cipher operation and complexity study," Contemporary Engineering Sciences-Hikari Ltd, vol. 3, no. 3, 2010, pp. 97–111.

[19] Z. Liu, P. Longa, G. Pereira, O. Reparaz, and H. Seo, "Fourq on embedded devices with strong countermeasures against side-channel attacks," Cryptology ePrint Archive, Report 2017/434, 2017. 28, 29, Tech. Rep.

[20] M. Brown, D. Hankerson, J. López, and A. Menezes, "Software implementation of the nist elliptic curves over prime fields," Topics in Cryptology—CT-RSA 2001, 2001, pp. 250–265.

[21] D. J. Bernstein, "Curve25519: new diffie-hellman speed records," in International Workshop on Public Key Cryptography. Springer, 2006, pp. 207–228.

Dilemmas of Branding for Start-ups

The Opportunities and Challenges in the Digital Era

Amirhossein Roshanzamir
Bradford University School of Management
Bradford, UK
Email: A.H.Roshanzamir@bradford.ac.uk

Abstract – **Most of the start-ups have challenges in building up their corporate brand as they have no resources, such as money and internal structure, nor do they have customers or even a consistent idea how the end-product should look like. Having a strong brand enables start-ups to increase their visibility and ensure a certain level of quality which ultimately increases their chance of success. Nonetheless branding, as a growing field, focuses mainly on well-established firms who are already successful as opposed to start-ups whose business model involves lots of risks and their success is still uncertain. Digitalization provides immersive opportunities for the start-ups to engage and communicate with their potential customers and stakeholders. The tremendous success of the new wave of start-ups, such as Facebook, Uber, Airbnb, and Coursera, which are now revolutionary brands, testifies the critical impact of digitalization on start-up brand building. This paper reviews the opportunities and challenges which start-ups face in building up their brands in the digital era and suggests a conceptual model with three notions including emotion, innovation, and co-creation to address these dilemmas. Later, Coursera is reviewed as one of the most successful education-focused technology start-ups in order to illustrate the application of the model. This paper highlights the vital role of branding for start-ups in the digital era and the findings contribute to the literature by articulating a three stages modular and incremental approach to build a start-up's brand from scratch.**

Keywords–Start-up; Branding; Digitalization; Digital disruption; Emotion; Innovation; Co-creation

I. INTRODUCTION

The new wave of start-ups fueled by information technology has flourished throughout the world, where leading companies emerge unexpectedly and cause what is state-of-the-art today to become outdated tomorrow [1]. We see start-ups like Uber valued at $68B [2] and Airbnb valued at $31B [2] in digital technologies, which are transforming the business environment, igniting major changes in the way we buy, sell, consume, communicate and even work and ultimately standing among the most valuable and beloved brands. The trend is also strong in other places of the world wherein those developing economies, start-ups are addressing local problems through creative technologies and solutions [3].

Meanwhile, it is important to note that, in today's world, everybody including customers increasingly face more choices with less time to make them and that is where a strong brand plays a major role to simplify decision making, reduce risk, and set expectations [4]. Customers are surrounded by alternatives in every step of the way and the companies need to stand up, get customers' attention, and deliver the message they want them to hear [5].

Reputation and brand are considered as pivotal engines for growth and financial asset for any organization which fosters business development [6]. Though there is an increased attention towards branding and also the term start-up and disruptive innovation are widespread, however, the intersection of these fields is still not thoroughly explored especially in the digital era. In other words, there are few papers on the branding of start-ups and the main focus remained on large and successful companies and recently on medium-sized enterprises (SMEs) [7]. The major reason perhaps is that most academics and practitioners take a holistic and result-oriented approach and prefer to study the brand of the companies who are successful as opposed to those whose business model involves lots of risks. However, branding plays a vital role during the start-up growth phases, when the company is seeking to make the first impressions, building the reputation in the public, attracting investors and ultimately securing the long-term loyalty of the customers.

In fact, for a start-up, "visibility creates Opportunities", the faster it gets visible the closer the possibility of a business success is [8]. Moreover, the digital era has provided start-ups with tremendous opportunities to communicate and engage with their potential customers and stakeholders but substantial risks at the same time. Young ventures have specific branding needs due to their lack of resources [9], lack of internal structures and processes [7], and fundamental need to build a reputation [10] in order to find customers and investors.

This paper, therefore, aims to explore the corporate branding of start-ups by reviewing the extant literature in order to identify the opportunities and challenges these new ventures face in building up their brand in the digital context. It further suggests a conceptual model with three notions including emotion, innovation, and co-creation which are built upon each other. The paper is structured in six sections where Section 2 reviews literature and works related to start-up branding and identifies gaps. Section 3 is dedicated to the impact of digitalization. In Section 4 the notions that correspond to start-up branding and implications of digitalization on each are reviewed. In Section 5, the findings to be discussed and a conceptional model is suggested to deal with the corporate branding of start-ups. In Section 6, Coursera is reviewed as one of the most successful education-focused technology start-ups in order to illustrate the application of the model. The conclusion summarizes the findings, discusses limitations and suggests further domain for research.

II. LITERATURE REVIEW

The term "start-up" is widespread and has grown in recent years especially in line with the great success of San Francisco new ventures. Yet, the term is not limited to Silicon Valley and Seattle, since start-ups and incubators have been popping up in other places including Barcelona, Shanghai, Sydney, and Bangalore who now rank among the world's top twenty start-up ecosystems, according to the Start-up Genome Project [1]. In many new industries, the most successful firms tend to be start-ups rather than established firms [11]. For example in IT field, it was newly established companies, such as Apple, Microsoft, Amazon, Google and more recently, Facebook, Twitter, Uber, and Airbnb who came up with outstanding ideas and solutions which mattered to our daily life. Start-ups have always been a symbol of change by devising a new way of doing things in a more efficient and cost-effective way. They crystalize ambitious team who are ready to take big risks and change the industries and classic business models with their creativity and innovation. We can observe that in just a few years, start-up companies like Facebook, Uber, and Airbnb have disrupted and changed the rules of business and stood among the top most valuable brands. These companies have become the new principal points of power and created influential social and financial impacts on how we live, think, work, and interact with each other—even how we feel and sense [3]. In fact, disruption is one of the most popular terms in management today and it is associated in part with the notion of "disruptive technology" outlined by Clayton Christensen [12]. Digital disruption can be defined as the change that occurs when new digital technologies and business models affect the value proposition of existing goods and services. These technologies often enter at the bottom of the market which is ignored by established companies and then start-ups grow and beat the old systems from that point.[12]. Jonikas [13] states that most start-ups even high-end innovation-based businesses face fearsome competition and must compete with the old ways of solving or simply ignoring the problem. He further insists on the important role of branding and argues that a solid brand can transform a business from an unknown start-up into a successful competitor and niche, or even market leader.

Tai [14] argues that all great brands over the last 100 years were born out of the creation of a new category. He further insists that the creation of a new category or a next-generation product is usually what makes the big brands successful in the first place and this ultimately enables them to cement their position as the leader of that category. Rode and Vallaster [7] argue that start-ups provide a specific context to research corporate branding, especially in its early stage, as the internal structure and process do not yet exist. It could be tempting for start-ups to skip branding in the rush to get a new product to the market [15]. Some research and interviews show that many entrepreneurs do not consider branding important at the early stage and see it as later stage luxury, a nice-to-have thing as against a must-have [16]. The major reason perhaps is that most entrepreneurs are as short on cash as they are on time and they don't think they can afford to spend either to attend to brand-building [15]. Others consider it a difficult and long process which does not create actionable results. Some people even mistake online presence on a few social media or even personal branding and PR program as a sufficient measure. Talbott [17] analyzes common reasons for the failure of a start-up in the article "Four Trends That Can Kill Your Start-up". Ruzzier and Ruzzier [18] summarizes these trends by highlighting the first one to be an incorrect or overly narrow understanding of brands, which is usually associated only with a nice, good-looking logo and some other design elements. Second, is the perception that customers buy your features instead of your brand (meaning how the product makes them feel). This is particularly common in engineering and tech start-ups. The third trend is related to the issue of brand differentiation, which most start-ups tend to seek through the most likable and trendy visual identity elements, while the fourth most common mistake concerns creativity and founder's perception, that creativity could be acquired on the market by hiring designers.

One of the recent streams in branding which has strong implication in start-ups is brand co-creation. Co-creation, which is developing as a new paradigm in the management literature, allows companies and stakeholders and customers to create value through interaction. It was first defined by Kambil [19] and further developed by Prahalad and Ramaswamy [20] where it is argued that the supplier needs to engage all stakeholders and create value with them rather than creating value for them. Schultz [21] defines brand co-creation as a process in which the company involves stakeholders to become part of designing, creating and innovating the brand. France, Merrilees and Miller [22] develop the customer brand co-creation model which discusses the influence of brand engagement, self-congruity, and involvement as antecedents to brand co-creation and identifies the moderating effect of brand interactivity and brand communities. The model actualizes the impact of brand co-creation upon the brand value and brand knowledge after all.

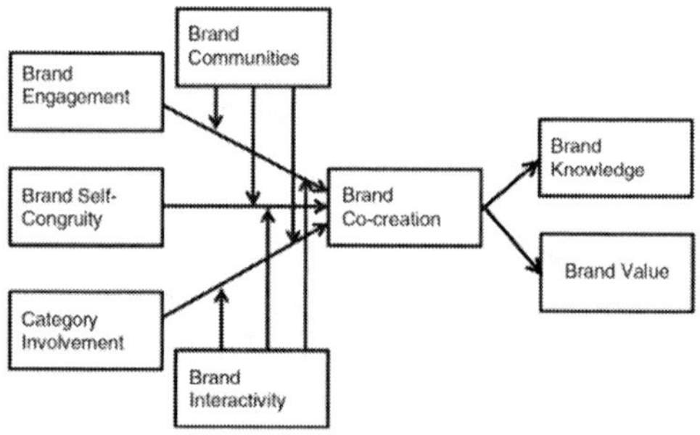

Figure 1. The customer brand co-creation model [22]

This is a solid framework for understanding the factors influencing customers to co-create and the impacts of customer co-creation on the brand. Though, it highlights the complexity of co-creation in contrast to traditional practices of marketing planning, yet, it ignores to take the other stakeholders into account within co-creation process. Also, the focus of this paper is not on start-ups. Another model which is developed by Juntunen [23] identifies internal and external corporate brand elements in B2B start-ups and argues that brand co-creation is a process that begins with the stakeholders inventing the corporate name before the company is established, and continues at the start-up phase by developing the new corporate name, updating the logo and communications material, and developing the product and business.

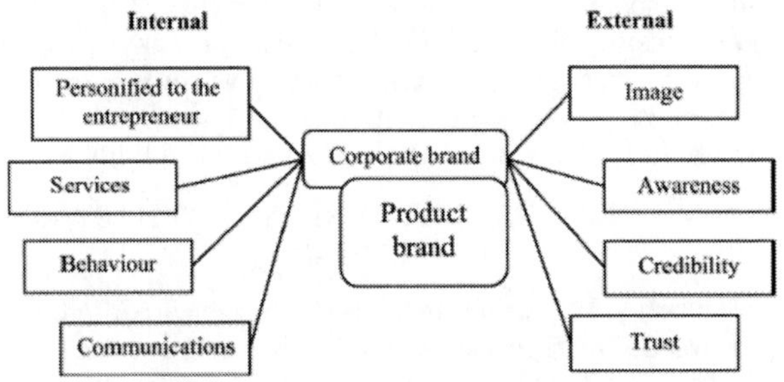

Figure 2. Corporate brand elements in B2B start-ups [23]

She addresses branding from superficial aspects and a visual viewpoint by concentrating on changes to corporate name and logo. Both internal and external elements of branding are identified with a focus on brand co-creation. Yet, less attention is given to exploring the ways to develope a great product and service which is at the core of the brand building.

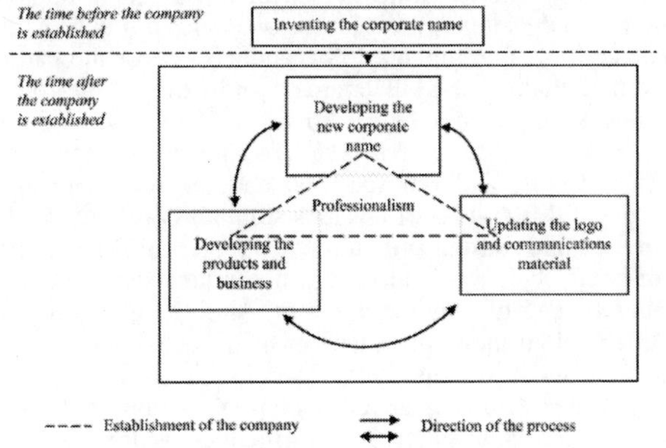

Figure 3. Corporate brand co-creation process [23]

Bresciani and Eppler [24] argue that branding is vital for the survival of start-ups, given their lack of resources and fundamental need to find and maintain clients. They propose a three phases development framework and key guidelines for start-up branding. First, the entrepreneur should define the brand strategy aligned to the strategy of the new organization before inception. Second, the brand strategy should be enacted through an appropriate brand design (name, logo, colors, and visual elements) in line with the brand mission and philosophy and finally, brand building activities should be developed carefully which entail using the power of the internet and also creating measurement tools [24]. This would enable start-ups to improve the branding strategy, in a continuous and iterative process [24].

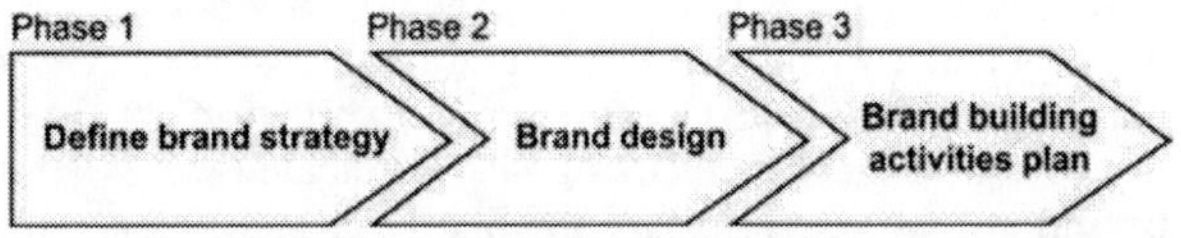

Figure 4. Brand creation sequences [24]

Each of the above-mentioned studies offers an important contribution to start-up branding and brand co-creation. We can also observe the importance of value co-creation from the early stage as well as creation sequences or development phases. Yet, emotion and innovation are two important notions which must be taken into consideration and their role in development phases to be identified. Meanwhile, none of the studies specifically reveal the role of the internet and digital marketplaces. With rapid growth and popularity of the internet, all companies including start-ups are forced to have a digital presence to connect with stakeholders in order to communicate and interact with them. Moreover, the platform is also an emerging business model that leverages digital technology to connect people, organizations, and resources in an interactive ecosystem in which amazing amounts of value can be created and exchanged [25]. Through these platforms and networks, companies like Google, Uber, and Airbnb are changing the structure of major industries and transforming businesses.

III. THE IMPACT OF DIGITALIZATION

The marketing communications environment, as Keller [4] argues, has changed dramatically in recent years, resulting in new challenges for marketers to build and manage their brand and reputation in the digital age. Digitalization which is defined as the mass adoption of Internet-connected digital technologies and applications by consumers, enterprises, and governments is a global phenomenon that touches every industry and nearly every consumer in the world [26].

The new technologies including machine learning, mobile, big data and social media, which are facilitated and promoted by internet connectivity, are driving companies beyond the boundaries of the local and traditional ways of doing business. We can observe that the world of marketing is shifting from mass market to customer networks in which the core behaviour of customers is focused on access, connect, engage, customize and collaborate [27]. Kotler [5] describes how marketing has evolved from product-driven marketing (1.0) to customer-centric marketing (2.0) to human-centric marketing (3.0) and now value-driven marketing (4.0) which leads to the convergence between digital marketing and traditional marketing and ultimately changes consumer's landscape to reach more customers. Today, social networks grow the power of connected consumers and put endless amount of information to share with each other and respectively interact with brands. Brands have less control over what is said about them in the digital era as online users are more autonomous than ever and have quick and easy access to other users, which heavily influence their opinions [28]. The successful start-ups in digital-born business have played the major role in digital disruption by suggesting new business models, new revenue streams, and new sources of competitive advantage not only possible, but in ways that are cheaper, faster, and more customer-centric than ever before [29][31]. For example, while many business executives seek solutions to digitally automate their existing operations, we observe start-ups like Uber and Airbnb find nontechnology improvement opportunities, simplify and standardize them and finally digitally automate the same [28].

Branding is as much about products and services as about everything that exists between the company and its stakeholders. Businesses throughout the world are interested to board digital transformation journey by engaging in e-commerce because they see digitalization an essential ingredient for growing their businesses, improving customer experience and upgrading their business models. Yet, senior business executives admit they are not sure how to do it, as Gartner found when it surveyed CEOs [30]. The reason perhaps is that digitalization is an emerging concept and there are few well-tried and known frameworks to guide companies through the digital transformation process. The author presumes "the five domains of digital transformation" described by Rogers [31] builds a good foundation to explains how digitalization is reshaping five key domains of strategy including customers, competition, data, innovation, and value. These domains are important ingredients of start-up branding. Table I. sets out strategic themes and key concepts as businesses move from the analogue to the digital age.

TABLE I. THE FIVE DOMAINS OF DIGITAL TRANSFORMATIONS [31]

DOMAIN	STRATEGIC THEMES
Customers	Harness Customer Networks
Competition	Build Platforms, not just products
Data	Turn data into assets
Innovation	Innovate by rapid experimentation
Value	Adapt value proposition

The first and most important domain is customers since digital technologies transform the whole customer experience. For example today a start-up can easily use social media and mobile apps for exploring customer's requirements, building communities of potential customers, using analytics to know them better and ultimately offering personalized sales and services. Further, the new technologies facilitated the power of the platform and today's most valuable companies like Facebook, Uber, and Airbnb are increasingly successful in building and managing platforms which are digitized, open, and participative that create commercially connected ecosystems of producers and consumers. Moreover, the possibility of direct interaction with customers offered via digital technologies, such as social media and mobile applications provide tremendous data and information about customers. The data can be analysed through data mining and machine learning techniques to know the customers' characteristics, buying patterns, spending, and other information. Digitalization and innovation facilitate the process and offer massive opportunities for visitors and potential customers through crowdsourcing and receiving feedbacks via social media and platforms. These are invaluable for designing new products and services and improving the existing one as Parker [25] argues innovation is no longer the province of in-house experts and research and development labs. Lastly, digital technologies enable start-ups to build, enhance, extend or reshape the customer value proposition with digital contents, insight, and engagement i.e. to offer better, cheaper, faster and personalized products and services. The digital transformation also underlies the success of many of today's biggest, fastest-growing, and most powerfully disruptive companies, from Google, Amazon, and Facebook to recent successful start-ups, such as Uber, Airbnb, and Pinterest.

IV. NOTIONS THAT CORRESPOND TO START-UP BRANDING

Talbott [17] indicates that it is not possible to differentiate in a crowded marketplace without a distinct brand. He further refers to a quotation from Rob Frankel who puts it best when he says, "Branding is about getting your prospects to perceive you as the only solution to their problem." The clear and consistent association with the defined category as Tai [14] argues is critical, especially when the brand is young and unknown to the world. There are a number of papers on SMEs in marketing literature but a few of it reflects on branding [32]. Rode and Vallaster [7] argue that literature on branding and corporate communication is rich, and studies about new ventures and entrepreneurship are also numerous, however, the intersection of these two fields is still an under-explored area. Abimbola [33] conducts one of the earliest explicit studies on SME branding and explores the role of branding as a competitive strategy. He further suggests SMEs, having fewer resources, require greater focus and effectiveness, and run specified and targeted campaigns. Though SMEs and start-ups look similar as they are small in revenue and staffing and built by entrepreneurs, they pursue different objectives and have a dissimilar business model, function and funding arrangement. An SME is a stable and structured business which focuses on the delivery of value to its already-known customers. Therefore, there is a base and foundation to build up a brand on top. A start-up, on the other hand, is a new, unstable, and unstructured business which is uncertain about its value proposition or even target customers and uses innovation to create new value.

Related research on SMEs is not applicable to start-ups, because they mainly focus on ongoing brand management [32], while start-ups face specific challenges, such as lack of resources and consistent idea how the end product should look like as well as the absence of reputation and customers.

So, a start-up goes through experimenting and testing its business model and lacks a base and build upon foundation especially in the early stage. Therefore, branding for a start-up would be more challenging since the business model and value proposition for potential customers are yet to be developed.

TABLE II. SMEs VS START-UPS DEVELOPED BY THE AUTHOR

SMEs	Start-Ups
Stable and Structured	Unstable, Risky
Final Products	Products are being developed
Delivery of Value	Create Value via Innovation
Known Customers	Seeking Customers

In this section, the major notions that correspond to start-up branding and implications of digitalization on each will be identified and reviewed.

A. Emotionally focused branding

Smith [34] says that branding is the creation of an idea, then communicating it in such a way that the market thinks and feels what you want them to know about you and your products. Talbott [17] argues that people often buy purely based on how a product makes them feel. However, we must remember that at the heart of a great brand is a great product or service [4], though, branding goes beyond features of the product and focuses on feelings of the consumers for the brand. The below matrix shows that the most beloved companies have both a fundamentally sound product and an emotionally connected brand [35].

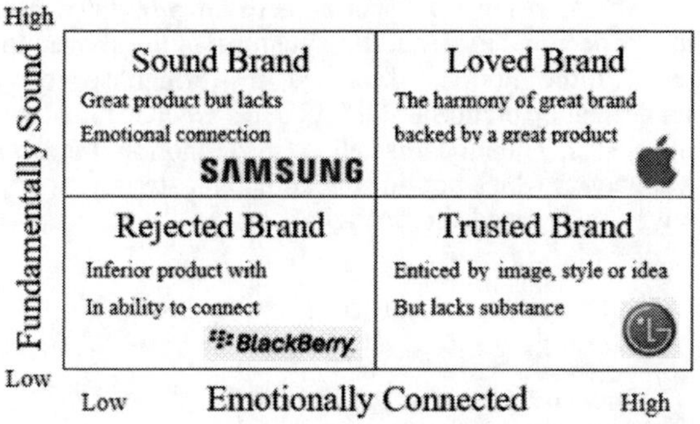

Figure 5. The matrix of Brand by Beloved Brands Inc [35]

Wasserman [36] argues that new ventures are usually labours of love for entrepreneurs, and they become emotionally attached to them using similar parenting language without even noticing. Therefore, start-ups need to sustain the high energy and determination to push the idea through the marketplace and that requires a powerful vision as argued by Maital and Seshadri [37] which excites the emotions, not just the power of reason [38].

The emotions and feelings can, therefore, play two roles in the branding of start-up. First, emotions and burning desire usually motivate an entrepreneur to initiate a solution and start a business and then he or she tries to create more authentic moments of customer engagement for example by story-telling and touching specific points which resonate with customer's requirements.

Li [39] argues that an entrepreneur's hope of creating a successful new venture significantly increases the attractiveness and perceived success likelihood of the new venture. Forgas [40] indicates that emotions influence individuals' judgment more strongly when the situation is ambiguous, information is limited, and decision making is intuitive rather than analytical. This is the case during the start-up process as decisions are made using emotions or rules of thumb, rather than systematic thinking during this stage. Kaplan [41] considers a passion or a cause as the common denominator among the innovators who organized around it and make things happen. Likewise, today we can see successful start-ups, such as Uber and Airbnb are built on a passion and clear point of view of their founders and then they fulfilled their promises on specific benefits, quality, and value by using credible, trustworthy, transparent media to communicate stories and information. All these ultimately cause the customers of these companies fall in love with brands, trust them, and believe in their superiority and feel emotionally connected. For example, the founders of Uber had trouble hailing a cab on a snowy Paris evening in 2008 and that is how they devised the idea of the tap a button, get a ride. Today, Uber connects people who need a reliable ride with people looking to earn money driving their car in 633 cities throughout the world with $6.5B annual revenue [42]. The Airbnb story is perhaps one of the most inspiring stories of the 21st century when the founders moved from New York with no job and had trouble paying their rent. They were looking for a way to earn some extra money and that is why they bought a few airbeds and set up a site called "Air Bed and Breakfast." to offer visitors a place to sleep and breakfast next day. Today, Airbnb has over 4 million lodging listings in 65,000 cities and 191 countries with $2.6B annual revenue [42].

The founder of Pinterest was inspired by the movie "Pirates of Silicon Valley," about Steve Jobs and Bill Gates, and got a job at Google in customer support because he was more excited than the previous applicant about the internet. He further quit his job and started Pinterest, a photo-collecting, sharing, and publishing site that allows users to "Pin" pictures they like and upload their own recommendations to their "pinboards". As of September 2017, the company has over 200 million monthly active users. All these success stories are full of persistence, determination and most of all fear and uncertainty but the founders seemed to crystallize this quote from Friedrich Nietzsche "He who has a why to live can bear almost any how."

B. Brand-driven innovation

The emotions and feelings are probably a good start to initiate a solution, devise an idea and get people together and connect them, especially at the early stage. Yet, after formation of a start-up, it seems that everybody is trying to speak the same emotional language today which fed up the customers. Margaret Thatcher says [43] "If you just set out to be liked, you would be prepared to compromise on anything at any time and you would achieve nothing." Joachimsthaler [44] suggests that trying to focus on emotions and being liked, cause a company to fall for everything and achieve nothing at the end. That is where creativity, invention, and innovation comes in. Having fewer resources are pushing start-ups to think differently and innovatively in order to solve problems, and get things done Yet, people normally equate innovation with creativity or invention. However, innovation is different from invention and creativity. Sloane [45] has defined these terms as follows: creativity is the capability or act of conceiving something original or unusual, the invention is the creation of something that has never been made before and is recognized as the product of some unique insights, while innovation is the implementation of something new. Payne [46] says that branding rarely gets a mention in the literature on innovation generally and co-creation especially. This was perhaps due to misconceptions about the terminology in the 1st decade of 21st century. Yet, brand-driven innovation, introduced by Abbing [47] helps companies grow in a way that fits their vision and values, and delivers a real and lasting value to their customers. In this light, the brand needs innovation to fulfill its promise, and innovation needs branding to define the relationship between the organization and its customers. The design thinking is the glue that creates the synergy between branding and innovation. For example, Nintendo's Wii or Apple's iPod re-defined what a video game means and how we listen to music [48] respectively. More recently, Uber and Airbnb utilized the power of digital disruption by crafting a unique perspective and massive brand awareness for their customers. Uber became a pioneer in the sharing economy and is the world's largest taxi company owns no vehicle. In the same token, Airbnb is the world's largest accommodation provider, owns no property. Both these companies are innovative companies who are redefining the rules and principles of taxi and hotel industry respectively. Uber and Airbnb have built and changed entirely new industry sectors by connecting the consumers and suppliers via technology. This requires a very strong brand supported by huge fans. Abbing [47] explores branding theory and argues that the brand both creates a frame for innovation and evolves as a result of innovation by consumers and other stakeholders. This is closely related to brand co-creation theme in start-ups in which innovation with brand strategy are intertwined whilst providing inspiration and guidance to engage all stakeholders in the process of creativity.

C. Brand co-creation

Steiner [49] investigates the corporate identity of young ventures and finds five factors that affect early corporate identity: vision, aesthetics, play, charisma, and trust.

In fact, the purpose of various statements, such as mission, vision, and values (which are called brand ideologies) is to connect stakeholders including employees and customers to a longer-term, purposeful yet abstract ideal model which brand hopes to achieve. Ind and Fuller [50] argue that a brand ideology creates a framework which guides the organization toward developing relevant products and services that are different from others. They further indicate that brands are fluid entities that are shaped by the interaction between employees, customers, and other stakeholders. The brands evolve because of the experiences and resulting expectations of people as they buy, use, adapt, discuss, interact with the brand and the absorption of those experienced by employees who in turn can use that knowledge to re-structure and re-present the brand [50]. This is, in fact, the co-creation of a brand which involves customer's active involvement and interaction with their supplier in every aspect, from product design to final product [24], [20]. It is particularly important for start-ups since they are pushed to listen to the stakeholders from early days and take their feedback and criticism seriously. Co-creation is now substantially facilitated by digitalization and has become a business norm. As manifested in Uber and Airbnb business model, co-creation blends business expertise and digital technology and ultimately creates a new value proposition together with partners and customers to shape a different future. Facebook is the most noticeable example in which the customers create all of the content and thus create the reason to engage as well as the value of the platform. Co-creation demands a mechanism and a platform to engage customers and inspire them to add their own content, opinions, code or connections.

V. MODEL DEVELOPMENT AND DISCUSSION

Joachimsthaler [44] suggests the building of brand substance in which companies must try to improve people's life by solving something, enabling people, delivering value, fitting into their lives and giving people time back.

These ingredients resonate with the ideology of most successful start-ups like Uber and Airbnb who have tried to improve people's life by addressing most of the above. In the line of three notions discussed in former section and considering the brand substance, the below conceptual model is suggested. The model is called EIC (Emotion, Innovation, Co-Creation) which provide a roadmap for start-up as how to build up their brands in the digital era.

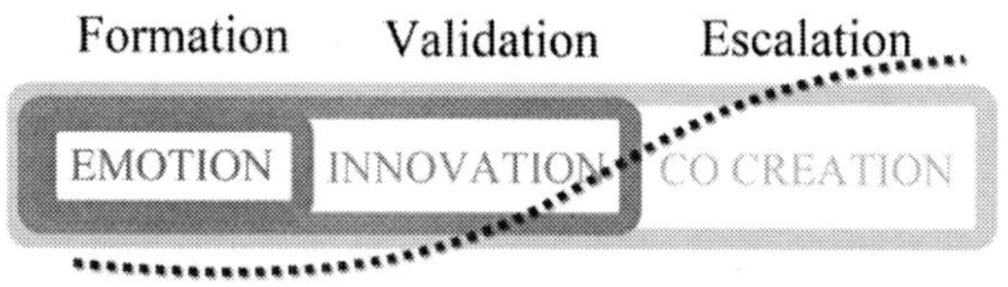

Figure 6. The EIC model for start-up branding in the digital era

We can see that there is a transition from start-up formation to validation and escalation by integrating three important notions including emotions and feelings which inspire a start-up to form, a brand-driven innovation which embraces creativity and invention to innovate something new and put into practice which can contribute into people's life. Ultimately, brand co-creation leverages the power of customers, stakeholders and their network in order to constitute a platform of a partnership between a start-up and its stakeholders. This is anchored by common goals, driven by a common vision to co-create values in order to meet the challenges of the new era. The blue line in the model shows the growth curve of a start-up and indicates the relationship between time on horizontal scale and growth or success on the vertical scale. Building on the matrix of the brand [35], the third dimension of co-creation is added to suggest 3 by 3 matrix of start-up branding. The most successful start-ups are emotionally connected, extremely innovative and highly co-creative and this is embodied in the shaded cubic.

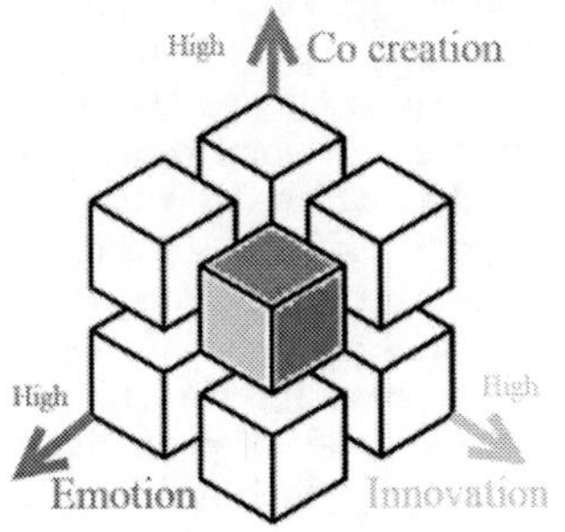

Figure 7. Three dimension matrix of start-up branding notions

The EIC model resonates with the Golden Circle developed by Simone Sinek in which he has been inspiring and challenging executives since his TED talk [51]. In his books [52] [53], he examines the emotional aspect of what makes employees and customers buy into a company.

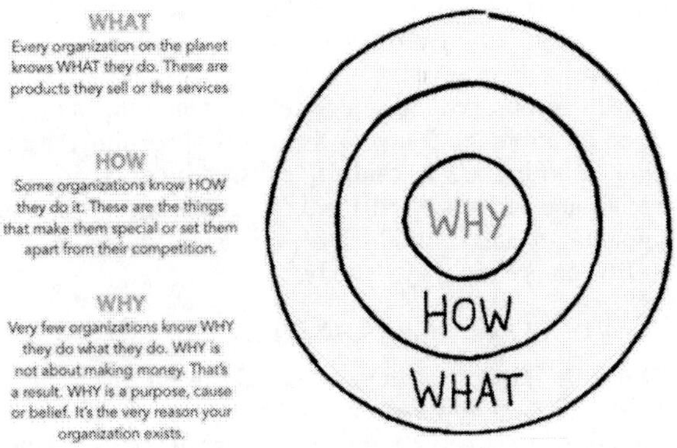

Figure 8. The Golden Circle [52]

Sinek [52] argues that when we're selling from the inside out, the WHY is the reason we might start and buy which correspondences with emotions. The HOWs are ''differentiating value proposition'' or ''unique selling proposition,'' which will be manifested in innovation as it is the implementation of something new. Finally, WHATs serve as the tangible proof of former stages to create value and become valuable as suggested by Thiel and Masters [54] which resonates with co-creating of products and service in EIC model

Today, we see Apple as one of the most successful companies in the world and it cannot be considered as a start-up anymore. Nonetheless, we can capture and share insights and best practices from the tremendous success of iPhone as a new and unknown product which was introduced by Steve Jobs on January 9, 2007. In fact, a very solid marketing strategy which controls over the consumer experience including the omnipresent advertising campaigns, the price positioning as a maker of premium goods, and the lingering nimbus of Steve Jobs's personal charisma all contributed to a perception that Apple offers products so good as to constitute a category of their own [52]. Moreover, the marketing success and brand strategy of iPhone can be simulated through the suggested model in the digital era. A burning desire and inspiration of the founder brought all the features of internet communication into one small and lightweight handheld concept. He then leveraged innovation to design a device which had a massive impact on worldwide communication and transformed people lives. Apple further utilized the power of co-creation by providing apple store platform in which the consumers could work with company-provided resources to produce their own value offering applications. The ongoing participation of active consumers in the production of new applications and exchanging value made the software even more important than hardware and created a huge source of income from marketing and selling apps and in-app advertisements both for Apple and its partners.

VI. CASE STUDY – COURSERA

Online learning has made huge changes in contemporary education and provided new opportunities for everyone who wants to learn something. Accelerated by the rapid and dramatic growth of the Internet, Massive Open Online Course (MOOC) emerged in 2012 when several well-financed providers, associated with top universities, including Coursera, Udacity, and edX were introduced. MOOCs penetrate the corporate environments and empower employee competencies and innovation [55] and provide an affordable and flexible way to learn new skills deliver quality educational experiences at scale,

Coursera which is one of the most successful MOOCs was founded in 2012 by two Stanford Computer Science professors who wanted to share their knowledge and skills with the world [56]. Today, Coursera has become as the world's leading and well-known brand in learning and education whose courses sought after by individuals and employers around the world because of evidence of mastery and verified certificates of completion. Coursera has built a platform where anyone, anywhere can learn and earn credentials from the world's top universities and education providers. With over 25 million registered users who have access to 2,000 courses by 149 partner universities, Coursera offers Specializations – collections of courses that build skills in a specific subject – as well as degrees and a workforce development product for businesses and government organizations [56].

Here, we briefly review Coursera case study and examine how it resonates with the conceptual model suggested in this paper.

A. Emotion

In the formation stage, we can observe that passion of the two founders is a bold contributor and a valid predictor of business creation as well as an outcome of their behavior. Daphne Koller and Andrew Ng were inspired by the experiences offering their courses online in fall 2011 at Stanford [56]. Specifically, Andrew, in 2011, led the development of Stanford's Massive Open Online Course platform and taught an online machine learning class that was offered to over 100,000 students - the initiative that led to the co-founding of Coursera [56] and offering the same there as one of the first courses. The founders' desire and passion to design, deliver and assure the high quality and integrity of their own courses embodied the reason and cause around which people showed up in Coursera as employees and developers. This also resonates with a research, in which it is argued that recruitment and a human capital building is vital to the survival and growth of new ventures [57]. The sense of purpose to help anyone to learn from top universities was so strong that attracted many students and courted the attention of other universities. Princeton, Stanford, the University of Michigan and the University of Pennsylvania were the first universities to offer content on the platform afterward [56]. Innovation and Co-creation mindsets are other important ingredients for successful brand building that were cultivated from early days since Coursera was perhaps the first MOOCs which started to provide universal access to the world's best education through partnering with top universities and organizations to offer courses online. These universities primarily expect branding and reputation benefits from participation [58]. Also, Coursera creates value through the design and engineering of the technological platform to facilitate access of students, which contains sophisticated search and recommender systems [59].

B. *Innovation*

Green [60] argues that MOOCs foster innovation by enabling both people with no formal education and those with a degree from a higher education institution to embrace the opportunities as these courses are provided for free or at low prices. Coursera like many other successful MOOCs, such as EDX and Udacity provides a platform upon registration which forms a diverse community of practice in which participants can share ideas and get deeply involved in the subject via a rich variety of synchronous and asynchronous online activities. Students at Coursera become engaged with the course, watching videos, communicating with peers, and accomplishing assignments. As of 2014, statistics show that only about 5 percent of students who enroll in MOOCs receive certificates of completion—a data point that has led many to conclude that online teaching is ineffective [25]. Nonetheless, Coursera has harnessed innovation and developed a community around its Courses by engaging learners and developing tools to facilitate their social interaction among each other [61] up to a level that some specializations in IT and programming can earn students a job in par with degree Carnegie Mellon and Caltech. Meanwhile, at Coursera, college credit is a "premium service" students pay extra for. This is the manifestation of brand-driven innovation in which Coursera delivers real and lasting values to the students and fulfills its promise to help anyone to learn and earn credentials from the world's top universities.

C. *Co-creation*

Co-creation practically happened in escalation stage when different stakeholders including individuals, organizations, and universities are brought together in order to produce a mutually valued output i.e. best education which benefits everybody. The platform, accessible upon registration allows learners to participate in thousands of courses offered and explore hundreds of contributions by other students, which often leads to further inspiration for their own and others assignment and even carrier experience. Freemium model, which is built on an expectation of converting a portion of free students to paying customers, increases the number of students and acts as a signal for content quality, thus increasing the legitimacy of Coursera's offering [59]. As the number of students grows, University partners have the benefit of predictive algorithms and data mining tools to identify their target students and evaluate the efficiency and effectiveness of their courses. All these are invaluable sources both for Coursera and university partners to design and introduce new courses as well as improving and enhancing the existing ones. Registering more free students increases the chance for payment and consequently increases the level of captured value (revenues, profit), thus raising the value creation capacity and ultimately reinforcing the societal value proposition [59]. Though every free student incurs costs to Coursera, each individual equally increases the societal value co-creation for Coursera, university partner and students themselves.

We can observe the integration of emotion, innovation and co-creation in Coursera as it envisions the future of online learning and challenges stakeholders including students and university partners to stretch and grow which ultimately excites (emotion), empowers (innovation) and benefits (co-creation) everybody.

VII. CONCLUSION AND FUTURE RESEARCH

Start-up branding cannot be addressed in a holistic approach since a new venture follows a growth curve where it goes through experimenting and testing its business model and lacks a base and build upon foundation especially in the early stage. The purpose of this paper was to provide a conceptual framework that helps to understand the vital role of branding in the digital era for survival and growth of start-ups. This has been met by articulating a three stages modular and incremental approach for building a start-up's brand from scratch.

First, founders must have a strong sense of purpose, cause or belief to solve a market need or take advantage of an existing market opportunity and cultivate innovation and co-creation mindset. Second, they need to innovate things that make them special and differentiate them from their competition. Third, they must seek to jointly create and develop value as the tangible manifestation of first two stages.

The paper is conceptual in nature and therefore future research is suggested to focus on validating and expanding the model through a qualitative research approach. Also identifying branding imperatives and developing quantitative metrics under each notion will be beneficial to measure the impact of a start-up brand in each growth stage.

REFERENCES

[1] H. Love "The Start-Up J Curve: The Six Steps to Entrepreneurial Success, "Greenleaf Book Group Press. Kindle Edition, 2016

[2] http://www.businessinsider.com/most-valuable-us-startups-10-billion-decacorns-2017-12#7-dropbox-1 [retrieved : Feb. 27, 2018]

[3] G. Ozkan "Tech Startups Touching Hearts," Design Management Review, Vol. 25, pp. 34–35. 2014

[4] K. L. Keller "Strategic Brand Management," 4th Edition Pearson HE, Inc. Kindle Edition. 2013

[5] P. Kotler, H. Kartajaya, and I. Setiawan, "Marketing 4.0: Moving from Traditional to Digital, " Wiley. Kindle Edition. 2017

[6] C. J. Fombrun and C. B. M. Van Riel " Fame & Fortune: How Successful Companies Build Winning Reputations" FT Press 1st Edition August 16, 2003

[7] V. Rode and C. Vallaster "Corporate branding for start-ups: the crucial role of entrepreneurs, "Corporate Reputation Review, Vol. 8 No. 2, pp. 121-135. 2005

[8] M. Nair "Why Is Branding Crucial For Start-ups ?" https://www.entrepreneur.com/article/279331 ; [retried Feb. 2018]

[9] T. Abimbola, and C. Vallaster "Brand, organizational identity and reputation in SMEs: an overview, "Qualitative Market Research: An International Journal, Vol. 10 Issue: 4, pp. 341-348. 2007

[10] A. P. Petkova, and V. P. Rindova, and A.K. Gupta "How can new ventures build reputation? An exploratory study," Corporate Reputation Review, Vol. 11, Issue 4, pp 320–334. 2008

[11] R. M. Grant, "Contemporary Strategy Analysis, " John Wiley and Sons. Kindle Edition. 2016

[12] C. M. Christensen "The innovator's dilemma: When new technologies cause great firms to fail, " Harvard Business School Press. 1997

[13] D. Jonikas, " Start-up Evolution Curve From Idea to Profitable and Scalable Business: Start-up Marketing Manual," Kindle Edition. 2017

[14] J. Tai " Brand Zero: The Complete Branding Guide for Start-Ups," Marshall Cavendish International Asita Pte Ltd. Kindle Edition. 2014

[15] D.L. Yohn "Start-Ups Need a Minimum Viable Brand," 2014; Available: https://hbr.org/2014/06/start-ups-need-a-minimum-viable-brand [retrieved: Feb. 27, 2018]

[16] A. Parida " Why Start-ups Need Branding? ," 2017; Available : https://www.entrepreneur.com/article/294595 [retrieved : Feb. 27, 2018]

[17] S. Talbott, "Four trends that can kill your start-up," Forbes. Published 2/ 06/ 2014 Available : http://www.forbes.com/sites/theyec/2014/02/06/four-trends-that-can-kill-your-start-up/ [retrieved : Feb. 27, 2018]

[18] M. K Ruzzier and M. Ruzzier " Startup Branding Funnel: Find Your Perfect Brand-Market Fit to Hack Your Growth Meritum l.l.c." Kindle Edition. 2015

[19] A. Kambil " Co-creation: A New Source of Value," Accenture Outlook pp. 38-43. 1999

[20] CK. Prahalad and V. Ramaswamy "Co-creating unique value with customers, " Strategy & Leadership Vol. 32, No. 3 pp. 4-9. 2004

[21] Schultz, Majken(2013), Co-creating brands with stakeholders, 2013 Available: https://www.youtube.com/watch?v=HZcT-hL6lOc [retrieved: Feb. 27, 2018]

[22] C. France, B. Merrilees and Dale Miller "Customer brand co-creation: a conceptual model," Marketing Intelligence & Planning, Vol. 33 No. 6, pp. 848-864, 2015

[23] M. Juntunen "Co-creating corporate brands in start-ups," Marketing Intelligence & Planning, Vol. 30 No. 2, pp. 230-249, 2012

[24] S. Bresciani and M. J. Eppler "Brand new ventures? Insights on start-ups' branding practices, " Journal of Product & Brand Management, Vol. 19 Issue. 5, pp.356-366. 2010

[25] G. G. Parker, M. W. Van Alstyne, S. P. Choudary " Platform Revolution: How Networked Markets Are Transforming the Economy and How to Make Them Work for You, " W. W. Norton & Company. 2016

[26] O. Acker, F. Gröne, L.Kropiunigg and T. Lefort "The digital future of creative Europe The impact of digitalization and the Internet on the creative industries, " 2015 Available: https://www.strategyand.pwc.com/reports/the-digital-future-creative-europe [retrieved: Feb. 27, 2018]

[27] D. Sanchez " The Importance of Brand Building in the Digital Age" June 20, 2016, Available : https://www.mediavisioninteractive.com/digital-marketing-2/the-importance-of-brand-building-in-the-digital-age/ [retrieved: Feb. 27, 2018]

[28] D. L. Rogers "The Network Is Your Customer: Five Strategies to Thrive in a Digital Age," Yale University Press. Kindle Edition. 2011

[29] W. Heitman, "It's time for IT teams to digitize like the start-ups do," CIO | Dec. 17, 2015

[30] M. Raskino, and J. Lopez " CEO and Senior Executive Survey 2013: As Uncertainty Recedes, the Digital Future Emerges" Gartner, Inc., p1-43. 2013

[31] D. L. Rogers "The Digital Transformation Playbook: Rethink Your Business for the Digital Age," Columbia Business School Publishing, Columbia University Press. Kindle Edition. 2016

[32] B. Merrilees "A theory of brand-led SME new venture development", Qualitative Market Research: An International Journal, Vol. 10 No. 4, pp. 403-415. 2007

[33] T. Abimbola "Branding as a competitive strategy for demand management in SMEs," Journal of Research in Marketing & Entrepreneurship, Vol. 3 No. 2, pp. 97-106. 2001

[34] S. Smith "Legally Branded," Rethink Press Limited. 2012

[35] http://beloved-brands.com [retrieved : Feb. 27, 2018]

[36] N. Wasserman "The Founder's Dilemma " Harvard Business Review, February 2008 Issue

[37] S. Maital and D.V.R. Seshadri "Innovation Management: Strategies, Concepts and Tools for Growth and Profit, SAGE Publications Pvt. Ltd. 2013

[38] J. Collins and J. Porras "Building Your Company's Vision," Harvard Business Review, September– October 1996.

[39] Y. Li, " Emotions and new venture judgment in China," Asia Pacific Journal of Management, Vol. 28, Issue 2, p277–298. 2011

[40] J. P. Forgas Mood and judgment: The affect infusion model (AIM), Psychological Bulletin, 117 p39-66. 1995

[41] S. Kaplan, S. "The Business Model Innovation Factory: How to Stay Relevant When The World is Changing Hardcover," Wiley 1st edition. 2012

[42] List of largest Internet companies ; Available : https://wikivividly.com/wiki/List_of_largest_Internet_companies [retrieved : Feb. 27, 2018]

[43] M. Fidelman "The Top 5 Leadership Lessons Margaret Thatcher Taught Us," April 10, 2013; Available: https://www.forbes.com/sites/markfidelman/2013/04/10/the-top-5-

leadership-lessons-margaret-thatcher-taught-us/#1711776b32d1 [retrieved: Feb. 27, 2018]

[44] E. Joachimsthaler " Love is Not Enough ! " at TEDx London Business School, 2013 ; Available: https://www.youtube.com/watch?v=drA-LBs4-Wk&t=334s [retrieved: Feb. 27, 2018]

[45] P. Sloane " The Innovative Leader: How to Inspire Your Team and Drive Creativity," Kogan Page. 2007

[46] A. Payne, K. Storbacka, P. Frow, and S. Knox " Co-creating brands: Diagnosing and designing the relationship experience," Journal of Business Research Vol. 62, Issue 3, pp. 379-389. 2009

[47] E. R. Abbing "Brand-driven innovation," AVA Publishing. 2010

[48] R. Verganti " Design-Driven Innovation: Changing the Rules of Competition by Radically Innovating What Things Mean," Harvard Business Review Press. 2009

[49] L. Steiner "Roots of identity in real estate industry," Corporate Reputation Review, Vol. 6 No. 2, pp. 178-96. 2003

[50] N. Ind and C. Fuller " Brand Together: How Co-Creation Generates Innovation and Re-energizes Brands," Kogan Page; 1st Edition. 2012

[51] S. Sinek "Start with why -- how great leaders inspire action "TEDxPugetSound; Available https://www.youtube.com/watch?v=u4ZoJKF_VuA&vl=en [retrieved: Feb. 27, 2018]

[52] S. Sinek "Start with Why: How Great Leaders Inspire Everyone to Take Action Paperback" Portfolio; Reprint edition. 2011

[53] S. Sinek, D. Mead and P. Docker "Find Your Why: A Practical Guide for Discovering Purpose for You and Your Team " Penguin Publishing Group. 2017

[54] P. Thiel and B. Masters " Zero to One: Notes on Start-ups, or How to Build the Future," The Crown Publishing Group. Kindle Edition. 2017

[55] S. Karnouskos "Massive open online courses (MOOCs) as an enabler for competent employees and innovation in the industry," Computers in Industry, Vol. 2017, pp. 1-10. 2017

[56] www.coursera.org ; [retrieved : Feb. 27, 2018]

[57] K. J. Moser, A. Tumasjan and I. M. Welpe "Small but attractive: Dimensions of new venture employer attractiveness and the moderating role of applicants' entrepreneurial behaviors, ' Journal of Business Venturing, Vol. 32, Issue 5, pp. 588-610. 2017

[58] S. Porter "The economics of MOOCs: a sustainable future?", The Bottom Line, Vol. 28 Issue: 1/2, pp. 52-62. 2015

[59] K. Täuscher and N. Abdelkafi ' Scalability and robustness of business models for sustainability: A simulation experiment," Journal of Cleaner Production Vol. 170, pp. 654-664. 2018

[60] S. Green (2015) " Pedagogy of MOOCs And Benefits For Modern Professionals," 2015; Available on http://elearningindustry.com/pedagogy-of-moocs-benefits-modern-professionals ; [retrieved: Feb. 27, 2018]

[61] R. Casadesus-Masanell and K. Hyunjin Kim. "Coursera," Harvard Business School Case pp. 714-412. 2013

Towards a Secured Authentication Based on an Online Double Serial Adaptive Mechanism of Users' Keystroke Dynamics

Abir Mhenni*‡, Estelle Cherrier†, Christophe Rosenberger† and Najoua Essoukri Ben Amara‡
*ENIT, University of Tunis El Manar, BP 94 Rommana 1068 Tunis, Tunisia
Email: abirmhenni@gmail.com
†Normandie Univ, UNICAEN, ENSICAEN, CNRS, GREYC, 14000 Caen, France
Email: estelle.cherrier@ensicaen.fr
Email: christophe.rosenberger@ensicaen.fr
‡LATIS- Laboratory of Advanced Technology and Intelligent Systems, ENISo
University of Sousse, BP 526 4002 Sousse, Tunisia
Email: najoua.benamara@eniso.rnu.tn

Abstract—**Password based applications are commonly used in our daily lives such as in social networks, e-mails, e-commerce, and e-banking. Given the increasing number of hacker attacks, only the use of passwords is not enough to protect personal data and does not meet usability requirements. Keystroke dynamics is a promising solution that decreases the vulnerability of passwords to guessing attacks by analyzing the typing manner of the user. Despite its efficiency in the discrimination between users, it remains non-industrialized essentially due to the tedious learning phase and the intra-class variation of the users' characteristics. In this paper, we propose a double serial mechanism to adapt the user's model over time. An important property of the proposed solution relies in its usability as we only use a single sample as user's reference during the account creation. We demonstrate that the proposed method offers competitive performances while keeping a high usability.**

Keywords–Passwords; Authentication; Password security; Keystroke dynamics; Adaptive strategy.

I. Introduction

Numerous applications used in daily life are based on password authentication. However, these passwords might be easily forgotten. That is why we generally opt for a unique password or simplified ones to remember all of them. But this strategy, although widespread, increases the vulnerability of passwords to guessing attacks. Besides, password composition policies calculate the complexity of the used passwords and advise users to combine symbols, numbers and letters to make them more complex and unguessable so as to avoid hacking attacks [1], [2]. Moreover, many studies explored the passwords length to evaluate their security [3].

Keystroke dynamics consists in analyzing the user's way of typing to decide if he/she is genuine or not. It is an interesting solution which enhances the security of password-based applications [4] regardless of the size and complexity of the password. In addition to the use of a syntactic verification of the password, the way of typing it must be similar to the legitimate user. Keystroke dynamics belongs to behavioral biometric modalities that vary over time. The characteristics describing the users' typing rhythms are mainly extracted from the latencies between the pressing and releasing moments of two successive keys.

Even if this modality has proved its efficiency in several scientific research papers, it is still not fully adopted in industrialized applications, unlike other morphological modalities such as the fingerprint (*e.g.*, fingerprint scanner [5], Touch ID [6], etc.) and the face (*e.g.*, video cameras on consumer devices [7], etc.). This is basically owing to the need of several typing captures during the enrollment phase to create the reference template that describes the typing rhythm of the users. It is not the case for real applications for which the password is usually requested only once, when creating an account. In [4], the reader can find a recent state of art on keystroke dynamics. As shown in Table I, for all the published research papers, the learning phase requires a large number of samples which generally exceeds 20 according to [8].

TABLE I. Number of samples required for enrollment phase for some systems in literature.

References	[9]	[10]	[11]	[12]	[13]
Number of samples	15	40	50	112	200

Besides the problem of the tedious enrollment phase, keystroke dynamics particularly suffers from large intra-class variation, as well as other behavioral modalities. In fact, the typing manner of the users is affected by different parameters [14]–[16] like emotional state, activeness, acquisition conditions, and keyboard changing.

Adaptive strategies [17], [18] are promising solutions in order to solve these problems. Indeed, they aim to update the reference template during the use of the authentication system. Therefore, they take into account the variations in the typing manner of users as time elapses. In this paper, we put forward an adaptive strategy based on a single sample for the enrollment phase of the initial reference template. The reference template is enriched thanks to the proposed adaptive strategy. The maximum size of the adapted reference template is set to ten samples. The proposed method makes possible the general use of keystroke dynamics on Internet as an efficient and usable logical access control to Web services. We demonstrate the benefit of the proposed approach on different datasets from the state of the art.

The remainder of this paper is organized as follows. Section II presents the literature work on the adaptation strategies applied to the keystroke dynamics modality. Section III describes the proposed methodology and the contributions of this paper. Section IV details the experimental protocol, the used databases and the obtained results. Section V presents the main conclusion of this work and some perspectives.

II. Related Work

The literature has shown that the adaptive strategy is one of the most suitable solutions to cope with intra-class variation, which is inherent to the keystroke dynamics modality. This strategy generally depends on five parameters according to [19]:

- Reference modeling: It consists of choosing the representation of the biometric reference. The reference template is generally composed of several samples. In this case, it is referred to as a gallery. To our knowledge, no work considers a single sample as reference for keystroke dynamics.
- Adaptive criteria: The adaptation process is initiated only if this criterion is verified. Different criteria have been proposed in the literature. We can cite the double threshold [20], the quality index [21], the context-sensitive [22], and the temporal errors distribution [23].
- Adaptive mode: It defines how to label the presented queries. It can be done in a supervised way or in a semi-supervised one.
- Adaptive periodicity: It details how often to apply the adaptation process, either immediately after the query acceptance, or after having collected a specific number of samples.
- Adaptive mechanism: It concerns how to modify the reference to update it. Different mechanisms have been suggested, like the additive mechanisms [24], the replacement mechanisms [25], [26] and the combined ones [27], [28].

Let us discuss some adaptive mechanisms given they belong to the most interesting step for the whole strategy. In fact, among the additive mechanisms, the growing window [29] is well known and frequently used [30]. The process consists in adding each accepted query to the reference gallery. Concerning the replacement mechanisms, the sliding window [29] is also commonly employed. It consists in replacing the oldest sample by the newly accepted query. Moreover, both of these mechanisms are generally combined to operate together. For example in [31], three combined mechanisms were proposed. All of them are based on two sub-references. These sub-references are managed as follows:

1) Parallel sliding: One biometric sub-reference is never updated, and the other one is updated with the sliding window.
2) Parallel growing: One biometric sub-reference is never updated, and the other one is updated with the growing window.
3) Double parallel: One biometric sub-reference is updated using the sliding window, and the other one is updated using the growing window. Later, Pisani et al [30] proposed an improved double parallel that limits the size of the sub-reference adapted with the growing window based on a statistical classifier.

According to [31], after 5 adaptation sessions the parallel growing, parallel sliding and double parallel mechanisms present respectively an Error Equal Rate (EER) higher than 20%, 15% and 10%.

As a main contribution, we combine two mechanisms, namely growing and sliding. The novelty lies in the fact that they are applied to a unique reference and they operate sequentially: The growing window is firstly applied, then the sliding window occurs. The obtained results show that this approach actually enhanced the performances.

III. Proposed Approach

In this paper, we put forward a novel keystroke dynamics authentication method that fits the industrial application conditions such as to secure the logical access control to a service on Internet. The main interest is to consider only the password sample introduced when creating an account. Furthermore, thanks to our adaptation strategy, the intra-class variation is taken into account over the use of the system in a transparent way. In what follows, we describe the main steps of our approach: enrollment, verification and adaptation. Figure 1 represents the overall scheme of the suggested approach.

A. Enrollment phase

In this work, the initial user's reference template $\mathcal{G}_j$ of the user j is composed of a single typing capture, the one introduced to save the user's password. A simple JavaScript code embedded in the service provider login page is sufficient for this task. From this single sample, we extract four characteristics which are time information between two successive keys:

- Time duration between two successive pressure events
- Time duration between two successive release events
- Time duration between one key press event and the successive key release event
- Time duration between one key release event and the successive key press event

These characteristics are commonly used and provided by the majority of available public databases of keystroke dynamics [32]–[34].

B. Verification phase

The classification is ensured with the K Nearest Neighbor (KNN) classifier. It is one of the most used classifiers for the keystroke dynamics modality that demonstrates good performances [35]. Knowing that the KNN classifier can be used with different distance metrics, we propose to evaluate its performances with different metrics described below:

- Statistical distance: It is based on extracting statistical values from each retained biometric feature (mean and standard deviation). This distance is well known for its competitive performances and its calculation speed while being used for the keystroke dynamics authentication [36].

$$D_{STAT} = 1 - \frac{1}{n}\sum_{i=1}^{n} e^{-\frac{|q_i - \mu_i|}{\sigma_i}} \quad (1)$$

- Hamming distance: It consists in calculating the percentage of different coordinates between the novel query and the reference samples.

$$D_{HAMMING} = (\#(q_j \neq \mathcal{G}_j(k))/n) \quad (2)$$

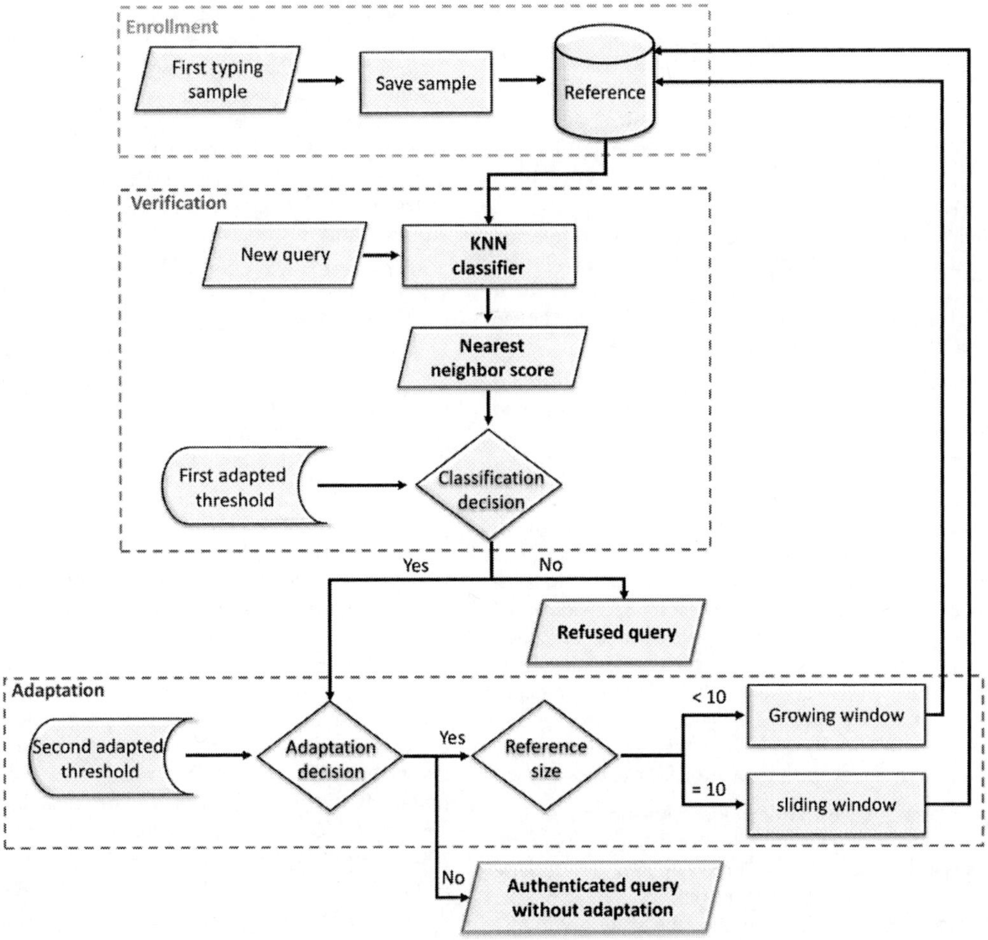

Figure 1. Description of the keystroke authentication process

- Euclidean distance: It is a simple distance metric usually used with the KNN classifier.

$$D_{EUCLIDEAN} = \sqrt{\sum_{k=1}^{m}(q_j - \mathcal{G}_j(k))^2} \qquad (3)$$

- Manhattan distance: It calculates the sum of the differences of the corresponding components of the new query and the reference samples.

$$D_{MANHATTAN} = \sum_{k=1}^{m} |q_j - \mathcal{G}_j(k)| \qquad (4)$$

where:
q_j is the claimed query of the user j, $\mathcal{G}_j(k)$ is the kth reference sample of the user j, m is the number of the samples in the reference $\mathcal{G}_j$, μ is the mean vector of the reference, and σ is the standard deviation vector of the user reference, and i varying from 1 to n where n is the length of the password.

C. Adaptation phase

The adaptation phase is required to remedy the problems of intra-class variation. It is ensured during the use of the authentication system to enhance its performances. For the proposed approach, we opt for the following choices:

- Reference modeling: To facilitate the enrollment phase task, the user is asked to only type the password once. This is a great advantage in term of usability. Thus, the user's gallery is initially composed of a single sample. Each accepted query is therefore added to the gallery, to enrich the typing manner description. The maximum size of the gallery is equal to ten. We chose not to enlarge the reference, to facilitate the communication of the web server with the database.
- Adaptation criterion: The decision to update the reference is taken according to the adapted thresholds criterion which has already been proposed in [37]. It is based on the double threshold criterion [20]. Two thresholds are considered: The first one decides whether to accept or to reject the query, while the second one decides to use the accepted query whether to update the reference or not. All studies implementing the double threshold criterion, have generally used fixed thresholds [8], [31]. For our adaptation criterion, the thresholds are updated during the use of the system

according to (5):

$$T_j^{i+1} = T_j^i - e^{-\frac{\mu_j}{\sigma_j}} \quad (5)$$

where μ_j and σ_j are respectively the mean and standard deviation vectors of the reference of the user j, and T_j^i is the threshold of the user j in the adaptation step i.

- Adaptation mode: The chosen mode for the suggested method is the semi-supervised one. The labels are assigned thanks to the KNN classifier. We apply it combined with different distance metrics to choose the optimal distance (best performances).
- Adaptation periodicity: The adaptation is performed online whenever a query is accepted by the adapted thresholds criterion.
- Adaptation mechanism: We propose the double-serial mechanism for our experimentations. At the beginning, the growing window mechanism is applied. Actually, each accepted query is added to the reference as long as the size of the gallery $\mathcal{G}_j$ is less than 10 samples. Once the size of the reference reaches 10 samples, the sliding window mechanism is launched to replace the oldest sample in the reference gallery with the last accepted query. The adaptation mechanism continues by updating the reference without any supervision by simply and efficiently considering the temporal variations in the keystroke dynamics.

As a consequence, once the decision criterion is verified, we update both the reference and the thresholds in a real time way. Thanks to the double-serial mechanism, the growing window mechanism serves to enrich the modeling of the keystroke dynamics of the users, whereas the sliding window is subsequently used to track the intra-class variation of the user's typing manner.

IV. Experiments and Results

We validate our adaptation approach of the keystroke dynamics on two public databases. The evaluation is done based on two commonly used metrics: the Error Equal Rate (EER) and the Area Under Curve (AUC) performance metrics. The experimentations and the achieved results are presented in the following.

A. Datasets

We choose the *GREYC 2009* [33] and *WebGREYC* [32] databases for the validation of the proposed method. In GREYC 2009, 133 users participated in the creation of this database. We are interested in only 100 users, those who participated in five acquisition sessions during 2 months and provided 60 samples per user. For the Web GREYC, 118 users were involved in its creation. Only 45 among them participated in five sessions and provided 60 patterns. For both databases, we only consider users who provided 60 samples.

B. Experimental methodology

To better describe the adopted methodology, we depict the used data stream generation. We have 60 samples per user. Thus, to assess the performances of our method, we define an evaluation protocol. For that purpose, we divide the process into sessions. At each session, we present eight new queries to the system. They are composed of five genuine samples and three impostor ones. According to the literature, the number of genuine samples per session is generally up to ten. Differently, we opt in our work for only five genuine samples, which allows precisely controlling the approach performances. The genuine queries are presented according to the chronological order of the database capture; whereas, the impostor queries are randomly introduced.

As a result, we obtain 12 adaptation sessions (60 genuine samples / 5). Since we store the first sample as reference in the enrollment phase, during the last session we present only 4 genuine samples. Three impostor attacks are randomly generated in each session by the samples of other users of the database. The biometric data stream is then divided into 37.5% (3/8) of impostor samples and 62.5% (5/8) geniune samples. The attack rate is higher than that generally used in keystroke dynamics studies [10], [31] (70% genuine and 30% impostor).

The initial thresholds are set for an EER equal to 3%. Then, after each query acceptance, the reference is updated according to the double serial mechanism, and the decision thresholds are adapted based on Equation (5).

C. Results

Although the reference initially contains only a single sample, the obtained results are promising. Figure 2 depicts the Receiver Operating Characteristic (ROC) curves with the associated EER and AUC performances for the twelve adaptation sessions of the different experimentations applied to the GREYC 2009 database. Figure 3 illustrates the ROC curves and the performances (EER, AUC) of the first and the last adaptation sessions obtained using both databases.

We choose four distance metrics to associate to the KNN classifier because we test a very large number of distances, but those that demonstrate competitive performances are hamming, statistical, euclidean and Manhattan. Comparing the metrics with each other, we note that the hamming distance and the statistical one perform better than others for the two considered databases.

We compare our approach with that of Giot *et al* [8], in which the authors applied the average mechanism based on 3 different classifiers: Support Vector Machine (SVM), neural network and statistical distance. Thereby, an examination of the classifiers' performance is essential. Table II summarizes the compared results.

TABLE II. Comparison of the chosen classifier with those of previous work for GREYC 2009 database.

Adaptive mechanism	Reference size Minimum	Reference size Maximum	Classifier	EER	AUC
Double serial mechanism	1	10	KNN (Hamming)	6.1%	0.013
	1	10	KNN (Statistical)	6.3%	0.017
	1	10	KNN (Euclidean)	7.8%	0.033
	1	10	KNN (Manhattan)	8.9%	0.031
Average mechanism [8]	5	15	SVM	6.96%	-
	5	15	Neural network	8.75%	-
	5	15	Statistical	10.75%	-

The best performance achieved in [8] is an EER equal to 6.96%, while using an SVM classifier and the reference was composed of 5 samples as minimum size and 15 samples maximum. In the present study, we use the same database as

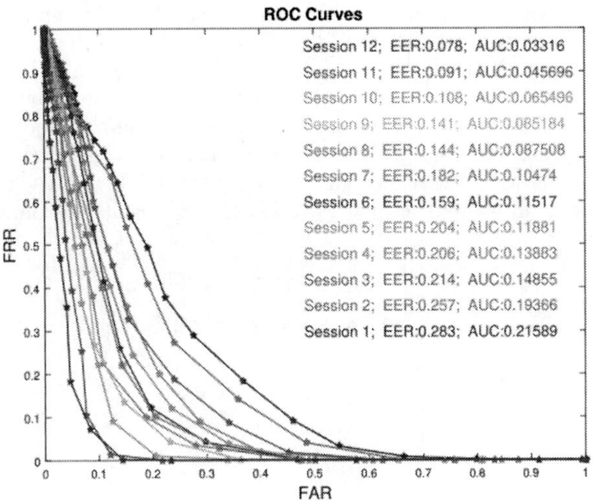

(a) Euclidean distance

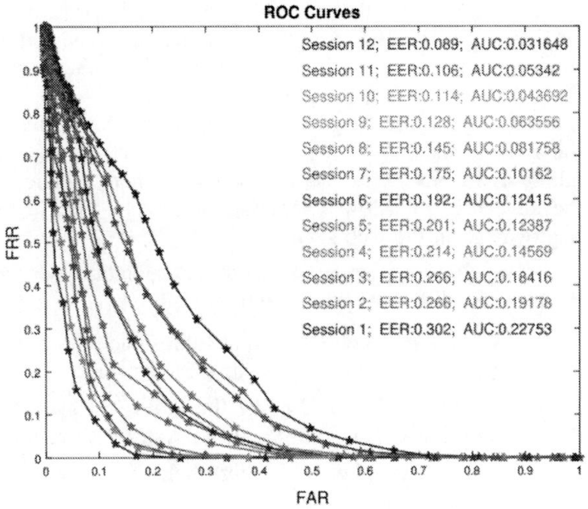

(b) Manhattan distance

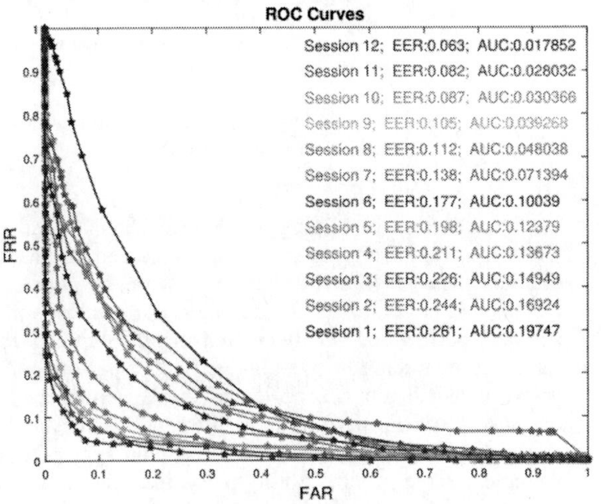

(c) Statistical distance

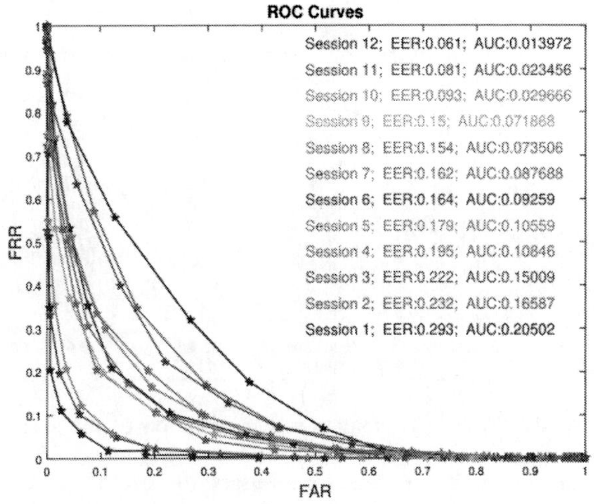

(d) Hamming distance

Figure 2. Roc curves evolving overs all adaptation sessions (GREYC 2009 database) and the associated performances (EER, AUC)

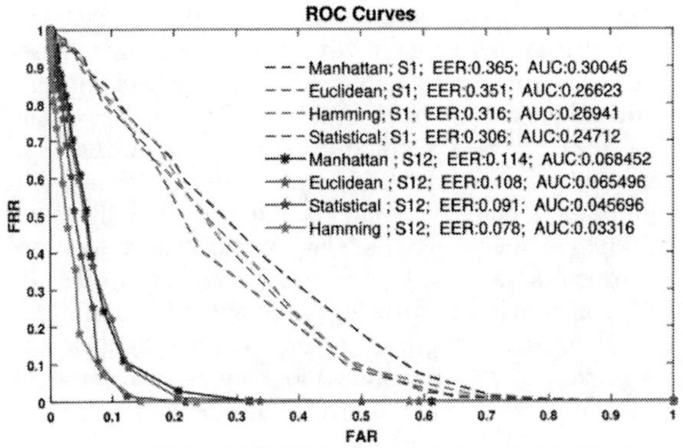

(a) WEB GREYC

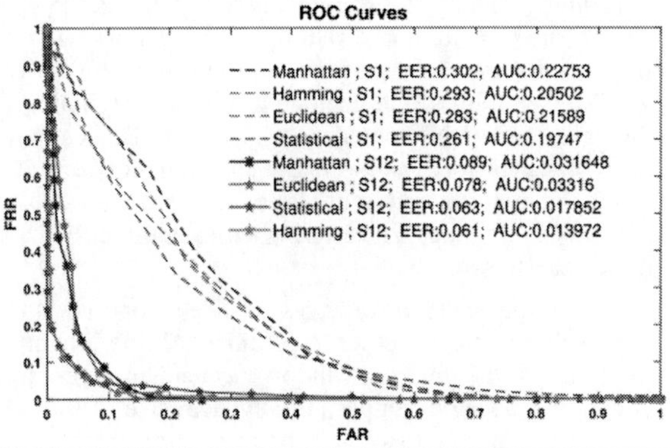

(b) GREYC 2009

Figure 3. Roc curves of the first and the last adaptation session (S1,S12) and the associated performances (EER, AUC)

in the work of [8], thus obtaining two better performances: an EER equal to 6.3% using the KNN based on the statistical distance, and 6.1% using the KNN based on the hamming distance. We will benefit from the minimisation of the size of the reference while keeping better performances to facilitate the industrialisation of the keystroke dynamics modality. In addition, the KNN classifier compared to other classifiers, has the advantage of a low computing time which facilitates its deployment on the web server.

To highlight the benefit of the chosen adaptation criterion, we also test different types of thresholds:

- Global thresholds: A single threshold is set for all users and during the use of the password.
- Individual thresholds: The thresholds are user dependent but remain set during the system utilization.
- Variable thresholds: The thresholds vary according to users and over time.

As demonstrated in previous work, [37], the variable thresholds are performing better, as provided in Table III.

TABLE III. COMPARISON OF OBTAINED RESULTS (EER) WITH DIFFERENT THRESHOLDS.

Distance metrics	Thresholds	GREYC 2009	WEB GREYC
Hamming	Variable	6.1%	7.8%
	Individual	7.3%	9.5%
	Global	8.1%	10.7%
Statistical	Variable	6.3%	9.1%
	Individual	6.9%	10.4 %
	Global	7.6%	11.7%
Euclidean	Variable	7.8%	10.8 %
	Individual	8.4%	12.8%
	Global	9.7%	14.2%
Manhattan	Variable	8.9%	11.4 %
	Individual	9.3%	13.6 %
	Global	10.1%	15.3 %

For our experimentation, the evolution of the size of the reference over time is significant. Since the number of accepted queries is not the same for all users, the size of the reference differs from one user to another at the end of the session. Table IV shows the minimum size and the maximum size of users' references in each session. As the maximum number of samples in the reference (10 samples) is rapidly reached, we therefore deduce that the growing window phase is quickly interrupted. Hence, the sliding window phase is more sustainable. Moreover, we notice that the slower the growing window phase is, the lower the performances are. In fact it is due to the weak recognition of the geniune user at the beginning. This is the case of the KNN based on Manhattan distance, unlike the other distance metrics especially the statistical one. Besides, user's having the minimum reference size are those whos keystroke dynamics is suffering from intra class variations more than the others.

To enforce the advantages of the proposed adaptation approach we tested other algorithms of the literature. We firstly tested the growing window mechanism with a reference containing a single sample initially. The size of the reference increases infinitely thanks to the adaptation mechanism. Secondly we applied the sliding window mechanism based on a reference sized 10. Thirdly the double parallel mechanism is conducted using two sub-references. One of them contains a single sample initially and it is adapted with the growing window mechanism. The other comprises 10 samples initially and it is adapted with the sliding window mechanism. Finally we also tested the proposed double serial mechanism while the reference is initialized to 5 samples and its maximum size is fixed to 10. Figure 4 summerizes the variations of the reference size for each of the tested adaptation mechanisms. All of these mechanisms are implemented by the KNN classifier with 4 distance metrics. The obtained results are summarized in Figure 5.

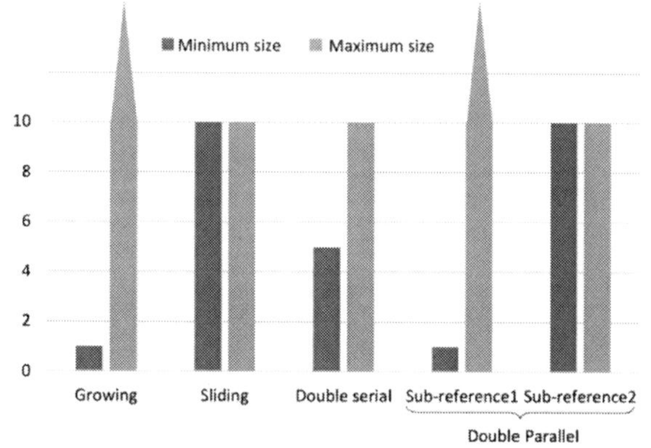

Figure 4. The minimum and the maximum size of the reference for the compared mechanisms.

By applying the sliding window mechanism and growing window mechanism separately, the obtained results are less efficient. The performance achieved with the double parallel mechanism is good. But the double serial mechanism remains the best performing. While increasing the initial size of the reference by 5 samples we obtained better performances. This is due to the larger description of the keystroke dynamics of the users. But the performance difference at the final session is not very large. This is why we chose an approach based on a single sample in the learning phase in order to familiarize it with the industrial applications environment.

V. CONCLUSION AND FUTURE WORK

This paper investigates a novel method, which considers the conditions necessary for the application in real life of the keystroke dynamics modality especially for web services. In fact, in spite of its great advantage to reinforce the security of the password-based applications facing hacking attacks, this modality has not been industrialized yet. The main interest of the proposed method is that it minimizes as much as possible the number of samples used in the learning phase. Indeed, a unique sample is required initially. Besides, we adopt the double serial adaptation mechanism to remedy to the intra-class variations of the users' characteristics: It consists in combining the growing window and the sliding window mechanisms. The growing window serves to enlarge the users' galleries so as to capture more intra-class variability. After reaching the maximum size of the reference, which is fixed to 10, the sliding window mechanism takes place. It permits describing and following the temporal variation of the users' keystroke dynamics. Also, the adaptive threshold criterion has a great impact on the improvement of the obtained results. It is adapted to the gallery variation of each user. Thanks to

TABLE IV. EVOLUTION OF THE USERS' REFERENCE SIZE FOR EACH DISTANCE METRIC OVER ALL ADAPTIVE SESSIONS: ILLUSTRATION OF THE MINIMUM AND THE MAXIMUM SAMPLES NUMBER.

Number of adaptive sessions	Min-Max number of samples in the reference							
	GREYC 2009 database				WEB GREYC database			
	Hamming	Statistical	Euclidean	Manhattan	Hamming	Statistical	Euclidean	Manhattan
1	2-4	2-5	2-4	2-4	2-5	2-5	2-4	2-4
2	6-10	5-10	4-8	3-7	5-9	6-9	4-8	4-8
3	**10-10**	7-10	7-10	6-10	8-10	7-10	7-10	6-10
4	10-10	**10-10**	**10-10**	9-10	**10-10**	**10-10**	**10-10**	9-10
5	10-10	10-10	10-10	**10-10**	10-10	10-10	10-10	**10-10**
6	10-10	10-10	10-10	10-10	10-10	10-10	10-10	10-10
7	10-10	10-10	10-10	10-10	10-10	10-10	10-10	10-10
8	10-10	10-10	10-10	10-10	10-10	10-10	10-10	10-10
9	10-10	10-10	10-10	10-10	10-10	10-10	10-10	10-10
10	10-10	10-10	10-10	10-10	10-10	10-10	10-10	10-10
11	10-10	10-10	10-10	10-10	10-10	10-10	10-10	10-10
12	10-10	10-10	10-10	10-10	10-10	10-10	10-10	10-10

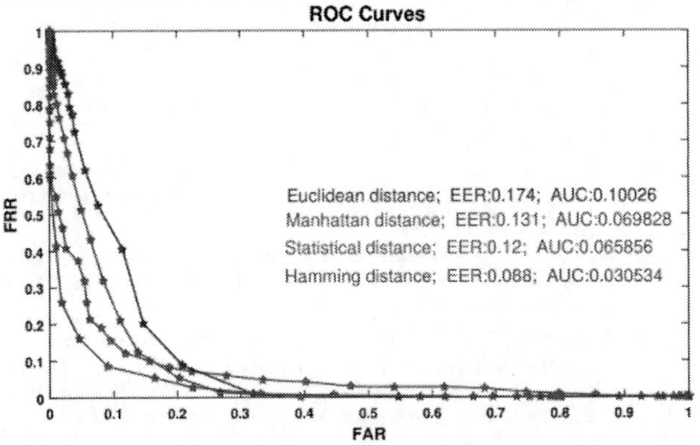

(a) Growing (1 features)

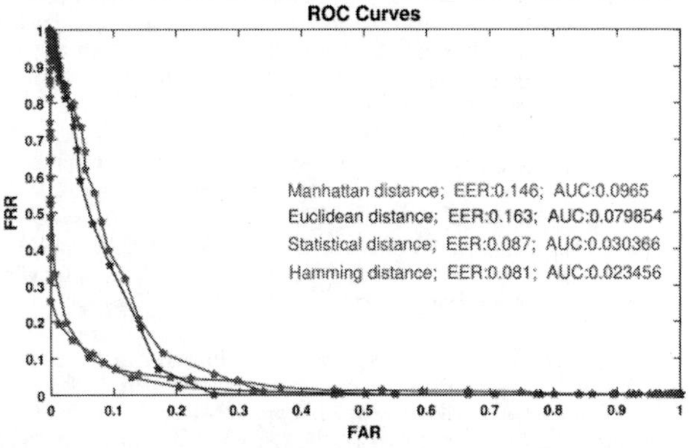

(b) Sliding (10 features)

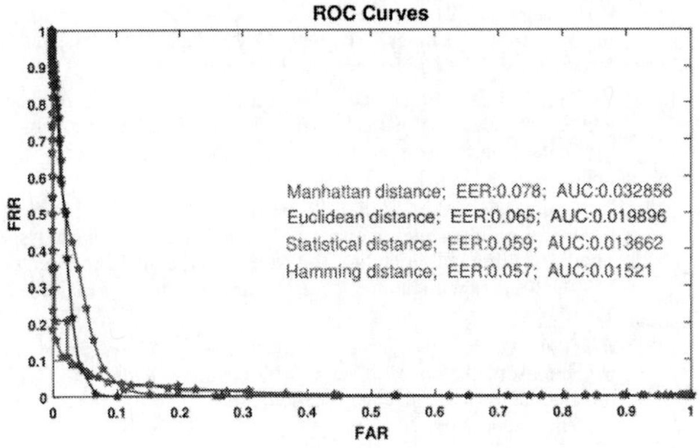

(c) Double serial mechanism (5 features)

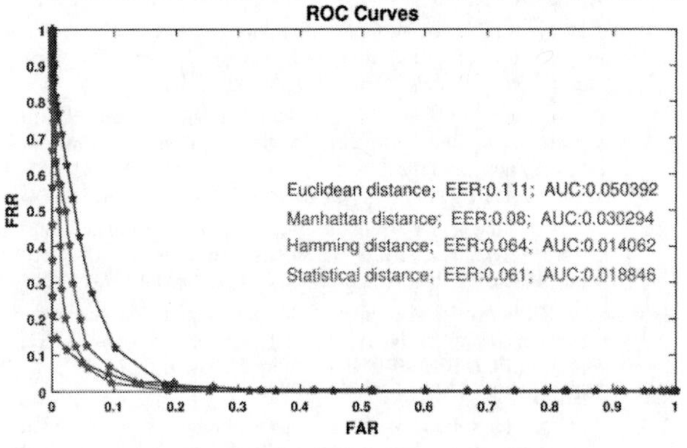

(d) Double parallel mechanism (10 features)

Figure 5. Roc curves of the last adaptation sessions and the associated performances (EER, AUC) of different adaptation mechanisms applied to the GREYC 2009 database

all these choices, we have obtained a competitive performance with a minimal size of the reference template (one sample for the enrollment and ten for the maximum size of the reference gallery). The accomplished results have improved the state of the art results by more than 0.8% going up to 4%. The achieved comparison of the different metrics combined with the KNN classifier have been also interesting. In fact, it reveals which metric provide the best results. Eventually, the hamming and statistical distances are the most efficient compared to others. We also implemented the double serial mechanism with different reference sizes and compared it to the double parallel, the growing window and the sliding window mechanisms. The double serial mechanism demonstrated the best performances.

We are interested in investigating an improved method that achieves better performance from the first sessions. Thus, preliminary experiments of a user specific adaptive mechanism are being conducted. In addition, further works will concern long term validation on real web services.

REFERENCES

[1] M. L. Mazurek and et al., "Measuring password guessability for an entire university," in Proceedings of the 2013 ACM SIGSAC Conference on Computer & Communications Security, ser. CCS '13. New York, NY, USA: ACM, 2013, pp. 173–186. [Online]. Available: http://doi.acm.org/10.1145/2508859.2516726

[2] B. Ur and et al., "Measuring real-world accuracies and biases in modeling password guessability." in USENIX Security Symposium, 2015, pp. 463–481.

[3] R. Shay and et al., "Can long passwords be secure and usable?" in Proceedings of the 32nd annual ACM conference on Human factors in computing systems. ACM, 2014, pp. 2927–2936.

[4] P. H. Pisani and A. C. Lorena, "A systematic review on keystroke dynamics," Journal of the Brazilian Computer Society, vol. 19, no. 4, 2013, pp. 573–587. [Online]. Available: http://dx.doi.org/10.1007/s13173-013-0117-7

[5] B. Fernandez-Saavedra, R. Sanchez-Reillo, R. Ros-Gomez, and J. Liu-Jimenez, "Small fingerprint scanners used in mobile devices: the impact on biometric performance," IET Biometrics, vol. 5, no. 1, March, pp. 28–36(8). [Online]. Available: http://digital-library.theiet.org/content/journals/10.1049/iet-bmt.2015.0018

[6] E. Marasco and A. Ross, "A survey on antispoofing schemes for fingerprint recognition systems," ACM Comput. Surv., vol. 47, no. 2, Nov. 2014, pp. 28:1–28:36. [Online]. Available: http://doi.acm.org/10.1145/2617756

[7] D. F. Smith, A. Wiliem, and B. C. Lovell, "Face recognition on consumer devices: Reflections on replay attacks," IEEE Transactions on Information Forensics and Security, vol. 10, no. 4, April 2015, pp. 736–745.

[8] R. Giot, M. El-Abed, B. Hemery, and C. Rosenberger, "Unconstrained keystroke dynamics authentication with shared secret," Computers & security, vol. 30, no. 6, Sept 2011, pp. 427–445.

[9] H. Çeker and S. Upadhyaya, "Adaptive techniques for intra-user variability in keystroke dynamics," in 2016 IEEE 8th International Conference on Biometrics Theory, Applications and Systems (BTAS), Sept 2016, pp. 1–6.

[10] P. H. Pisani, R. Giot, A. C. De Carvalho, and A. C. Lorena, "Enhanced template update: Application to keystroke dynamics," Computers & Security, vol. 60, July 2016, pp. 134–153.

[11] E. Yu and S. Cho, "Keystroke dynamics identity verification its problems and practical solutions," Computers & Security, vol. 23, no. 5, July 2004, pp. 428 – 440. [Online]. Available: http://www.sciencedirect.com/science/article/pii/S0167404804000963

[12] M. S. Obaidat and B. Sadoun, "Verification of computer users using keystroke dynamics," IEEE Transactions on Systems, Man, and Cybernetics, Part B (Cybernetics), vol. 27, no. 2, April 1997, pp. 261–269.

[13] K. S. Killourhy, R. Maxion et al., "Comparing anomaly-detection algorithms for keystroke dynamics," in Dependable Systems & Networks, 2009. DSN'09. IEEE/IFIP International Conference on, IEEE. IEEE, 2009, pp. 125–134.

[14] C. Epp, "Identifying emotional states through keystroke dynamics," Ph.D. dissertation, University of Saskatchewan Saskatoon, 2010.

[15] A. N. H. Nahin, J. M. Alam, H. Mahmud, and K. Hasan, "Identifying emotion by keystroke dynamics and text pattern analysis," Behaviour & Information Technology, vol. 33, no. 9, May 2014, pp. 987–996.

[16] C. Gonzalez, B. Best, A. F. Healy, J. A. Kole, and L. E. Bourne, "A cognitive modeling account of simultaneous learning and fatigue effects," Cognitive Systems Research, vol. 12, no. 1, March 2011, pp. 19–32.

[17] L. Didaci, G. L. Marcialis, and F. Roli, "Analysis of unsupervised template update in biometric recognition systems," Pattern Recognition Letters, vol. 37, February 2014, pp. 151–160.

[18] N. Poh, A. Rattani, and F. Roli, "Critical analysis of adaptive biometric systems," IET biometrics, vol. 1, no. 4, December 2012, pp. 179–187.

[19] A. Rattani, B. Freni, G. L. Marcialis, and F. Roli, "Template update methods in adaptive biometric systems: a critical review," in Advances in Biometrics. Springer, 2009, pp. 847–856.

[20] A. Rattani, "Adaptive biometric system based on template update procedures," Dept. of Elect. and Comp. Eng., University of Cagliari, PhD Thesis, 2010.

[21] N. Poh, J. Kittler, S. Marcel, D. Matrouf, and J. F. Bonastre, "Model and score adaptation for biometric systems: Coping with device interoperability and changing acquisition conditions," in 2010 20th International Conference on Pattern Recognition, Aug 2010, pp. 1229–1232.

[22] C. Pagano, E. Granger, R. Sabourin, P. Tuveri, G. Marcialis, and F. Roli, "Context-sensitive self-updating for adaptive face recognition," in Adaptive Biometric Systems. Springer, October 2015, pp. 9–34.

[23] A. Serwadda and et al., "Scan-based evaluation of continuous keystroke authentication systems," IT Professional, vol. 15, no. 4, July-Aug 2013, pp. 20–23.

[24] A. Rattani, G. L. Marcialis, and F. Roli, "Biometric system adaptation by self-update and graph-based techniques," Journal of Visual Languages & Computing, vol. 24, no. 1, February 2013, pp. 1–9.

[25] B. Freni, G. L. Marcialis, and F. Roli, "Replacement algorithms for fingerprint template update," in Image Analysis and Recognition. Springer, 2008, pp. 884–893.

[26] T. Scheidat, A. Makrushin, and C. Vielhauer, "Automatic template update strategies for biometrics," Otto-von-Guericke University of Magdeburg, Magdeburg, Germany, 2007.

[27] F. Roli, L. Didaci, and G. L. Marcialis, "Template co-update in multimodal biometric systems," in Advances in Biometrics. Springer, 2007, pp. 1194–1202.

[28] A. Rattani, G. L. Marcialis, and F. Roli, "Capturing large intra-class variations of biometric data by template co-updating," in Computer Vision and Pattern Recognition Workshops, 2008. CVPRW'08. IEEE Computer Society Conference on. IEEE, 2008, pp. 1–6.

[29] P. Kang, S.-s. Hwang, and S. Cho, "Continual retraining of keystroke dynamics based authenticator," in Advances in Biometrics. Springer, 2007, pp. 1203–1211.

[30] P. H. Pisani, A. C. Lorena, and A. C. de Carvalho, "Adaptive approches for keystroke dynamics," in Neural Networks (IJCNN), The 2015 International Joint Conference on, 2015, pp. 1–8.

[31] R. Giot, C. Rosenberger, and B. Dorizzi, "Hybrid template update system for unimodal biometric systems," in 2012 IEEE Fifth International Conference on Biometrics: Theory, Applications and Systems (BTAS), Sept 2012, pp. 1–7.

[32] R. Giot, M. El-Abed, and C. Rosenberger, "Web-based benchmark for keystroke dynamics biometric systems: A statistical analysis," in Intelligent Information Hiding and Multimedia Signal Processing (IIH-MSP), 2012 Eighth International Conference on. IEEE, 2012, pp. 11–15.

[33] R. Giot, M. El Abed, and C. Rosenberger, "Greyc keystroke: A benchmark for keystroke dynamics biometric systems," in 2009 IEEE 3rd International Conference on Biometrics: Theory, Applications, and Systems, Sept 2009, pp. 1–6.

[34] K. Killourhy and R. Maxion, "Why did my detector do that?!" in International Workshop on Recent Advances in Intrusion Detection, vol. 6307, Springer. Springer, 2010, pp. 256–276.

[35] Z. Akhtar, A. Ahmed, C. E. Erdem, and G. L. Foresti, "Biometric template update under facial aging," in Computational Intelligence in Biometrics and Identity Management (CIBIM), 2014 IEEE Symposium on. IEEE, 2014, pp. 9–15.

[36] S. Hocquet, J.-Y. Ramel, and H. Cardot, "User classification for keystroke dynamics authentication," in International Conference on Biometrics. Springer, 2007, pp. 531–539.

[37] A. Mhenni, C. Rosenberger, E. Cherrier, and N. E. B. Amara, "Keystroke template update with adapted thresholds," in International Conference on Advanced Technologies for Signal and Image Processing (ATSIP), 2016.